Therapy with Families of Sexually Acting-Out Girls

Therapy with Families Of Sexually Acting-Out Girls

ALFRED S. FRIEDMAN

JOHN C. SONNE   ROSS V. SPECK

JEAN P. BARR   JEROME E. JUNGREIS

IVAN BOSZORMENYI-NAGY   GERALDINE LINCOLN

GERTRUDE COHEN   GERALDINE SPARK

OSCAR R. WEINER

SPRINGER PUBLISHING COMPANY, INC.

NEW YORK

Acknowledgments

The United States Office of Juvenile Delinquency and Youth Development, Welfare Administration, provided the grant support for the training, curriculum development and demonstration project entitled "Family Counseling for Sexual Behavior Problems of Adolescent Girls" (Grant number 63205) on which the experience of this book is based. The project, directed by Dr. Alfred S. Friedman, was conducted at the Philadelphia Psychiatric Center. We wish to thank Dr. Jack Otis, former Chief of the Training Section, Office of Juvenile Delinquency and Youth Development, for providing consultation and assistance in planning the training program for the project.

We are indebted to Dorothy Lewis for her valuable editorial assistance and to Tybie Levit, who was most helpful in the preparation of the manuscript and various other phases of the work.

Chapter 2, "The family and female sexual delinquency: an overview of the problem," is reprinted, by permission of the editors and the publisher, from A. S. Friedman, "The family and the female delinquent." In O. Pollak and A. Friedman (eds.), *Family Dynamics and Female Sexual Delinquency*, Palo Alto, California: Science and Behavior Books, Inc., 1969.

Printed in U.S.A.

Preface

Family therapy is a relatively new and rapidly growing form of intervention in the mental health field. In its first phase, free-wheeling experimentation with new techniques and approaches was (properly) the order of the day, and up to now there has been little effort to document systematically the detailed process of family treatment or to formalize and structure the techniques employed. This book is such an effort. It is an attempt to present concisely and comprehensively the rationale for treating — as well as the method of treating — whole families together.

In our earlier book, *Psychotherapy for the Whole Family,* we presented detailed case histories of schizophrenic families. Similarly, this new book concentrates on one particular class of family problems; that is, on families who have problems related to the sexual behavior of their daughters. The specific forms of behavior for which the girls were referred to us by courts and social agencies were: running away, vagrancy, promiscuity, pregnancy out of wedlock, homosexuality, and incest. Our basic orientation in conceptualizing the sexual behavior of adolescent girls, as well as individual behavior in general, is that much that is important and crucial in the individual psyche develops from a shared family experience. Case examples of families with some of these problems are included in this book. These are detailed reports of the process of family therapy including the problems as well as the progress.

This book also approximates a guide to practice by reporting on the learning process of the beginning family therapist and on the role of his supervisor. While we are not suggesting that one can become a mature and skilled family therapist or family counselor by reading this or any other book, we do believe that our experiences provide techniques and insights about the problems of families that can be of assistance to those in the mental health profession and other helping professions who are now beginning to cope with problems of whole families. Therapists, counselors, family case workers, or psychiatric case workers who are already professionally mature can appropriately apply, with supervision, some of the techniques presented here in beginning family therapy or counseling.

We recognize that it may seem premature to present a book on techniques in this early and exploratory phase of the family treatment approach. Any outline, procedure, or formula is necessarily an oversimplification of the complex and subtle operations required for treating a family. Structuring treatment and applying a technical formula is to some extent artificial, since every family and every family therapy session is unique, demanding insight, sensitivity and art on the part the clinician; nevertheless, a guide to practice or a manual of operation can allay the anxiety of the beginning family therapist or family counselor by giving him something to hold on to and by putting him one step ahead of the family he is trying to help.

A practice book such as this should not just state that an individual's symptom is part of a family pathological system, but illustrate this; it should not just say how treatment should be conducted, but should give details of the procedures.

One of the special features of this book is the presentation of the process of family treatment as perceived by the beginning trainee therapist and by the experienced supervising family therapist.

The pioneers in the field of family therapy worked before any formal training was available. They used informal training methods. They trained each other by observing each other in action, either through the one way mirror or as they worked together in co-therapy teams with families. They accepted the challenge of dealing candidly with the significance of the therapist's personality in the process of therapy. Such was the experience of the authors of this book. As a result of this experience, family therapy is presented here as a co-therapy team process, and the teaching of family therapy is presented as a team process as well.

This volume had its origin in a training, curriculum development, and demonstration project entitled "Family Counseling for Sexual Behavior Problems of Adolescent Girls," which was conducted during the two-and-one-half year period from 1963 to 1965. The project was directed by Alfred S. Friedman and administered under the auspices and partnership of the Philadelphia Psychiatric Center and the United States Office of Juvenile Delinquency and Youth Development. It was funded by a federal grant from the latter agency. In the training and demonstration part of the project the families were treated and counseled in sessions by co-therapist teams consisting of a trainee and his supervisor. The trainees were experienced senior social case workers from the staffs of family service agencies, psychiatric clinics, and child guidance clinics. The authors of this book (with two exceptions) were the teaching and supervising therapists.

In addition to becoming part of a co-therapy team working with families, the trainees had two types of seminars. One of these was a technique seminar in which questions were raised and cases, issues, and problems were reviewed. Some of the content of this seminar is reported in the chapter entitled "Answers to Typical Questions of the Trainee Family Therapist." The other seminar was theoretical, and dealt primarily with such issues as: the family as a system, the family impact on personality development and on female sexual behavior, attitudes toward pre-marital sexual behavior, and principles of conjoint family therapy. The trainees attended this seminar in order to integrate their new family therapy experiences with theoretical material, and to clarify their thinking regarding the pertinent areas of family life.

The specific objects of the entire training program were:

1. To provide training in the concepts of family dynamics and in the principles and methods of family therapy and counseling as it relates to sexual delinquency in adolescent females.

2. To develop and refine a training curriculum for a course in family therapy for the specific problem of sexual delinquency.

3. To provide training in making a comprehensive diagnostic evaluation of a family with this type of problem.

4. To interest relevant community social agencies and clinics in the need for training professional staff to become qualified family therapists and family counselors.

It is anticipated that the methods and training experiences described in this book can be applied constructively in working with problems of adolescents, boys as well as girls, "delinquent" or otherwise; and that they can also be applied to family therapy in general. Some of the concepts of family therapy and some of the essentials of this training could also be made available to clergy, teachers, school counselors, pediatricians and other professionals who share community responsibility for fostering family life and growth.

We see our work as part of the current effort to achieve a new perception of family living, and to develop more adequate concepts of family functioning and a theory for family treatment. We do not believe we have final answers to offer, but we try to offer a variety of exposures or windows through which to glimpse family treatment in process.

Whitaker* has said, "What the therapist writes about therapy is often a kind of monologue understandable only to the speaker, whereas teaching is a dialogue that is geared to the student." The fact that this enterprise involved the moving process of teaching family therapy to other professionals, and of giving them new experiences and insights, made it a stimulating and rewarding experience for the teachers who are the authors of this book.

We must here add a sad note by reporting that our retrospective view of the pleasure we had in sharing this venture as good friends together is marred by the memory of the untimely death of our colleague, Jerome J. Jungreis. A part of our indebtedness to him can be seen in the two chapters he wrote for this book. He was also the coordinator of the practicum part of our training project and contributed much more than is readily apparent here.

ALFRED S. FRIEDMAN
JOHN C. SONNE
ROSS V. SPECK

Philadelphia, Pennsylvania
August, 1970

* Whitaker, Carl, Foreword in *Family Dynamics and Female Sexual Delinquency*, O. Pollak and A. S. Friedman, eds. Palo Alto, Calif.: Science and Behavior Books, Inc., 1969.

The authors

ALFRED S. FRIEDMAN, PH.D., Director of Research, Philadelphia Psychiatric Center; Project Director, Family Treatment for Sexual Behavior Problems of Adolescent Girls; Consultant in Family Therapy, Philadelphia Child Study Center.

JEAN P. BARR, ACSW, Assistant Professor and Director of Social Work Education, Department of Psychiatry, Hahnemann Medical College, Philadelphia, Pennsylvania.

IVAN BOSZORMENYI-NAGY, M.D., Director of Family Psychiatry Division, Eastern Pennsylvania Psychiatric Institute; Consultant in Family Psychiatry, West Philadelphia Community Mental Health Consortium; Associate Professor of Psychiatry, Jefferson University, Philadelphia, Pennsylvania.

GERTRUDE COHEN, Case Coordinator, Family Treatment Project, Philadelphia Psychiatric Center.

JEROME E. JUNGREIS, ACSW, Family Therapist, Philadelphia Psychiatric Center; Mental Health Coordinator, Philadelphia Child Guidance Clinic (Deceased May; 1967).

GERALDINE LINCOLN, M.ED., Family Therapist, Philadelphia Psychiatric Center; Senior Clinical Instructor, Department of Psychiatry, Hahnemann Medical College, Philadelphia, Pennsylvania.

JOHN C. SONNE, M.D., Staff Research Psychiatrist, Philadelphia Psychiatric Center; Director of Family Therapy, Institute of the Pennsylvania Hospital; Assistant Clinical Professor of Psychiatry, Hahnemann Medical College, Philadelphia, Pennsylvania.

GERALDINE SPARK, ACSW, Associate Director and Chief Social Worker, Division of Family Psychiatry, Eastern Pennsylvania Psychiatric Institute, Philadelphia, Pennsylvania.

ROSS V. SPECK, M.D., Staff Research Psychiatrist, Philadelphia Psychiatric Center; Consultant in Family Social Networks, Philadelphia Child Guidance Clinic; Head, Section of Social Psychiatry and Clinical Associate Professor, Hahnemann Medical College, Philadelphia, Pennsylvania.

OSCAR R. WEINER, M.D., Head, Section of Family Therapy and Study, Department of Psychiatry, Hahnemann Medical College, Philadelphia, Pennsylvania.

Contents

Female sexual behavior and "delinquency" in a changing society

Ross Speck, John Sonne, and Alfred S. Friedman

Chapter

1

This book has grown out of our experiences with the families of sexually acting-out girls. Soon after beginning our project, we began to realize that we were in the middle of a social revolution that made the definition of sexual "delinquency" difficult. The families we worked with were concerned about the sexual behavior of their adolescent daughters and were struggling with the problem of reconciling stereotypical traditional sexual mores with the rapidly changing mores of the day, which all families must do. However, "our" families were approaching the task already crippled by depression, marital disharmony, and mechanisms of denial, projection, and family isolation. Since our project was completed in 1965, and since our treatment population was represented mostly by lower-class families, their daughters did not have the middle-class options of going to college or escaping to the "hippie" scene. Instead, they and their families remained "trapped" within the psycho-social matrix of the family. Already in 1965 some girls from middle-class families had fled from their homes to "do their own thing," which often meant engaging in sexual behavior within their own peer social network and with peer social approval. The minority of girls in our project who came from middle-class homes apparently did not have this freedom of movement or the desire to avail themselves of those escapes. We will see why this was so as we review some of these cases in the ensuing chapters of this book.

The word "delinquency" derives from a Latin word that means "to fail," "to do wrong," or "to leave."* In today's affluent society, middle-class girls have a new-found freedom which allows them to leave the traditional family contraints and thus, perhaps, escape from a pathological family system. The older generation then sometimes labels this leaving or desertion of themselves as "delinquency."

Throughout this book, terms such as "sexual promiscuity," "sexual acting-out," "sexual delinquency," and so forth are not used pejoratively, but rather because they represented at the time the study was being done

---

* The word "delinquent" is from de Latin *delinquens - entis,* present participle of *delinquere,* to fail, do wrong, from *de+linquere,* to leave.[1]

1

— and still do to an extent — terms used by professionals in ordinary clinical communication. We are fully aware of the danger in "labelling" another person's behavior, but the families comprising our research population had already been so "labelled" by others because of their daughters' sexual misbehavior. Our therapy teams sought to alleviate distress among family members and to change family system operations in the hope that potential for growth and participation in the human experience would be released. We were interested in the phenomenology of the processes in the family which led them to be referred to us and to accept family treatment with us. We saw ourselves as offering help in a therapeutic situation which contained an awareness of rapidly changing social mores and flexible attitudes about sexual behavior. We were often more interested in working on a girl's emotional immaturity and unreadiness to integrate her sexual experiences, and on the family's complicity in this condition, than in representing society's traditional mores to our clients.

A word of caution is necessary at this point lest we forget that we are living in an age of cybernetics, computerization, and automation. The past fifty years have seen more progress in human technology than has the preceding two thousand years. The rate of change in our culture is following an asymptotic curve which is affecting all of our social institutions.[2] When social values and mores are undergoing rapid change, one might easily question what is "sick" both in the individual and in the family. Deviance just might be up for re-definition as well. Many of today's unmarried young girls who are having sexual relations do not think of themselves as being delinquent or as engaging in "immoral" or illegal behavior. Instead, they see the traditional attitudes of the society, their parents, and the "establishment" as being unfair and dishonest and thus "immoral."

In conducting family therapy in cases of middle-class delinquent boys or girls, we have often been impressed by the contrast between the defensive hypocrisy of the parents and the openness and emotional honesty of the acting-out offspring. Our observation of many of these families agrees with Ackerman's observation that "The acting-out is a resistance to a spurious pattern of control and conformity in the family. There is a deep split between the external facade of the family, the mask that the family presents to the wider community, and its inner life. The family looks respectable on the outside but is rotten on the inside."[3] Since these youths derive their self-esteem from conforming to the new behavior standards of their young peer group, they are validated and supported in their sexual behavior, which enables them to stand up to the accusations of the traditional society and to reflect back the "sick" or "deviant" or "delinquent" label.

Sometimes the girl's sexual acting-out appears to be self-destructive and against her own best interests, but quite as often it may be the best available path toward solving her problem with her family. Family treatment may reveal that she has personality strengths and signs of emotional health which her parents lack. Her sexual acting-out, aside from being a personal escape, may be a signal that the family's integrity and health are in danger and may serve to alert community agencies to the fact that there is a crisis in the family and that it needs help.

If the sexually active adolescent female leaves her family to join the "hippie" subculture, she *may* not suffer loss of self-esteem, and *may* not be considered sick by herself and others. Similarly, if her parents put her on the "pill" or accept her pregnancy, little loss of self-esteem or deviant labelling by others is likely to occur.

The term "delinquency" is primarily a sociological and legal concept. It refers to certain actions regarded as destructive or dangerous to others and therefore to be proscribed by the community. It is clearly not a psychiatric or psychological diagnosis, nor even a personality trait.

Much behavior that has been labelled "delinquent" is considered by many sociologists not to be deviant or maladjustive behavior but to have its origin in the social structure derived from individual or family dynamics and to be determined by economic, social, and cultural factors. The "cure" for such "delinquent" behavior, particularly in the economically and socially disadvantaged lower classes, would be broad social reforms, new social and political attitudes, and massive economic programs for the poor, including tax reforms, etc. Such theorists might regard family therapy (and individual psychotherapy as well) as a sop provided by the "establishment" to distract the poor, the rebellious young, and the black "ghetto" population from participation in organized efforts to obtain equal opportunities and improved conditions. While there may be a validity to this position, we as family therapists generally adopt a neutral position in regard to these sociological issues in delinquency. Similarly, we are generally neutral as to whether the sexual "acting-out" behavior of an unmarried girl is "delinquent," morally "bad," or "deviant."

A girl's premarital sexual behavior may not at first appear to have the same sociocultural and socioeconomic origins as does male delinquent behavior such as stealing, assault, etc. Yet for many teen-age girls, sexual acting-out may well be an expression of rebellion against authority and a vehicle for discharge of anger at parents and society. A girl's parents are very personally involved in, and concerned with, how she uses her body, and the immature girl, although perhaps not ready to derive pleasure or satisfaction from sex, learns in some vague way that she can use her body to retaliate against her parents and to get some of the things she wants from boys.

Premarital sexual relations in teen-age girls tends to have a different significance in socioeconomically deprived families than in the families of the advanced middle or upper classes.

That premarital sexual behavior has socioeconomic and cultural origins and cannot always be construed as psychologically deviant behavior is shown by the prevalence of sexual behavior and motherhood out of wedlock among the lower socioeconomic Negro girls of the urban "ghettos." Their behavior is part of the "legitimate" pattern of their family structure which has been historically determined, a legacy from slavery, and has its own acceptability and validity. An early psychiatric study of "habitually promiscuous" women that was conducted during World War II in San Francisco found that only 44 percent of the Negro females, compared to 77 percent of the white females studied were "actively conflicted" or "maladapted."[4] The fact that significantly more of the Negro females were free of neurotic symptoms and unstable character traits is consistent with the idea that historical, cultural, and economic factors play an important determining role in so-called "promiscuous" behavior.

REFERENCES

1. Webster, N. *Webster's Collegiate Dictionary*, Fifth Edition. Merriam Company, 1944, p. 266.
2. Gioscia, Victor. LSD Subcultures: Acidoxy Versus Orthodoxy. *Amer. J. Orthopsychiat.* 39 (3):428-435, April 1969.
3. Ackerman, N. A. Sexual Delinquency Among Middle-Class Girls. Chap. 5 in *Family Dynamics and Female Sexual Delinquency*, O. Pollak and A. S. Friedman, eds. Palo Alto: Science and Behavior Books, Inc., 1969.
4. Ernst, C. et al. An Experiment in the Psychiatric Treatment of Promiscuous Girls. Annual Report of Department of Public Health, San Francisco, 1945, pp. 19-20.

The family and female sexual delinquency: an overview of the problem

Alfred S. Friedman

Sexual delinquency in adolescent girls is a problem of central concern to society, for it involves economic health, legal, religious, moral, and ethical problems. Promiscuous pre-marital sexual behavior raises questions of the moral code and society's interest in controlling the sexual impulse, and in maintaining the family system. There is tragic evidence that female sexual delinquency is far more self-destructive and irreversible in its consequences for girls than is true for most types of male delinquent behavior. As Blos points out, "The sexually delinquent girl violates the caring and protective attributes of her maternal role in a way which will harm her and her offspring for the remainder of her life."[1] Even in ethnic and social-class groups where illegitimacy is less a social stigma than in white middle-class groups, the girl, her illegitimate baby, and her family usually face additional handicaps in achieving economic and family stability. It would be well if the predisposing conditions for female sexual delinquency could be recognized and dealt with in its latent or predelinquent stage, before the full onslaught of puberty pushes the girl into acting-out behavior and before the consequences of sexual delinquency bring additional stress to the already vulnerable personality of the adolescent girl. (An out-of-wedlock pregnancy affects the future lives not only of the girl, the baby, and the boy who fathers the baby, but of the two families involved, and the future spouses of the boy and the girl.) A progression of emotional, mental, social, and economic problems, and of unstable family conditions accrue to the second generation from one out-of-wedlock pregnancy.

For many girls, promiscuous behavior reflects a superficiality in human relationships; sexuality for them is often an empty gesture, with personal satisfaction totally lacking. A vain search for pleasure, a sense of personal inadequacy, a desire to escape, fear, and an inability to establish an appropriate identity are often determining factors. In her pubescent need for the affection that is not forthcoming from her parents, and in her desire to be accepted, the girl may confuse sexual popularity with bona fide concern and care. Negative values in human relationships, and

5

immature and exploitative attitudes, on the part of one or both partners toward the other, are often involved in promiscuous sexual behavior. Of course, premarital sexual relationships can also occur on a mature, constructive, and satisfactory level, and it should be made clear that we are not labelling all pre-marital sexual relationships as promiscuous or delinquent.

While the young male delinquent shows a wide variety of anti-social forms of behavior, the girl usually possesses a quite limited delinquent repertoire. By and large, her legally defined offenses consist of running away, stealing, and sexually acting-out. Unlike delinquent boys, girls do not usually engage in car stealing, assault, burglary, robbery, vandalism, etc. In 1963 sex offenses constituted the largest single group of complaints against adolescent girls in the Philadelphia courts. More than 25% of the girls who came to the attention of the County Court of Philadelphia were directly charged with sexual misbehavior.[2] Many additional cases involving sexual waywardness in girls were not so clearly charged. S. Robinson reports from a survey of court practice that girls guilty of sex offenses "are customarily designated as ungovernable or as having deserted their homes."[3] Reports of the United States Children's Bureau, supported by local surveys, indicate that among girls the two most frequent infractions are "ungovernable behavior" and sexual offenses. Although police are largely responsible for bringing boys to court, in cases involving girls the petitioners are usually the parents. There are many cases of sexual promiscuity and sexual delinquency that never reach the court; these are privately handled by psychiatrists, private agencies, psychiatric out-patient clinics, private schools, and the like. Block and Flynn report that commitment or referral to agencies and institutions for sexual misbehavior is far more frequent for girls than for boys."[4]

At Sleighton Farm School for Girls, a state-supported institution near Philadelphia, a survey revealed that 32 percent of the 190 girls were admitted primarily for sexual promiscuity and that 76 percent of all the girls had some history of sexual delinquency, ranging from contacts with only one boy to the relatively few cases where a girl was delinquent with as many as 50 different men and boys.[5] Only three of the girls had been known to engage in prostitution. A not unusual case was the girl who had had sexual relations with only one boy and claimed to love him and to want to marry him. Her parents disapproved of the marriage and preferred that she be institutionalized. In such a case it is a question of whether the institutionalization is more for the purpose of solving the parents' problem than the girl's.

High schools have reported the sexual behavior of some of their female students to be an increasingly acute problem. For example, the existence of an "N.V." (non-virgin) club was revealed, through a clinic, in a suburban school district of our metropolitan area. The girls underwent "initiation rites" in which they lost their virginity, through the courtesy of several high school boys and service men from a nearby Army installation. The girls were required to undergo this initiation in the presence of other girls who were already members. In some gangs, the peer culture even requires homosexual contacts between girls for membership status.

It is difficult to define sexual promiscuity scientifically or for society to agree on the degree of sexual contact or the type and amount of sexual behavior which is to be classified as delinquent. There has been little organized community effort to correct it, and there appears to be an unresolved complex of social attitudes surrounding it. It may be, also, that society as a whole is somewhat more ambivalent about its desire to terminate sexually promiscuous behavior in young girls than it is about its desire to terminate the destructive behavior of delinquent boys directed against property and other persons.

In contrast to other forms of delinquency, female sexual delinquency has received relatively little systematic study and evaluation. As far as we can find, there are virtually no adequate studies of the problem or of its treatment in the literature. For example, we do not know whether or not there is the same incidence of sexual promiscuity in Negro girls as in white girls of the same socio-economic class, nor how the two groups compare in their values, aspirations or attitudes toward premarital sex. We know that there is a higher incidence of unwed motherhood among Negro girls than among white girls when the socio-economic class variable is not controlled. We do not know how much of lower class Negro family instability and illegitimacy is due to current conditions of Negro socio-economic inequality nor, conversely, how much of current Negro inequality is the result of illegitimacy and unstable family structure.

The ability to form relationships with boys and to be attractive to them are determining factors in the development of self-identity and sex-role differentiation and in the peer status of adolescent girls. Butman has considered a number of areas as being crucial in affecting adolescents' approach to heterosexual relationships, interactions with the opposite sex, and attendant sexual behavior, among which are: (1) orientations and attitude to cross-sex relations such as "fun morality" versus "puritanism," etc., and the degree of dependence on cross-sex relations to satisfy affiliative status needs; (2) opportunities for sexual behavior and the control structures determining whether sexual behavior occurs, including external restrictions and internalization of standards and restrictions regarding sex; (3) information and attitudes regarding sexual behavior conveyed by significant others and by social and religious authorities. This includes the nature, depth and openness of sex information available to the adolescent.[6]

There is a clear need for development of further systematic approaches to the prevention and treatment of sexual delinquency in girls, as well as for controlled studies to evaluate the effectiveness of various forms of treatment.

Sexual delinquency among girls often reflects the breakdown of parental control, a generation gap and rebellion against authority, and an acute disturbance in the parent-adolescent relationship, just as do many other forms of juvenile delinquency. It has been noted that delinquent

girls generally appear to be more seriously emotionally disturbed than
do delinquent boys. Many such cases are referred for psychiatric study
and treatment. Monachesi's findings with the Minnesota Multiphasic
Personality Inventory support the view that delinquency in females in
a predominately white sample is a manifestation of personality difficulty,
rather than only a demonstration of subcultural standards or group
norms.[7]

Some authors have speculated that certain factors of cultural change
in the United States may be contributing to increased sexual acting-out
and illegitimate pregnancies. Such factors may include the prevalence of
a pattern of maternal dominance in American homes, the disappearance
of the autocratic, "strong" type of father, and the higher divorce rate.
These factors result in the absence of a strong father figure, both as an
identification model and as a love object, in the lives of American girls.
Much has been written about the serious implications of the absence
of a strong father figure for the American boy, particularly the Negro
boy, and how this has contributed to juvenile delinquency. The need
of the girl for a strong father may be just as important. Dame et al
have speculated that this need results in a delay in the resolution of the
Oedipal problem for girls — the wish for a strong father is never sufficiently satisfied, nor is there an adequate opportunity to learn to control
or delay the wish for the father. The Oedipal relationship may be so
lacking or exist so exclusively in fantasy that there is no possibility of
working it through. This yearning for a strong father, combined with
anger at the mother for chasing the father away or for emasculating him,
is seen as resulting in the girl's sexual acting out. Her negative dependency on her mother may be transferred to dependency on a rebellious,
aggressive, or delinquent boy who acts out for her the aggression she
has suppressed in herself.[8]

In addition to the family constellations characterized by passive, weak,
or absent fathers, we found in our own study and treatment of families
of sexually acting-out girls a type of father-daughter relationship which
appears, at least on the surface, to be quite different: the father's behavior
toward the girl is incestuously toned and is accompanied by a restrictive
attitude toward her. Threatened by her pubescence, and because of guilt
over his partially repressed sexual interest in her, he projects the sexual
impulses onto her and becomes angry and restrictive. By accusing her
of sexual misbehavior with boys, he justifies his restrictiveness. The girl,
disappointed by being pushed away by her father, flouts his authority
and seeks outside sexual objects. Although this constellation is quite
different from the first one described here, they have in common the lack
of a substantial father-daughter relationship based on trust, warmth,
and affection.

Following are some of the observations of family dynamics we made
on the first group of 24 families we treated on the project. Most of the
fathers were seen as dependent, needy, and demanding, and as wanting
their wives to assume mother roles for them; many were demanding,
hostile, and restrictive toward their daughters. Further, the fathers were

seen (1) as seductive to their daughters, (2) as caught up in the daughters' unresolved Oedipal feelings, and (3) as seeking an unusual amount of attention from the daughters. In our family therapy work we have seen adolescent daughters pushed to the brink of promiscuous sexual behavior by their fathers' provocative and suspicious questioning. One of the fathers would check the speedometer and the amount of gas in his daughter's car before and after she went out on a date. He would then interrogate her regarding her actions until he reduced her to tears and anger. She sometimes reacted to the repeated accusations with the attitude "If I have the name, I might as well have the game." The father did not realize that his obsession in this matter was an unwitting provocation to sexual acting out in that he was impressing on his daughter the picture he had of her as being a sexually misbehaving girl.

Another father who was obsessively preoccupied with his attractive daughter's relationship with boys continuously made suggestive remarks about what she must be doing on her dates. His manner indicated that he was jealous of the boys, and also that he was excited by the fantasy of their sexual behavior with his daughter. He would say to her, "Well, you know what boys want. If you don't give it to them, they're not going to be interested in you." In one session, the daughter told of a fantasy she had of getting her own apartment and earning money by having men come over. She said she had thought about it but of course she would never do it. The father then said, "Oh, yes, that is something to think about." While he may have intended this to be mildly sarcastic, she could not know for sure whether he wanted her to be promiscuous or not.

We found that mothers as well as fathers were unduly suspicious of their daughter's dating activities. Nearly all the mothers had excessive emotional investment in their daughters; at the same time, most of them saw their daughters as very much unlike themselves. The mothers' own neediness, while not superficially apparent, was shown by struggles with the daughters over who should be the parent: about half of the mothers were trying to make their daughters take over some significant aspects of their own mothering roles. When both parents are weak, the entire family becomes emotionally needy and puts pressure on the oldest or next to the oldest daughter to assume the mother role.

Gehrke et al recently made the following clinical generalizations, some of which are consistent with our own observation above, based on their family therapy observations of families with sexually acting-out daughters: The parents have an unnatural fear of the child's developing sexual impulses, and a fear that grownup sexuality is dangerous. The "weaker," more immature parent needs to use the spouse or the daughter as a parent to an unusual degree because he fears he could not survive the aggressive sexual impulses perceived in his partner. This parent derives secondary gain in terms of his or her own sexual feelings, which can be more safely expressed, in fantasy, toward this child than toward the marital partner, who might, in his fantasy, abandon or devour him. The function of the identified patient is to relate and behave in a way to protect this weaker, child-like parent.[9] These authors also observe that, while the parents may argue and blame each other, they will nevertheless be in accord in their projection onto the identified patient as the scapegoat and the real cause of the family difficulty. While the parents have seduced this daughter into being the scapegoat, she responds to the stimulation she is receiving from them with mixed feelings, and she is tempted also by the fact that the situation enables her to obtain a controlling and important position in the family. This kind of family can seldom agree on what the rules should be in the family, or how they should be carried out.

One might wonder whether there is a connection between the increasing number of sexually acting-out girls and the observation that the classic picture of hysterical neurosis described by Freud has become a relative clinical rarity. The classical hysterical reaction was characterized by guilt and contained both hidden wish and punishment. The modern female is less prone toward feeling guilty about sex; and with the changing western cultural attitudes toward more positive acceptance of sex and equality for women, she may also be less likely to derive masochistic gratification from submitting sexually in her fantasy, whether consciously or unconsciously, to a male. She has been more accustomed to submitting to her mother than to her passive father.

Giffin, Johnson, and Litin describe a subtle form of parental seduction or inappropriate sexual temptation of children which occurs under the guise of parental love and tenderness. This disguised tempting by a parent, stemming from poorly integrated forbidden impulses in the parent, "confronts the child with an ambivalent, genital passion which he or she cannot understand or begin to integrate. The child becomes unconsciously aware of and absorbs the parent's hostile, guilty, shameful feelings, and experiences genital frustration, confusion, fear of detection and anxiety. In cases of perversion, we always see the overstressing, usually by the mother, of at least one aspect of polymorphous sexual proclivities of the young child, such as to lead to unusual selective hypertrophy."[10] Thus the parent is consciously, or more often unconsciously, permissive and inconsistent in stimulation of the small child. The parent later achieves an unconscious vicarious gratification of his own inadequately repressed instinctual needs in the acting out of the child. For example, inordinate curiosity regarding an adolescent daughter's experiences on dates with boys carries with it implied sanction; too exciting discussions about sex in the family may constitute unwitting approval; and the parent's warnings and accusations against sexual behavior may, when occurring simultaneously with the intense curiosity and excitement of the parent, result in blocking the child's natural development of an adequate conscience and standard of behavior. Szurek observes that "if the discipline of the parent is administered with guilt, it permits the child to act out, and to subtly blackmail the parent until the particular issue is befogged with irrelevant bickerings."[11]

Blos has pointed out that Johnson's dynamic formulation of sexual delinquency in terms of the child's acting out the unconscious wishes of the parent can only take place when the emotional separation between parent and child is pathologically incomplete. In fact, he considered the continuation of the symbiotic tie between the mother and the child and the continued need for immediate object possession, to constitute the preconditional factor for sexual acting out.[12] Blos presents, in psychoanalytic terms, a comprehensive psychodynamic formulation of female sexual delinquency in which he describes three "typical constellations" of female sexual delinquency.[1] He sees the sexual acting-out as a defense against regression to the intense attachment to the pre-Oedipal mother, which results from a failure in the pre-adolescent task of emotional liberation from the pre-Oedipal mother.

Some cases develop into a compulsive form of promiscuity described by Bychowski.[13] Because of being too filled with the object of her earliest unsatisfied wishes and because of disappointments in relationships with parents, the girl, according to this formulation, is fearful of committing herself to a new love relationship. She may, depending on other factors, either avoid all heterosexual contact, or still having insatiable desires, develop a partial depersonalization in the area of sex, splitting the experience and sensations of the physical sexual contact off from emotional object relationships, which latter permits promiscuous sexual behavior.

Kaufman, Peck and Taguiri found that the incest could not be explained in terms of the personalities of the father or daughter alone.[14] Rather, both parents were involved in a pattern of unconscious stimulation and permission of the incestual behavior, the mother from the unconscious desire to place the daughter in a maternal role. The girl reacts to this desire of the mother's by developing a pseudo-maturity, and by seeking gratification from the relationship with the father. The parents do not provide adequate controls or adequate assistance in reality testing and superego formation for the girl. Robey noted quite a similar pattern to the above in young girls who run away from home and act out sexually with one or more boys.[15] Robey did not see quite the depth of pathology in the family of the runaway girls as Kaufman et al reported for the incest cases. He speculated that it was because of the girl's strength that, when she was given the choice of taking over the mother's role or running away, she chose the latter as a method of fighting off the incestuous wishes unconsciously shared by all members of the family. The immediate or superficial conflict from which the girl runs away is often between herself and her father, although there often appears to be an equally important underlying conflict with the mother.

Since every family must develop controls for intrafamilial sexual incestuous impulses and feelings, it is obviously not sufficient to postulate that the incest threat within a family is the immediate precipitant to a girl's running away and acting out sexually. We do not yet know how the intensity of the incest threat and the way of defending against it differ in the various types (delinquent, schizophrenic, and "normal") of families. This could be a matter for future research.

Ernst et al of the San Francisco Department of Public Health studied 139 "habitually promiscuous" women by psychiatric interview and history, and classified them according to their "motivations" in the following four groups:

1. *Actively-conflicted group.* Promiscuity is an expression of intra-psychic, neurotic conflict (55 percent of the white females and 28 percent of the Negro females studied).

2. *Dependent group.* Promiscuity is an expression of dependency and immaturity causing relatively little concern since responsibility for behavior is placed on the sexual partners (14 percent of the white and 28 percent of the Negro females studied).

3. *Maladapted group.* Promiscuity is part of an unstable character formation that is characterized by the absence of a sense of responsibility and an unawareness of social restraints, but with no evidence of internal conflict (22 percent of the white females and 16 percent of the Negro females studied).

4. *Non-conflictual group.* Promiscuity appears to be primarily a means of satisfying sexual desires, with no conflicts revealed within the self or with the social group (3 percent of white females and 20 percent of Negro females studied).[16]

In summary, some of the family dynamics considered in the literature to contribute to so-called female sexual delinquency are: primary emotional deprivation, and an unfulfilled need for closeness and tenderness in the girl; rejection by parents, particularly by the father; excessive strictness by the father; over-stimulation or seduction; over-permissiveness and inconsistent parental controls; hostility, provocation, suspicion and accusation by parents; confusion over sexual identity resulting from inappropriate role relationships in the parental marriage; a defense against regression to the infantile relationship with a nurturing mother; a defense against homosexual threat; a flight from incest threat within the family; a tendency to fulfill a parent's dire prediction; identification with a pregnant mother, a sister, or friend, or with a promiscuous mother; a longing for a missing father; an attempt to rectify a distorted past, and combinations of the above factors.

While there is not complete agreement, there are a number of consistent elements of family dynamics which recur often in the descriptions of the observers reviewed above.

There clearly are enough available ideas, speculations, and theories from which one might, if he wanted, select working hypotheses for treating such cases. We also should not forget, while formulating concepts of psychopathology and psychodynamics, that we should not lose sight of normal coping mechanisms, and the fact that sexual behavior in adolescence has natural and non-pathological sources, both biological and psychological, such as natural curiosity, pleasure-seeking, need for self-expression and self-assertion (need to prove personal adequacy and success in the peer social group), imitation of adults, desire for love and acceptance, and adolescent striving for autonomy and freedom from parental control.

Teen-Age Illegitimate Pregnancy

The problem of the pregnant unmarried girl is an increasing one that requires special attention. During the 22-year period from 1938 to 1959, the national illegitimacy rate for 15- to 19-year-old girls almost doubled. The total number of officially reported unmarried mothers during the single year of 1965 was 291,000. It has been speculated that, including unreported cases, somewhere between a half million and a million unmarried girls were pregnant in 1968, and that 200,000 illegal abortions were performed, constituting, in a sense, a social emergency for our national community.

Herzog of the U. S. Children's Bureau has pointed out that these figures do not necessarily represent a sudden crisis, or a teen-age revolution in sex mores, but represent a chronic problem, a long-term trend and steady increase in the number of cases over the past 40 years. She calls for coordinated planning of long-term comprehensive basic services. She estimates that in 1965 less than one-third of all unmarried mothers, and only about one-tenth of non-white cases, received any social or psychological services at all and, when they did receive services, it was usually only around the time of childbirth. About 70 percent of white babies and less than 10 percent of non-white babies born out of wedlock are legally adopted. She concludes: "It seems obvious that we must find ways to bring needed services to a larger proportion of our unmarried mothers, with less selectivity based on those painfully intertwined factors, class, color and income; and that these services should be designed not only to tide over the period of pregnancy and childbirth, but also, where indicated, to provide support and training that will lead toward the possibility of becoming adequate mothers and adequate citizens. . . ."[17]

High school and college teachers today are faced increasingly with the problem of the presence of pregnant single girls in their classrooms. The absence of these girls from their courses, as well as their presence in the classroom, pose problems to be solved. In Chicago, Visotsky reports that less than 30 percent of the lower socioeconomic class girls excluded from elementary school because of pregnancy return after the enforced absence, and that the termination of their schooling will undoubtedly have serious consequences for their future lives.[18]

In addition to the need for facilities, there is a need for developing a more adequate rationale for the treatment of this problem. The problem is multiply-determined and requires a broad approach in its understanding and treatment. There is evidence that cultural, religious, and educational values, differential intrafamilial relationships, differential peer experiences related to dating and heterosexual contacts, and the personality dynamics of the individual girl are all involved in the occurrence of illegitimate pregnancy, as well as in the girl's subsequent decision to keep or surrender the infant.[19]

Butman conducted a controlled research comparison of girls who dropped out of school because of illegitimate pregnancies with other girls of similar background in the same school. She found the following factors to differentiate the girls who became pregnant: 1) A low self-image reflected in a low estimate of their own competence in meeting performance expectations, 2) inadequate and inaccurate sex information obtained from personal experience, boyfriends, or books, 3) a perception of boys as definitely expecting sex relations, 4) orientation to marriage as an immediate goal and 5) psychological involvement in and commitment to a relationship with a boy.[6]

Young found that 48 out of 100 unmarried mothers she studied had dominating and rejecting mothers, and 20 of those who had fathers had dominating and rejecting fathers, and that the girl's relation to the dominant parent "was a battleground on which a struggle was fought, and the baby was an integral part of that struggle." She also had the impression that all of the girls were neurotic, unhappy, and had poor interpersonal relations; only a few of them made constructive use of their native ability in work, and none had genuinely cared for or been happy with the father of her baby. The tendency to self-punishment and self-destruction was found to be a deeply ingrained and powerful force in these girls.[20]

In a controlled study of pregnant unmarried girls, Vincent found a large subgroup who had either been rejected by, or had withdrawn from, their parents to a considerable degree. The only major difference he found between these pregnant girls and non-pregnant girls from similar backgrounds who had also been rejected or had withdrawn from their parents, was that the girls who had not become pregnant were able to identify with a teacher or with another adult in the community from whom they learned and internalized traditional sex mores. The pregnant unmarried girls were guided almost exclusively by the permissive sex mores of a small peer group upon whose acceptance they were dependent in the absence of positive meaningful relationships with a parent, a teacher, a minister, or another adult friend.[21]

Some observations of attitudes and characteristics of lower socio-economic Negro girls who become unmarried mothers are reported by Visotsky as follows: 1) They believe they will go crazy if they don't have sexual relations before adulthood. 2) While mothers set up many verbal prohibitions against sexual acting out, and sex is not a "nice" thing to talk about, there seems to be acceptance by mothers of the likelihood of sexual relations occurring with the girls at the onset of menstruation regardless of age. The mothers see themselves as having little control over their own fate or their daughters' sexual behavior. 3) Women demand little in the relationship with men over and above sexual gratification. The girls are stimulated sexually within the family by observing sexual acts involving older children as well as adults. There is a corresponding lack of other substitute gratifications and other forms of impulse expression, since economic circumstances and mothers' attitudes do not permit the gratification of dependent and childlike needs. 4) Dating is less permitted than in middle-class homes because of the expectation that it is likely to result in sex relations. 5) There is pressure within the peer group to have sex relations, and it is considered the way to prove that one is a female and is attractive to males. 6) There are frequent misconceptions regarding the reproductive process, such as a) pregnancy will not occur at time of first intercourse, b) pregnancy will occur only when intercourse occurs during menstruation, or c) only when the boy is older.[18]

In our own work thus far with lower socio-economic families in which a girl gets pregnant, we have seen some, but not all, of these attitudes occurring in white as well as Negro families. A key differential factor appears to be the more established responsibility of the father in the middle-class families, whether white or Negro, and the greater expectations from him, and correspondingly from young peer males, for authority, control and for satisfactions other than sex.

The girl brought up in a rather strict middle-class home who becomes an unmarried mother may tend to be, on the average, emotionally sicker than the girl who comes from a more permissive lower-class home and becomes an unmarried mother. The circumstances of illegitimate pregnancy in middle-class white families typically bring additional stress to already highly conflictual family relationships. The girl may withdraw further from family ties and from outside friendships. She often hides the fact of her pregnancy from one parent and sometimes from both. The home, instead of being a haven during this period of stress, is experienced as a place of exile — the family feels that the girl should "hide" from the community and exist in oblivion until the pregnancy is terminated. It is clear that there is an acute need for counseling with the whole family in regard to their attitudes and roles in this problem. It is also clear that when the girl comes to an agency for help she should be encouraged more often than occurs in current practice to face the problem openly with her parents and family, rather than to hide it from them. Loesch and Greenberg conclude that, following termination of their pregnancies, the majority of unwed mothers re-enter the world having made little emotional change, remaining still in conflict with their families and capable only of dependent, or hostile, or chaotic relationships with men.[22]

Most psychoanalytic studies emphasize the unconscious "purpose" of the act of becoming pregnant. Although the girl does not plan consciously and intentionally to bear an out-of-wedlock child, she does act in such a way that this becomes the almost inevitable result. After she is pregnant, she often continues to behave as though she were not. The act of insemination is described by Young as a dissociated episode in the lives of the girls: "They conceive without knowing it, and as it were from no one; they bear and deliver as easily as the most fortunate of their married sisters, but they relinquish the new-born child to their mothers"[20] as a gift they hope she will accept. Characteristically, the mother is ambivalent about accepting the gift. The girls' strong, unconscious need to become pregnant is motivated by the need for a love object they never had. The longing for a baby is a dominant unconscious fantasy in the sexual acting out, although the girl may consciously believe she does not want to get pregnant. This longing for a baby may be considered to represent the unconscious wish to have a child with the mother, and is essentially an undoing of a disappointment in the mother; the mother-child unit thus becomes re-established by proxy. Greenberg, Loesch and Lakin found that the pregnancies frequently appear to occur subsequent to the loss of an important love object by the girl – a death of a parent, or separation from a boyfriend or a significant relative, loss of a valued job, and so on. The emotional state during pregnancy is also often dominated consciously by the girl's conflict over the coming loss of her future infant.[23]

Observations from Family Treatment of Families with Sexually Delinquent Girls

We have conducted family therapy in the special demonstration and training project at Philadelphia Psychiatric Center with a group of families with sexually acting-out adolescent girls. We have also conducted family therapy with a group of families with either adolescent schizophrenic girls or adolescent schizophrenic boys. These two experiences have afforded us an opportunity to develop some impressions regarding the differences and similarities between these two types of families. Since our therapeutic contact with the families of sexually acting-out girls was of shorter duration and perhaps of lesser depth than that with the schizophrenic families, our impressions, listed below, must be considered as only tentative hypotheses which deserve more careful and controlled evaluation:

1. We do not see in the sexually delinquent families the intense and overwhelming pathological dyadic relationship and symbiosis between the mother and child that we see in the schizophrenic family. The schizophrenic child has less capacity to break out of the symbiosis and to form real or intimate relationships with peers on the outside. The delinquent perhaps can also relate somewhat more simultaneously to both mother and father in a triadic relationship, at least in a tentative way, than can the schizophrenic. If there is more of a real marriage between the parents in the acting-out family and a less complete emotional divorce, then it follows that there will be less freeing of the generational lines, and that a less intense and pervasive symbiotic bind will develop between the mother and daughter. It appears that the fathers of the sexually acting-out girls are able to give their daughters something which the schizophrenics' fathers are not able to. Perhaps the key difference is that the former treat their daughters more as though they were real people. The schizophrenic daughters often cannot obtain any confirmation of themselves or their feelings from their parents.

2. The parental marriages in both types of families can be characterized by intense conflict. Nevertheless there seems to be more hope in the marriages of the acting-out families, in that they are still struggling to work out their differences, whereas the parents of the schizophrenics

THE FAMILY AND FEMALE DELINQUENCY

seem more resigned to their schism and to their hostile feelings. Prior to marriage, the parents of the acting-out families appear to have had some degree of satisfying relatedness to the community; but their marriage and the appearance of children were sometimes regarded as unhappy interruptions of those earlier rewarding experiences.

3. The acting-out families are livelier and more mobile, less predictable and repetitive, less stereotyped and are not as frightened by sex. Indeed, in some of our "delinquent" families where the girl's sexual promiscuity was not very extreme, the instability in the family organization was not very marked. The schizophrenic families often appear more funereal and "dead," and sex is often a forbidden, frightening thing to them. In addition to the feeling of an underlying reservoir of loss, mourning, and resignation, some of the schizophrenic families are just plain boring. This is the result of massive denial, repression, superficiality and rigidity. (This is consistent with the finding of Meyers and Roberts, who report that their female schizophrenic patients, regardless of class status, were sexually inhibited, and their female neurotic character patients were sexually "hyperactive, which represented a rebellion against the strictness and control of parents."[24]) We also agreed here with the finding of the Stabenau study that the schizophrenic child is more "inactive" than the delinquent.[25] At one level the parents of schizophrenics want the child to be inactive, conforming and suppressed. However, at another level in some of these "dead" families, the schizophrenic child represents the life or the "id" of the family, and the parents need this for their own pleasure.

4. Part of the reason for the above difference is that the fathers in the acting-out families have more and somewhat livelier relationships in the outside world than the fathers in the schizophrenic families. They are generally more worldly, interesting to talk to, have a wider range of interests, interact more spontaneously in the treatment, and are not as withdrawn, vague, and concealing. The family system is thus more open and more people are allowed to interact not only with the father but with all family members. Because they have more to do with the outside world, the acting-out families may not have the excessively important and influential "peripheral persons" which many schizophrenic families have and depend on. These latter families form pathological dyadic relationships with such a significant peripheral person.

5. The fathers of acting-out girls may tend to be more overtly aggressive, spontaneous, and labile in affect expression, with temper outbursts and rages, than the schizophrenic fathers (particularly fathers of male schizophrenics), many of whom we have described as "cardboard" fathers. They can become punitive, authoritarian, restrictive, and critical towards their daughters. This overt behavior may cover feelings of inferiority and underlying passive-dependent wishes toward their wives and daughters, but nevertheless the overt behavior may be aggressive. We did not find as much difference in regard to the assertiveness and the aggression of the mothers in the two groups of families as we did in regard to the fathers.

6. The delinquent girl, not having had the shared past of a crippling symbiotic relationship with her mother, and not having been arrested at the level of the submissive, inert child as has the schizophrenic girl, finds her status with her father too much that of a peer or rival with her mother to remain comfortably at home. Consequently, her rebelling and acting-out outside of the family in an aggressive sexual fashion serves to shore up the incest taboo.

The Oedipal involvement of the daughter with the father has a more real quality here and does not appear in a pseudo or fantasy fashion as it does between the schizophrenic girl and her father. In the acting-out families the parents have less delay of impulse gratification. They are more prone to have conscious fantasies of acting-out sexually. While the parents of the schizophrenics may not admit these fantasies into consciousness, the family acts as if, should they wait long enough, sex and other pleasures will be delivered within the family unit. One does not have to look outside; in fact it is "taboo" to look outside, the reverse of what is considered normal.

The incest threat is probably reacted to differently in the two types of families, and we do not know the combination of subtle factors which causes the delinquent girl or boy to run away from the family and from the incest threat and to act out while the schizophrenic remains stuck at home and preoccupied, consciously or unconsciously, with his incest fantasies.

7. The roles of "badness" and "madness" in the family derive from tendencies which the parents either had themselves in their early life, or feared having, and which they defensively denied in themselves, and now project onto their offspring. The "good sibling" of the delinquent child, who, because of their tendency to dichotomize and oversimplify is unrealistically idealized by his parents, may be analogous to the "well sibling" in the family of the schizophrenic. Accordingly, the "good sibling" deserves special study and should be made a part of the family's therapeutic commitment.

8. In the schizophrenic case the family, particularly the mother, tends to dwell on symptomatology and on helping the sick or problem child. It may be that the presence of symptoms seals the symbiosis and that, as long as symptoms can be talked about, the symbiosis is fortified. In the acting-out families there may be less of a need to continue the disturbing behavior over a long period of time, or to continue talking about it in treatment sessions. We believe that, since the acting-out is a bid for attention and results from the child doubting the parents' interest in her, the family's coming to treatment might make the acting-out less necessary.

We postulate that the family image in the schizophrenic families is distorted or defective. The family image in the delinquent family may also be to some extent distorted but, more specifically, there may be a deficit, an absence of an adequate family image, a lack of a consciousness among the family members of themselves as constituting an integrated family unit. Each member of the family finds himself at a particular level of arrested development and immaturity beyond which the family cannot foster growth.

Stabenau et al reported that delinquent families, in a systematic comparison with schizophrenic families and normal families, manifested more loose, unstable family organization, shifting of family roles, under-control of affect, open conflict among family members, artificial affect, and superficial and impersonal parent-child interaction. "The demand was for expedient action, and when the parental 'standards' were not met, the child was automatically rejected."[25]

REFERENCES

1. Blos, Peter. Three Typical Constellations in Female Delinquency. Chap. 10 in *Family Dynamics and Female Sexual Delinquency*. O. Pollak and A. S. Friedman, eds. Palo Alto: Science and Behavior Books, Inc., 1969, pp. 78-86.
2. 50th Annual Report of County Court of Philadelphia, M. L. Matt, ed. Department of Statistics and Research, Philadelphia, 1963, p. 116.
3. Robinson, S., What is Delinquency? Chap. I in *Delinquency: Its Nature and Control*. New York: Henry Holt and Co., 1960, pp. 8-9.
4. Block, H. A. and Flynn, F. T. *Delinquency: The Juvenile Offender*. New York: Random House, 1956, p. 27.
5. Annual Report, Sleighton Farm School for Girls, Darlington, Pa., 1961, pp. 7-11.
6. Butman, J. W. Summary, Conclusions, and Implications. Chapter in *The Social, Psychological and Behavioral World of the Teen-Age Girl*, a final report to the Department of Health, Education and Welfare, Social Security Administration, Institute for Social Research, University of Michigan, June, 1965, pp. 152-158.
7. Monachesi, E. D. and Hathaway, S. R. *Analyzing and Predicting Juvenile Delinquency*. Minneapolis: University of Minnesota Press, 1953, pp. 38-53.
8. Dame, et al. Conflict in Marriage Following Premarital Pregnancy. *Amer. J. Orthopsychiat.* 35:407, 1965.
9. Gehrke, S. and Kirshenbaum, M. Survival Patterns in Family Conjoint Therapy. *Family Process* 6:67-80, 1967.
10. Giffin, M., Johnson, A., and Litin, E. The Transmission of Superego Defects on the Family. Chap. 50 in *The Family*, N. Bell and E. Vogel, eds. Glencoe, Ill.: The Free Press, 1960, pp. 634-635.
11. Szurek, S. Some Impressions from Clinical Experience with Delinquents. In *Searchlights on Delinquency*, E. Eissler, ed. New York: International Universities Press, Inc., 1949, pp. 125-127.
12. Johnson, A. and Szurek, S. The Genesis of Anti-Social Acting Out in Children and Adults. *Psychoanal. Quart.* 21:322-343, 1952.
13. Bychowski, G. Object Relationships in Women. Scientific Proceedings, *J. Amer. Psychoanal. Assoc.* 9:580-581, 1961.
14. Kaufman, I., Peck, A., and Taguiri, C. The Family Constellation and Overt Incestous Relations Between Father and Daughter. *Amer. J. Orthopsychiat.* 24:266, 1954.
15. Robey, A., Rosenwald, R. J., Snell, J. E., and Lee, R. E. The Runaway Girl: A Reaction to Family Stress. *Amer. J. Orthopsychiat.* 34:4, 1964.
16. Ernst, C., et al. An Experiment in the Psychiatric Treatment of Promiscuous Girls. Annual Report of the Department of Public Health, San Francisco, Calif., 1945, pp. 19-20.
17. Herzog, Elizabeth. Families Out of Wedlock. Chap. 7 in *Family Dynamics and Female Sexual Delinquency*, O. Pollak and A. S. Friedman, eds. Palo Alto: Science and Behavior Books, Inc., 1969, pp. 64-77.

18. Visotsky, H. M. A. Community Project for Unwed Pregnant Adolescents. Chap. 8 in *Family Dynamics and Female Sexual Delinquency*, O. Pollak and A. S. Friedman, eds. Palo Alto: Science and Behavior Books, Inc., 1969, pp. 78-86.
19. Jones, W. C., Meyers, J. K., and Borgotta,, E. F. Social and Psychological Factors in Status Decisions of Unmarried Mothers. *Marriage and Family Living* 24(3):228-230, August, 1962.
20. Young, L. R. Personality Patterns in Unmarried Mothers. *The Family XXVI:* 296-303, December, 1945.
21. Vincent, Clark E. *Unmarried Mothers*. New York: The Free Press, 1961, Chap. 5, pp. 106-120.
22. Loesch, J. G. and Greenberg, N. H. Some Specific Areas of Conflict Observed During Pregnancy: A Comparative Study of Unmarried Pregnant Women. *Amer. J. Orthopsychiat.* 32:628-630, July, 1962.
23. Greenberg, N. H. J., Loesch, J., and Lakin, M. Life Situations Associated with Onset of Pregnancy. *Psychosomatic Med.* 21:296, 310, 1959.
24. Meyers, J. K. and Roberts, B. H. *Family and Class Dynamics in Mental Illness.* New York: Wiley, 1959, pp. 123-124.
25. Stabenau, James R., Tupin, Joe, Werner, Martha, and Pollin, W. A. Comparative Study of Families of Schizophrenics, Delinquents, and Normals. *Psychiatry* 28(1):58-59, February, 1965.

The rationale and the plan of the treatment method

Alfred S. Friedman

**Chapter
3**

There is impressive evidence that delinquent adolescents fail to respond to individual psychotherapy and other traditional forms of treatment. Many professional workers have observed the difficulty of establishing a constructive therapeutic relationship with these youths, and it has been postulated that the cause lies in their not having developed any relationship of trust early in life with an important other person.

The results of using traditional psychoanalytically oriented individual psychotherapy with the teen-age promiscuous and sexually delinquent girl have generally not been impressive, and the course of the transference and countertransference has often been precarious. The girl acts out, misses appointments, and handles the stress of the treatment in the same way she always handled anxiety and tension – by running away. The therapist, particularly a male therapist, may feel empathy with her, but he often finds the one-to-one therapeutic relationship very difficult in the face of her seductive, impulsive, fickle, insincere, and vengeful behavior.

In general, methods and problems of treatment for the sexually delinquent girl have received much less attention than for the delinquent boy. In recent years, modifications of group psychotherapy and of group socialization programs have been used for the treatment of delinquent boys, and these, in a few instances, have been tried with sexually delinquent girls. Concurrently, there is a growing professional consensus that the treatment of juvenile delinquents is more likely to be successful if the parents are included in the treatment process and if a combination of psychological and environmental approaches is employed. The Surgeon General's Ad Hoc Committee on Planning for Mental Health Facilities stated in its 1961 report: "The treatment of juvenile delinquency should include work with the families since the program should remain child-centered and community oriented with as little disruption of a normal environmental situation as possible."[1] A conference of social welfare leaders in Westchester County, New York, declared that "parental delinquency must be treated for a long-term reduction in the incidence of teen-age deviant behavior."[2]

As far back as 1915, Healy stressed the etiological importance of the "family drama" in delinquency.[3] In the late fifties, Reiner and Kauf-

21

man studied and treated 80 parents of juvenile delinquents at
the Judge Baker Guidance Center in Boston.[4] They described the majority of the parents as having "impulse-ridden character disorders," and
they reported some success with their long-term casework and counseling approach to these difficult cases. They speculated that delinquency
is an attempt to deal with early deprivation and object-loss by striking
out at and taking from the environment. They saw their initial therapeutic goal as helping the delinquent and his parents to shift from
adjusting by denial of affect to awareness of an underlying depressive
action.

Nathan Ackerman has reported that while he, like others, found
the "delinquent" psychopathic adolescent virtually untreatable in isolation from his family and community, he could "successfully alleviate
psychopathic behavior in adolescents when oriented to it as a family
process, with the adolescent representing a symptom of the psychopathological warp of his family group, or a component of psychopathic
behavior in the family structure."[5] This conviction was derived from
clinical experience and obviously has yet to stand the test of a controlled evaluation.

Hallowitz has reported on a family group counseling project that
focused on "restoring damaged lines of communication" in 60 families of "character-disordered" boys from 12 to 16 years of age. About
half of the boys had been in Children's Court, and all of them had
been suspended from school. The approaches employed included:
1) Providing the family with extra support and reassurance at times
of crisis, 2) assisting the family to set realistic goals and to work co-
operatively toward them, 3) uncovering long-suppressed hostile feelings of the members toward each other, and 4) helping the members
to understand and resolve their feelings about each other instead of
attacking and counter-attacking.[6]

An evaluation of the milieu and family therapy program for delinquent boys at Wiltwyck School was conducted by McCord et al,
who speculated that the various features of the treatment program
operated to achieve positive change in the following ways: 1) Adult-
child rapport facilitated the capacity for increased internalized guilt;
2) permissiveness decreased aggression toward authority; 3) group
influence increased behavioral control; 4) individual counseling increased the boys' realistic self-perception.[7]

Family Therapy and Delinquency

The rationale for employing the conjoint family treatment approach
in cases where the presenting problem is the delinquent sexual behavior of an adolescent girl is quite the same as that which has been
developed for treating a wide variety of other individual symptoms
and family problems. Family therapy finds its explanation in family
system theory. The sexual delinquency of a daughter is assumed to be

an expression of a particular combination of family system disfunctions or pathological family dynamics. It is helpful in our orientation to therapeutic work if we focus on the family as a system that should give satisfaction to its members in the here and now as well as preparing them for the future.

In family therapy the family is the unit of treatment, and the counseling or treatment of the delinquent girl is considered to be an integral part of the total family group treatment. Since the term "family therapy" has been used loosely in the literature to connote a variety of therapy arrangements, we define it as a procedure in which all the members of the nuclear family of procreation, as a minimum, meet and work together with the same therapist or co-therapy team, and in which the designated family problem member is not seen in separate individual therapy except possibly for a special reason. The terms "family therapy," "conjoint family treatment," "family group treatment," and "family unit treatment" have all been used to designate the same approach and to distinguish it from "family oriented" collaborative forms of treatment in which individual members of the family are seen separately by either the same or a different therapist.

The following schema, suggested by V. Freeman, is useful for categorizing the possible types of approaches and techniques that could be referred to as "family treatment": 1) Treatment of the "patient" in the presence of other family members, using traditional analytically oriented psychotherapy and focusing specifically, but not exclusively, on the patient. 2) Treatment of the family group as *individuals,* with content focused on overt member interactions. There may or may not be a specific designated "patient." 3) Treatment of the family group as *individuals,* but with the additional use of group process to facilitate insight development. This approach would most closely approximate traditional *group psychotherapy.* 4) Treatment of the family group *as individuals,* using group process both interpretively and manipulatively. This approach would most closely approximate traditional *social group work.* 5) Treatment of the family as a group, the group system itself being the object of therapy — consequently, there can be no therapeutically designated "patient." In this last approach, group problems and group goals are of *primary* concern and family system process is the predominant methodologic frame of reference, with the intent being to exclude the "one-to-one" therapist-individual interventions.[8]

In addition to the parents and children, the therapy unit membership may include grandparents, aunts, uncles, or any significant relatives or nonrelatives who share the living experience together under one roof. We have also found that there often are "significant others" or "significant peripheral persons" who exercise influential and controlling roles in relation to a family and are an important part of the family system. At appropriate times, we include such a significant person in the family therapy sessions, whether he is a married sibling, a close friend of the family, a boyfriend of the mother, the "delinquent" adolescent girl's boyfriend, the family attorney or clergyman, etc.

Many therapists now realize that, when they treat a single individual, a part of the total problem is not visible, and that sometimes their client or patient will not or cannot change if the family does not do likewise. Individual treatment may bog down because the primary emotional investment of the client lies outside the treatment situation, in the family relationships, and not in the therapeutic "transference." In some families it appears that the designated problem member is needed by the family as a "scapegoat," and that the delinquent acting-out may serve a purpose in maintaining a particular system of family relationships.

Adelaide Johnson and S. Szurek have developed the thesis (documented clinically from their work with parents and their adolescent children with behavior problems) that the parents' unwitting sanction, indirect encouragement, or provocation is a major cause of, and the specific stimulus for anti-social behavior.[9] Parents sometimes express their poorly inhibited anti-social impulses by unwittingly and unconsciously provoking their offspring into delinquent behavior which they then overtly find most objectionable. Deprivation, neglect, lack of interest, lack of parenting, rejection, and intensely immature relationships and attachments of parents to children and of parents to grandparents have been observed to exist in cases of adolescent behavior disorder and social maladjustment.

The inadequacies and defects in the delinquent adolescent's social values and social perceptions, in his self-image, and in his ways of communicating and relating are derived, through identification, modeling, learning, and other socialization processes, in large part from characteristics of the family social system. What he learns in the family may conflict with the mores of society, which are rapidly changing today. The adolescent, by engaging in or experimenting with new behavior, often starts opening the family to the culture and, although he is presented as the problem, he may turn out not to be the most difficult or the "sickest" member of the family.

In the family system view, the presenting behavior problem is not considered to be the "fault" of the delinquent child or due to the mother's "bad influence" or to the father's inadequacy or lack of role responsibility. Instead, the whole family system is viewed as being disordered or deficient; the whole system must be influenced to change if any of the elements are to change. In a time of social change, rigid and closed family systems are particularly vulnerable and are in special need of openness to the culture.

The stance or orientation which we are taking here is that a substantial part of the problem derives from elements in the *social setting*. We make the assumption that sexual behavior, whether symptomatic or not, is learned, and can be unlearned or replaced, if indicated, by interventions within the total social context. Accordingly, the treatment model we apply is not the traditional medical one of attempting to cure the symptoms of a particular girl, but rather to engage in operations to enhance the functioning of the small social system, which includes the family and relevant peripheral individual and community influences on the family. (We realize that the relevant peer social system, which has its own standards, also has a powerful influence on the adolescent girl who is our designated problem, but we do not have her extra-familial peer group available for treatment. A broader social network treatment approach, such as reported recently by Speck, might have the advantage of treating some of the members of the girl's relevant peer group, either together with her family or in a separate setting.[10]) This social matrix or small social community system is perceived and dealt with as a unit or as an organic whole instead of treating separate isolated individuals. The goal of the treatment is not necessarily to influence the individuals to approximate some traditional ideal of a "normal," socially-adjusted (i.e., conforming) model, but to enable them to live more comfortably and effectively by pragmatic rearrangements of the social context, plus, hopefully, some new understanding and perceptions of additional options by the members.

The method focuses on the interactional effects of the emotional disturbances and social deficits within the family group. In this concept, parents are not regarded as sources of contagion or as destructive influences, but are approached as responsible agents and encouraged to apply whatever strengths they have in a positive way to make the system work more satisfactorily. Rather than confronting the parents with the part of the problem which they might be contributing, consciously or unconsciously, on a neurotic basis, to the maintenance of the child's self-defeating behavior, one can support and encourage the parents to approach the child more positively, to institute changes in the home, and to learn new techniques of behavior shaping and control.

The Home Setting

In many of these situations, family group interviews in the home are the quickest, most effective way of assessing the situation. Friends and neighbors and local community agencies who have had contact with the family can also be interviewed. We have found that working with the whole family in their own home adds a new dimension of reality and meaning to the therapeutic experience. The therapist, as a participant-observer, can experience directly the emotional climate of the home and see through to the underlying unverbalized family problems. Families are more relaxed and natural in their homes, and usually drop some of the facade of adjustment which they present to the outside community and in the doctor's office. As the therapist observes the family within its usual life-space and surroundings, he is presented with rich material for a quick understanding of the dynamic forces that act upon, and the problems that beset, its members. We have held sessions in every room in the house — kitchen, dining room, living room, bedroom, bathroom, and on the patio outside the house.

Henry justified observing and treating families with psychotic children in their own homes in a challenging way: "The parents, blinded by their own disorientation, confusion, and misery, sometimes half mad themselves, made dreadful mistakes; but only an observer who sees these with his own eyes can really know exactly how the tragedy was prepared. How can a parent who is psychologically blind perceive what he did to his child? How can he recall for a psychiatrist his innumerable acts, especially since most people are unaware of what they are doing?"[11]

The home setting for family treatment has the advantage of more easily involving the fathers and all other family members in the treatment. Often the fathers and stepfathers of delinquents have abdicated the responsible authority role in the family. When the treatment team comes to the home, some fathers may at first feel uneasy about being faced with their family problems, but we have found that they eventually become involved actively in the treatment.

Treatment of culturally deprived lower-class families obviously requires a flexibility of role adaptation by the middle-class therapist and an acceptance of the family's way of life. This can be expressed by such procedures as bringing a six-pack of beer to the family therapy session and relaxing over a can of beer with the father while involving him in a discussion of the family problems. In working with such families it is often best to keep verbal interpretations and abstract conceptualizing to a minimum. Some of the essential elements of the treatment approach are: Modeling and demonstration of constructive role fulfillment, activity, intervention, guiding family discussion, and assisting in solving of reality problems.

It is our assumption that the family treatment approach can 1) help the delinquent girl control her self-defeating promiscuity or cope more effectively with an out-of-wedlock pregnancy, 2) achieve a more adequate family life, and 3) make illegitimate pregnancy and sexual delinquency less likely to reoccur. We have found that family treatment can in some cases be conducted successfully with multi-problem, so-called "hard-core" families of low socioeconomic status and low education. For example, we found that, in many cases where the family continued in treatment for several months or longer, the girl's maladjustive sexual acting-out either stopped completely or diminished considerably. We hypothesized that the parents' commitment to make a serious effort in treatment was perceived hopefully by the girl as their intention to be more responsible parents, to take more of an interest in her, and this made it less necessary for her to run away or act out.

Referrals and Scheduling of Treatment

The referrals of cases and families to this treatment demonstration project came mostly from the Women's Division of the Philadelphia County Court and from a number of private community family service and children's service agencies. Since our trainee group were mainly senior level social case workers employed as supervisors in family and children's agencies, they made many of the referrals themselves from their own agencies.

In most instances we accepted cases only where the family was intact and living together, and where both of the parents or step-parents of the designated problem girl agreed to participate in the treatment. We usually had all the siblings included in the treatment unit, but on occasion we agreed to make an exception of an older married sibling, a sibling who was away at college, or of very young siblings where it was particularly difficult for the family to bring them along. This might be the case with a poor family without a car who would have to bring the young childern to the clinic on public transportation if we were not conducting the treatment in the home. We preferred to have the young children in for diagnostic purposes, particularly to see how the parents related to them and handled them, even if these young children became restless during the session and disrupted the discussion.

While a number of middle socioeconomic level families were included in the sample, the majority were "working class" — lower-middle and lower socioeconomic level families. The fees charged to the families for treatment sessions were based on ability to pay and were most often small or nominal. No fee was charged to a number of the poorer families in the sample.

Our plan of treatment was to schedule regular weekly sessions of one and one-half hours' duration in the clinic or in the home. Special additional arrangements were made as required to guide the family in the handling of an acute problem or crisis. In some cases where the girl was pregnant, the treatment was transferred to the maternity home (Booth Memorial Hospital) when she was admitted to the hospital, usually during the seventh month of pregnancy. We have even initiated family treatment in the Detention Home of the Juvenile Court of Philadelphia when the girl was retained there before coming to trial for sexually delinquent behavior. It is advantageous to initiate work with a family during a crisis precipitated by the girl's delinquent behavior (e.g., after her arrest by the police), since most families are anxious for change at that time.

In the initial session, the concept of the problem family, as distinct from the problem individual, is discussed, and the composition of the family treatment group is determined. We attempt to orient the family to the ideas of working as a whole family on the solution of their problems, accepting responsibility for self and for appropriate family roles, and initiating new, more positive, future-oriented goals for the family.

Therapeutic Use of Social Authority

What should the policy be with regard to parents of sexually delinquent girls who are not interested in the offer of family treatment, who do not see it as an opportunity to get help, and who do not wish to participate in an effort to help their problem daughters? We have thus far actually had relatively few families refuse treatment, particularly when home visits were offered. But resistance to the recommendation of family treatment does occur. Our recommendation is usually presented in a brief, simple, matter-of-fact suggestion that the whole family come in to see us or be at home to talk over the problem. If this fails, or too many alibis are offered by the family, we sometimes consider invoking the authority of the Court and initiating the family treatment on a compulsory basis.

It is a generally accepted principle that efforts to force psychotherapy on individuals are inappropriate and useless. There is supposed to be an intrinsic contradiction between the motivation necessary for psychotherapeutic change and enforced treatment, whether primarily in the interests of society, the family, or the girl. Nevertheless, when we ignored this principle and experimented with having the Juvenile Court order families to participate in family treatment with us, we were pleasantly surprised. We found that several families who started treatment on this basis fairly soon developed positive therapeutic relationships and worked consciously on their problems.

The family therapy approach may pose new questions for judges regarding their responsibility in ordering treatment in lieu of punishment. An illustration of this is where an excellent Juvenile Court judge and a probation service entered into an unwitting collusion with a mother and daughter to keep the daughter's sexual delinquency a secret from the father, although the details of the delinquent acts had already been discussed in open court. The mother feared that the father would blame her and would punish the daughter if he were informed. The court in this case would not give us permission to invite the father to participate in family treatment unless we obtained permission from the mother and her attorney. Had we addressed the offer of family treatment to both parents, by mail, rather than telephoning it to the mother, we would have unwittingly exposed to the father the collusion which his wife and daughter had entered into with the attorney and the Court to keep him in the dark.

Our Family Therapy Method and Techniques

Family Process, the first journal devoted exclusively to family dynamics and family treatment, made its debut in 1962. Haley, the editor, in his lead article, compared nine different approaches or "schools" of family treatment. He identified these with such descriptive and humorous names as "The Dynamic Psychodynamic School of Family Diagnosis" (Ackerman), "The Dignified School" (Bell), "The Great Mother School" (Satir), "The Stonewall School" (Jackson), "The Brotherly Love School" (our Philadelphia group), "The Eyebrows School,"

"The Multiplication School," "The Total Push in the Tall Country School" (Galveston "Multiple-Impact Project"), and "The Hospitalize the Whole Damn Maelstrom School" (Bowen).[12]

In his book, *The Psychodynamics of Family Life,* Ackerman probably made the most substantial early contribution toward developing a rationale for family treatment and toward outlining the issues and methods of family treatment. He has described his therapeutic role variously as "playing an active and continually changing part in the stormy processes of family interaction," acting as referee in conflict, "playing favorites," "protecting weaker from stronger members," "undercutting defenses," etc. "The therapist is observer, participant, supporter, activator, challenger, and reintegrator of family processes." It is clear that Ackerman takes the center of the stage as a catalyst, making the family react to him as he reacts to the family, and taking complete and active control and direction of a family therapy session.[13]

Wynne describes the family therapist as needing to be active and aggressive enough to define and insist upon conditions that will allow family members to take the risk of free communication.[14]

Haley's description of his early work with Jackson in Palo Alto emphasized the manipulation of control as a technique in family therapy. The therapist must gain control of what happens in the therapy, and he does this by outmaneuvering the family, by posing paradoxical questions, by disinvolving himself of any responsibility, and by passive silence. He frustrates the attempts of family members to form coalitions with him, and he instructs the most actively controlling member of the family to take charge of the situation, thus making it impossible for that member, if he follows the instruction, to be in control of the therapist.[15]

Our own therapeutic techniques have usually not been quite as actively intervening and authoritative as those described by Ackerman[16] or as controlling and manipulative as those described by Haley and Jackson.[15] We permit or stimulate, as the case requires, considerable free interaction among family members, and do not keep the attention of the family focused on ourselves.

Although we have employed active techniques and have at times intervened in the family's relationships, some of our group have been classified, in a survey of family therapists by Beels and Ferber,[17] as being "reactors" rather than "conductors" in their therapeutic approach, since we do not appear to be controlling, directing, and manipulating the therapy session as much as those "conductors" or "star" performers mentioned above. The "conductors" have nearly always preferred to work solo, while we have tended to work in co-therapy teams.

The main operational procedure and dynamic of our therapeutic work, as described in our earlier book, has been along interactional and transactional lines, with analysis of family roles, expectations, misunderstanding, and delineation of the pathological family system.[18] Our rationale for engaging in a rather long-term form of family treatment is that we want to provide more than temporary symptomatic or be-

havioral change or relief from a family crisis, and do more than just
getting the pressure or focus of the family problems transferred from
one member to another member.

Haley has referred to our approach as the "Brotherly Love School,"
not just to identify us as Philadelphians but because we have gone
to families in their homes, have risked being on unfamiliar ground, and
have participated in family discussions in an empathic and supportive
way.[12] He suggests that the effects of the therapists' visits may tend
to persist — in that the therapists remain as "ghosts in the house" after
a session is over. (Whether we are working in the home or in the clinic,
some of our co-therapist teams do tend to become actively and em-
pathically involved with the families. This entering into, or getting
caught up in, the family transactional system provides therapeutic
leverage, but also poses some difficulties. The relative advantages and
disadvantages of such an involved approach can perhaps best be understood from the actual case reports of family therapy process to be
found in subsequent chapters of this book.)

Among the varied and flexible therapeutic methods and therapist
roles utilized by our group are: Neutral observing, reflecting, active
empathic participation, communication expert, problem-solving expert,
interpreting, confronting, and direct authoritative leadership. We may
also engage at times in uncovering the continuing effects on the current
family relationships of developmental crises, past conflicts, and family
myths from the parents' early lives in their families of origin.

Analysis of a fantasy, dream, or childhood memory often leads to
diminished denial and projection into a "here and now" family communication impasse. For example, a mother hounds her daughter for
chatting with boys. After the mother recalls how she herself had once
stopped talking with boys to regain favor with her adolescent girlfriends who had ostracized her for telling "dirty stories" she had heard
from boys, the mother's behavior changed. She dropped her denial in
this impasse, recognized her hostility toward her daughter's sexuality,
and no longer projected her problem on her daughter.

When a family's anger, tension, and hysteria escalates, the therapist
may temporarily adopt the role of a superego figure and authoritatively
restore order out of chaos. He may also give attention to real-life environmental problems, task assignments, job counseling, development
of motivational incentives and rewards, etc. In nonverbal families he
may facilitate expressive and interpersonal skills.

Our rationale for employing a variety of active techniques is that
these may speed up the therapeutic change process; and also that the
dysfunctional family habits and interactional cycles have an ingrained
and conditional character whose modification requires considerable
investments of time and effort on the part of the therapists. We join in
with the family as empathic participant observers, and do not always
strive to stay outside the boundaries of family life and interaction as
such therapists as J. Bell indicate that they attempt to do. We would
not agree with Bell that the therapist should always "relate to the

identified family group so as to strengthen the boundaries surrounding the group as a group."[19]

In our orientation toward positive family group goals, we use techniques that aim at: Making group goals explicit, affecting compromise and integration, improving communication within the family, helping members to express feelings, helping members to listen and to hear, correcting distortion, acting as a communication bridge, reflecting feelings of members toward each other, focusing attention on nonverbal reactions, providing feedback and mirroring, verbalizing for the group, and giving information. We make no attempt to adopt a uniform method or treatment technique to be applied to all families and adhered to by all therapists; this would be stultifying. The therapist makes constructive use of his own personality, his feelings, and his creativity. To the chaotic or destructive family he presents himself as a definite integrated personality and a factor to be reckoned with. To the stereotyped or apathetic family he presents the stimulating, involved, challenging, and exploring aspects of his personality for the family to respond to and deal with. We have attempted this intensive, flexible, and comprehensive approach in working with the families of sexually acting-out girls.

System Manipulation Family Therapy Versus Affective Family Therapy

There are "system purists" in the family therapy field who believe that one can't help an individual family member to change unless one first changes the whole family system, and that therefore one should work only with the total family system at once, and that one should not split the family up into individual members or dyads, to work with them part of the time, even within the total context of a family-oriented therapy plan. The question may resolve itself into which is the prior necessary condition to improvement. Can an individual family member who has been helped by the family therapist to understand his part in maintaining a dysfunctional family pattern initiate a change in that family pattern by changing his part in it, or will all family members have to be changed simultaneously before it is possible for an individual member to change? This may be an over-statement, and may not reflect accurately the way "system purists" and communicating theory system-oriented family therapists actually work with families.

Perhaps it is not possible to work with the whole family system, except for a small part of the therapeutic time, without first fitting together the parts of the jigsaw puzzle by working with the pieces — the individuals, the dyadic relationships, etc. To conceptualize a particular pattern of family dysfunction or a disturbed family system is one thing, to treat the family at every moment as though it were one biological organism is another and is unreal. We found fairly often that we could help the family member, whether a parent or a child, who was most emotionally mature and who was able to change, to make the first change. Then we had to support and encourage him not to regress to his former pattern when the other family members failed to reciprocate. Sometimes the change initiated by one member in response to the therapist eventually brought about a realignment of relationships and a new pattern in the family.

Changes in the family system, in the family as a unit, cannot in our view be separated from internal changes in each family member. This is like the question of whether an individual's behavior can improve before he changes his self-image, his internal attitude toward himself. Perhaps an individual who is forced, manipulated, or influenced to improve his behavior (as by rewards in behavior therapy approaches) will, as a result of experiencing this new success, improve his self-image. Thus the locus where the change is initiated can be either internal, in feelings, attitudes or insights, or external, in behavior or performance. The change, however, must have an effect in both places for it to be constructive and permanent, and without exacting some other cost from the individual. Accordingly, we cannot agree with those who believe that the solution to the problem lies solely in changing the living situation a person finds himself in, whether the family situation or the broader social situation, and that it is not necessary for the individual to change. We question whether the change in the system, which involves changes in the positions, roles, and stances of family members toward each other, can occur without involving internal changes in the individual members. We believe that the family therapist must be aware of the individuals' needs, and of what is needed to improve total family functioning. He must respect individual autonomy as well as family goals and family relationships.

Those who believe in working primarily by changing the family system by therapeutic manipulation also tend to work to improve channels of communication in the family by working with the "here and now" interaction to the exclusion of the intra-psychic, the past, affects, and fantasies. Our own therapy group did not take quite so extreme or restricted a position in its therapeutic approach. We probably did spend most of the session time in dealing with the "here and now" and with the interaction of the family, but we also did not shy away from using the intra-psychic expressions of feelings, the working through of key emotional conflicts and blocks, catharsis, and on occasion even fantasies and dreams. We were not interested in adapting psychoanalytic method to family therapy, or in maintaining allegiance to psychoanalytic doctrine. On the other hand, we had no need to rebel against psychoanalysis, and therefore to throw out old insights and methods which might be useful in a balanced, comprehensive family therapy approach, for the sake of just doing something new and different. We realize, however, that the unlearning process may be even more difficult for "old" therapists than the learning of new tricks, and perhaps we have a tendency to continue to do some of that with which we are familiar and comfortable. Nevertheless, we try to integrate what is relevant and useful from the old knowledge with the new concepts and new methods to achieve a balanced approach.

Frequently, a parent's disturbed reaction to a child's behavior is evoked by the parent's associating a problem or a feeling which he had in childhood toward his or her own parent over a similar issue. The affective release and insight which that parent experiences when encouraged by the therapist to recollect and relive the feelings associated with that early parent-child problem seem often to enable these parents to respond in a new way to their children's current behavior.

We do not know too much about what processes in family therapy actually cause change and make for improvement. Those who believe in system manipulation believe that change occurs when the therapist intervenes in certain ways to reorganize the family system, and that it is not necessary for the family members to know what is happening to them. These therapists do not believe that efforts to help family members understand themselves and how and why they relate to each other the way they do can make for change or accomplish anything toward improving the family situation or the lives of the individual members. In their view, it is more important that the therapist gain insight into what is dysfunctional in the family system than that the family members each gain insight. After achieving this insight he may use it to devise some prescription or manipulation for change in the family system such as a new role task arrangement, or negotiating a new contract, such as a different arrangement for the parents to work together in disciplining the children.

It is conceivable that the therapist's prescription or manipulation can induce new insight in the family members, if they adhere to it. Bell, for example, observed that after he made neutral observations of the nonverbal communication between family members, they did not become as defensive as when he made interpretations of their motives based on verbal content, and that after they became aware of how they were reacting nonverbally, they supplied their own "insight."[20] Beels and Ferber also described how action and change resulting in new affective levels of family interaction in therapy sessions might lead to insight more quickly than new insight would lead to change in family behavior patterns: "Whereas formerly we assumed that insight ultimately led to action by some unknown process, we have now concluded that action may be seen more fruitfully as coming before insight. Action has the primacy rather than insight. That is, insight and action do not take place in some parallel psychological processes, but insight is within the mainsteam of action. What is even more important, we have concluded that the action that leads to insight takes place with, for and because of others — that it is a process of and in a social group rather than of and especially within an isolated individual."[17]

Our own experience supports the idea that therapists' actions, interventions, and maneuvers can precede and lead to insight. We also have observed that focusing on the nonverbal behavior can frequently be more effective than restricting therapeutic attention to the verbal sphere, as Bell and Scheflen and others have observed.[20,21] We have not, however, had very much evidence as yet that action in the form of manipulation of family role relationships and task prescriptions has brought about a permanent improvement in family relationships when it was not accompanied by some corrective emotional experience between two or more family members and a new level of awareness. The following brief example may clarify this point:

An attractive 20-year-old girl, who was recovering from a psychotic episode and had recently returned home from the hospital, was having difficulty in getting out of bed and getting dressed in the morning. She was very anxious about resuming social relationships and about going out to look for a job. Her parents were involved in this anxiety, especially the mother, who felt that there would be some unknown terrible consequence or that the girl would regress and become psychotic again if she did not get up promptly each morning. The parents were afraid to leave the house and go to work while the girl was in bed. They would become angry and there was a major disturbance and scene in the home every morning. Essential to understanding this situation is the fact that both parents were poliomyelitis victims and were handicapped in their legs. They relied on their daughter, an only child, to run errands for them and to be their legs, so to speak. Her staying in bed also activated the unconscious envy and anger which they must have felt toward her and toward all persons with normal mobility. No amount of reassurance by me that the girl would not become psychotic again if she did not get out of bed in the morning would allay the parents' anxiety. After this situation had endured for two or three weeks I decided to use a therapeutic manipulation (according to the rationale given by Haley) — I instructed the girl to stay in bed as long as she could each day for a one-week period, and instructed the parents to support and encourage this effort, and not to try to get her out of bed. The result of this intervention was that by the third day the girl started to get out of bed promptly each morning, and initiated a well-planned campaign to get a good job for herself, in which she succeeded. Thus it appeared that the therapeutic action or manuever was effective whereas the prior effort to explore the feelings and the family pathological pattern related to the problem behavior did not succeed. There is, however, a sequel to this little story. The parents, particularly the mother, had become furious at me when I had given the instruction that the girl stay in bed all day. The mother had suppressed most of this anger at the time, as she felt she had no choice but to go along, and was genuinely looking for help in solving the problem. If the therapy had terminated at that point, the mother's anger, anxiety, and ambivalence regarding the therapist's collusion with her daughter might well have contributed to getting the daughter into a bind again over getting up in the morning, going out, and socializing. Since the therapy continued, the mother's anger at the therapist surfaced at a later time and we had the opportunity to work this affect through adequately.

REFERENCES

1. Surgeon General's Ad Hoc Committee, Planning of Facilities for Mental Health Services, U. S. Department of Health, Education and Welfare, Public Health Service, 1961, p. 11.
2. *The New York Times*, Vol. 112, #38, September 23, 1962, p. 72.
3. Healy, W. *The Individual Delinquent*. London: Heinemann, 1915, pp. 290-296.
4. Reiner, B. S. and Kaufman, I. *Character Disorders in Parents of Delinquents*. New York: Family Service Assn. of America, 1959, pp. 7-17.
5. Ackerman, N. Sexual Delinquency Among Middle-Class Girls. Chapter in *Family Dynamics and Female Sexual Delinquency*, O. Pollak and A. S. Friedman, eds. Palo Alto: Science and Behavior Books, Inc., 1969, pp. 45-50.
6. Hallowitz D. and Cutter, A. V. Diagnosis and Treatment of the Family Unit with Respect to the Character-Disordered Youngster. *J. Amer. Acad. Child Psychiat.* 1(4):610, October, 1962.
7. McCord, W. and McCord, J. *Psychopathology and Delinquency*. New York: Grune & Stratton, 1956, pp. 161-163.
8. Freeman, V. J. Differentiation of "Unit" Family Therapy. Approaches Prominent in the United States. *Int. J. Social Psychiat.*, Special Edition #2, pp. 35-46, August, 1964.
9. Johnson, A. and Szurek, S. The Genesis of Anti-Social Acting-Out in Children and Adults. *Psychoanal. Quart.* 21:322-343, 1952.
10. Speck, R. V. and Reuveni, U. Network Therapy — A Developing Concept. *Family Process* 8(2):182-191, September, 1969.
11. Henry, J. *Culture Against Man*. New York: Random House, 1963, p. 323.
12. Haley, J. Whither Family Therapy? *Family Process* 1:69-100, 1962.
13. Ackerman, N. W. *The Psychodynamics of Family Life: Diagnosis and Treatment of Family Relationships*. New York: Basic Books, Inc., 1958, pp. 274-307.
14. Wynne, L. C. The Study of Intrafamilial Alignments and Splits in Exploratory Family Therapy. In *Exploring the Base for Family Therapy*, N. W. Ackerman, ed. New York: Family Service Assn. of America, 1961, p., 102.
15. Haley, J. *Strategies of Psychotherapy*. New York: Grune & Stratton, 1963, Chaps. 6 and 7.
16. Ackerman, N. W. *Treating the Troubled Family*. New York: Basic Books, Inc., 1966, pp. 95-101.
17. Beels, C. C. and Ferber, A. Family Therapy: A View. *Family Process* 8(2): 293, September, 1969.
18. Friedman, A. S., *et al. Psychotherapy for the Whole Family*. New York: Springer Publishing Co., Inc., 1965, pp. 27-28.
19. Bell, J. E. A Theoretical Position for Family Group Therapy. *Family Process* 2:10, 1963.
20. Bell, J. E. Promoting Action Through New Insights: Some Theoretical Revisions from Family Group Therapy. Read at meetings of Amer. Psychol. Assn., Philadelphia, 1963. *Amer. Psychologist* 18:340, 1963.
21. Scheflen, A. E. The Significance of Posture in Communications Systems. *Psychiatry* 27:316-331, November, 1964.

Co-therapy as family therapy method and as a training method

Alfred S. Friedman

Chapter

4

We usually employed co-therapy teams. While it is possible to conduct family therapy solo we usually preferred having a partner, and felt that we did more effective work this way, particularly when working with a quite disturbed or chaotic family situation. Two therapists can support each other in finding meaning in a fragmented or disorganized sequence of family interaction, or by talking calmly with each other and with the family when there is intense anxiety or hostility in the family. Two therapists are also more able than one to devote attention to each family member as an individual person and to establish an empathic relationship with him or her.

In the co-therapy team approach, the interventive interaction is no longer limited to the relationship between therapist and client; it extends to interaction between therapist and therapist, and between therapy team and family. A team is less likely to be "swallowed up" by a disturbed family system, and the presence of a second therapist assists in checking countertransference reactions, whether positive, negative or ambivalent. A tightly integrated co-therapy team appears sometimes to be needed to counterbalance the force of an intensely interwoven family defense, or family pathology, system. This achieves a more adequate balance and is more like the traditional one-to-one therapy situation. As a disturbed family pattern of relationships continues to go round and round in its vicious cycle, the single therapist sometimes finds it difficult to see where the main locus or source of the problem is, and each contending or conflictual family member begins to sound completely reasonable in his attitude and behavior.

We prefer that the co-therapy team be composed of a male and a female therapist, as this provides a more natural model for identification for the therapeutic working relationship of the two team members. Each new heterosexual co-therapist pairing is like a new marriage, providing the opportunity for a new adventure in developing a relationship of intimacy and trust. If the co-therapists are eager to explore with each other, in an open-minded, nondefensive way, all the possible ways of understanding and treating a particular family, the work experience can be stimulating. Sonne and Lincoln, two members of our group, have described how, as a heterosexual co-therapy team, they cooperated in using their respective maleness and femaleness in helping a mother and a father work through some marital problems that were related to problems they had earlier had with *their* parents.[1] However, sex difference in the team is not required to obtain multiple mother and father transference reactions from family members. These occur regardless of the sex of therapist, but are easier to elucidate and discuss if the sex of the therapist is appropriate to the particular reaction. Teams composed of two male therapists have worked together successfully, but they are sometimes more susceptible in the beginning of their working relationship to competition for the leadership role. The family resistance can, consciously or unconsciously, exploit any failure in achieving a comfortable, smooth working relationship between the two team members. We have not yet tried working with teams of female therapists, although we have heard of a few instances where this arrangement has been successful.

Co-therapy partners share in the problems and decisions and learn from each other about the many things that happen simultaneously in a family therapy session. They confer with each other after each session and plan future strategy. Clinical observations are more reliable when the family has been worked with and observed by two professional persons rather than one. When two therapists become a harmoniously working team, they complement and assist each other in many ways. One of them may adopt the reassuring role of an observer while the other actively stimulates family communication and affective interaction. It is difficult for a solo therapist to perform the two disparate roles simultaneously of being an active instigator of affect and interaction in the family and of maintaining the calm, objective, uninvolved, and detached role of the neutral observer or the wise counselor. It is easier and more natural to divide these two therapeutic roles or approaches between two co-therapists. The co-therapists may also decide that it is more advantageous for one of them to take the lead in working on a certain problem with a particular family member. Also, with co-therapy, more avenues of action are open. Take, for example, the common American marital scene, often re-enacted in family therapy, in which the wife appears to be dominating and castrating the husband. One therapist might intervene to protect or rescue the husband from the wife's aggression; another might confront the wife with her behavior; another might seduce the wife into a more feminine and less castrating role; still another might ignore the behavior altogether, not consider it a problem, and focus on some other aspect of the family relationship; or a female therapist might show the wife how she can be happier if she behaves toward her husband in a less aggressive way and allows him to be the leader. This obviously does not exhaust all the possibilities of therapist response to such a situation. It does, however, indicate that the possibilities are so varied that a co-therapy team has more opportunity for achieving a flexible, multi-faceted approach and is less likely than a solo therapist to get stuck or stalemated in a single-track approach which may not happen to work for a particular marital couple.

If one of the partners disagrees with some particular intervention or procedure of the other in a session, he may choose to ignore it for the time being, but explain his disagreement to his partner later in a post-session review. Or, in the course of their development of a close-working team relationship, the team may develop mutually acceptable ways of adding to, modifying, and even correcting each other during the session and in the presence of the family. As they gain team maturity, these "corrections" can be made smoothly, spontaneously, and without anger, and without imposing any co-therapist team conflict or discord on the family. When they are secure enough in their respect for each other's opinion, it may even be helpful for them to discuss differing reactions to a particular family problem in the presence of the family. The family listens attentively to this professional conference on their problems, and to the serious respect with which each therapist regards the other's views. This exercises a strong control over the family system and permits effective therapeutic interaction. Both work toward a balance of their authority and support each other's position with the family when indicated. The family may tend to select one of the therapists at a particular time to be the leader of the therapeutic enterprise, but the therapists, realizing that this constitutes a neurotic need, a resistance, or a maneuver, need not necessarily go along with it. A major requirement for teamwork is the ability to trust the co-therapist and to respect him as a person and as a therapist. The degree to which a co-therapist accepts his partner's therapeutic behavior with understanding, rather than reacting with competitiveness, frustration, or criticism, depends upon the maturity of the two partners. If each co-therapist does "his own thing," that can be fine and effective as far as it goes. But if he remains closed, does not reveal himself to his partner, and does not engage in a shared, cooperative working relationship, the partner's enthusiasm and pleasure in the enterprise may be suppressed. We would agree in general with Heilfron's characterization of the interdependence relationship between co-therapists as including the following combination of independence and dependence: 1) If one therapist is the leader, controller, or actor involved in a particular theme of family interaction, "he feels free to let his own feelings and thoughts prompt his actions; and 2) if his partner is the main actor, he couples his awareness of the theme and of his partner's role with an evaluation of their appropriateness to the movement of the group. Conversely, when one therapist is actively engaged with the group, he is dependent upon his partner to be alert enough to help both him and the group should they get off the track by redirecting attention to relevant content. Co-therapy does not permit one therapist to relax while the other works."[2]

Supposing one co-therapist is working with the family on a problem and no family member responds to his efforts, or he gets into a deadlock with the family — should his partner bail him out? Such help appears to us to be indicated in most such situations, and is an essential part of a co-therapy relationship. But one partner should not be too quick to rush in to rescue the other; he should have enough confidence in the other to wait and see whether he tries a new tack or another way to break the deadlock before he intervenes. The family members will be impressed by the confidence the co-therapists manifest in each other. Also, they will not resent or envy the help one co-therapist receives from the other if they have seen that the co-therapists are just as likely to intervene to help out family members in resolving problems they have with each other. The family members will not perceive the close co-operative relationship of the co-therapists to be an alliance that leaves them out, or is entirely apart from them, or is against them. The co-therapist's loyalty to his partner does not have to be in conflict with his loyalty to the family.

Sharing the experience of a family session with a colleague and reviewing it with him later makes for a vastly more stimulating and meaningful professional relationship than does conducting a solo session and later reviewing it with a colleague or supervisor.

Use of a co-therapy team provides extra leverage for loosening up the tight formation of symbiotic family dyads. A child who has been pulled apart by conflictual parents and has learned that the only way he can preserve his integrity and gain power in the family is by keeping the parents split, can now learn to relate to an integrated co-therapy team, which presents a healthier parental marriage model to him. The co-therapists won't get anxious and compete with each other for this child if he appears to like one better than the other.

Whitaker has justified co-therapy as being necessary for the emotional support and equilibrium of each therapist when faced with the powerful and confusing impact of a whole family and its pathological system. The following quotation presents some of Whitaker's thinking on this issue:

We do not know enough, we are not clever enough, and God knows we are not mature enough, to be subjectively involved in a family and still be objectively perceptive of our own subjective involvement and its relationships to the family process. By implication, then, our task in family psychotherapy is to be available as a team to move as participants in the psychological and social patterns of this family, and thereby to aid the family unit in its auto-psychological reparative process. . . . We have been forced to admit that family psychotherapy can be effectively undertaken only by a team of two therapists. A good surgeon can do a routine appendectomy, but even a good surgeon wouldn't attempt a major abdominal operation without a colleague of equal adequacy across the table. We believe family psychotherapy is a major operation. Moreover, we are convinced that no team is powerful enough to 'handle' the family.[3]

Whitaker maintains that having a partner who can rescue him if he becomes too trapped in the family system enables the therapist to enter actively into the family, usurp the role of one of the family members, and to move in and out of the family at will while denying his involvement. This is similar to an approach reported by Jungreis in our earlier book in which he made a family an offer to take the place of their schizophrenic son and to allow himself to be "swallowed

up" by them, to be taken care of by the parents, and to be seduced
by the sister.[4] Regardless of whether a particular therapist stops himself
from getting lost in such a family role, or is stopped by his co-therapist,
the experience can be utilized to show the family how their group tendencies and dynamics contrive to "pull" the therapist into, or induce
him to play, the particular role. However, when a therapist conducts solo
family therapy and some of the family members resist him by joining in
an alliance against his particular therapeutic goal, he may be tempted
to look toward another family member to agree with or support what
he is doing. In such a case, it is better to have a partner to which the
therapist can look for support, as he will then be more capable of
maintaining objectivity and a therapeutic stance toward the family
member who is willing to be his ally or assistant therapist. Because
the co-therapy relationship is a small social system in its own right,
with its own healthy standards of relationship, the family has more
difficulty in ignoring, subverting, or changing it than they would have
with a solo therapist.

Not all family and group therapists have looked upon co-therapy
as the method of choice for conducting family therapy. Sager regards
it as an arrangement for anxious and inexperienced family therapists
who need to compensate for their lack of proper training by increasing
their numerical strength. He states that it "sometimes leads to spawning
a therapist subcultural group that is imposed on the family from
without and remains a foreign body irritant within the treated family.
Such a subgroup frequently has values that differ from those of their
patients."[5] The foregoing evaluation of co-therapy might be partly
justified by the position which some co-therapists take that agreement
between therapists and the co-therapy relationship vis-a-vis the family
should be like the parental marriage vis-a-vis the child, and should
always take precedence over either parent's relationship to the child
in regard to any questions of loyalty or intimacy. But not all co-therapy
teams follow this principle or relate to issues in terms of accepting
a choice between siding with either their co-therapist on the one
hand or with a family member on the other hand. Sager also questions
co-therapy advocates' claims that "two heads and four eyes are
presumed to be better than those of one person, and that different
co-therapists can act different roles — one being more critical than
the other, or one more analytical and the other more confronting, and
so on." He says: "It reminds me of the roles assigned to investigators
during the McCarthy period. One was supposed to use a hard sell,
the other a soft approach."[5] Sager implies here that those who prefer
to work as co-therapists tend all too frequently to regard the families
as a hostile, emotionally upsetting force against which the co-therapists
must band together to protect themselves while offering to aid this
sick unit of society. Such team countertransferences are, hopefully, put
in balance when the therapists become aware of them. These same
countertransference problems can also happen with a solo therapist
— and to a more serious degree if he is less secure working without a

partner; furthermore, he has less chance of becoming aware of his counter-transference.

Kuehn et al, in a recent statement regarding therapy, also questioned the value of the co-therapy method.

We suggest that the single most crucial issue in the utility of small group experiences revolves around the maturity, experience, and expertise of the leaders. Incidentally, there is some clinical evidence from our experience that the use of more than one leader is potentially even more antitherapeutic to group members unless the leaders themselves are closely supervised (particularly as regards the issue of reciprocal counter-transference). If this level of sophistication in supervision is not available where there is plural leadership, we would advise that the project as such be abandoned.[6]

This seems to say that if one leader can be bad, two together can be worse. We must state here that in our own experience we have had a number of pairs of co-therapists who succeeded in working out a smooth, efficient team relationship on their own without benefit of a supervisor. But this may not be such a usual or routine occurrence, and may take some working at the relationship to accomplish it. It in fact requires an extra commitment and an extra effort toward working out an emotional relationship between the two co-therapists, and this necessarily takes precedence over the consideration of theoretical issues and the development of techniques. This extra effort has its own reward in that it helps both co-therapists grow as human beings. They assist each other in dealing with feelings they experience toward the family during the session; they discuss the feelings they had toward each other during the session, and become more aware of, and accurate in, their perceptions of how they affect each other. As they become more comfortable with each other, they may be able to reveal areas in which they feel they have problems or weaknesses. One partner does not need to probe into the other's background to find what originally caused the problem or weakness, for the focus is on locating the here and now therapist behavior that hinders their achieving their full potential effectiveness as a co-therapy team.

REFERENCES

1. Sonne, J. C. and Lincoln, G. Heterosexual Co-Therapy Relationship and Its Significance in Family Therapy. Chap. 14 in *Psychotherapy for the Whole Family*. New York: Springer Publishing Co., Inc., 1965, pp. 213-227.
2. Heilfron, M. Co-Therapy: The Relationship Between Therapists. *Int. J. Group Psychother.* XIX (3):378-380, July, 1969.
3. Whitaker, C. A. *Acting Out: Theoretical and Clinical Aspects.* New York: Grune & Stratton, 1965, p. 191.
4. Jungreis, J. E. The Single Therapist in Family Therapy. Chap. 16 in *Psychotherapy for the Whole Family*. New York: Springer Publishing Co., Inc., 1965, pp. 232-238.
5. Sager, C. J. An Overview of Family Therapy. *Int. J. Group Psychother.* 18: 302-312, 1968.
6. Kuehn, J. L. and Crinella, F. M. Sensitivity Training: Interpersonal "Overkill" and Other Problems. *Amer. J. Psychiat.*: 108-112, December, 1969.

The plan of a structured training program for family therapy

Alfred S. Friedman and Gertrude Cohen

Chapter
5

Our training program, like most training programs, had three main components: 1) theory and cognitive knowledge, 2) development of skills, and 3) development of personality attributes and interpersonal sensitivity. The various procedures that we used to impart the necessary knowledge and skills to our trainees and to stimulate the therapeutic use of their personalities will be presented in this chapter. The methods by which we evaluated the trainees will be detailed and discussed later in Chapter 17.

There is as yet no sufficiently coherent theory of family therapy nor theory of action for a training program for developing family therapists that can be used as a basis for postulating that a specific combination of lectures, seminars, discussions, demonstrations, films, role plays, etc., will produce a more effective family therapist than some other combination. Until we have substantial research evaluation of the effects of family therapy, we cannot know whether one particular approach or technique is more effective than another (e.g., new task or role assignment by the therapist versus affective catharsis or versus new self-awareness by family members). In the meantime, we can organize a training program only by selecting knowledge and techniques which we have found useful and effective in our own clinical experience. For teaching, we tend to select the particular methods and techniques in which each of us is most skilled and which come naturally to our individual personalities.

Some of the topics, issues, and methods which we presented to our trainees in systematic fashion as part of our training program were:

1. Family therapy theory; classical papers; and a review of "schools" of family therapy.

2. Comparison of the family therapy approach with individual therapy and group therapy approaches.

3. Composition of the family therapy unit; the problem of absent members; partial family therapy; "multiple-impact" family therapy.

4. Implications of culturally and socially determined family roles in family therapy.

5. The importance of relatives and friends who have close relationships with, and important influences on, the family, and the need to include them in the family therapy.

6. Testing limits and motivation for family therapy; orienting the family to the therapy procedure, to its purpose, and to their role and the role of the therapist in it.

7. The discussion of family "secrets" and of sexual history and behavior in the family.

8. Family system analysis versus psychodynamic, intrapsychic approach in family therapy. How to view symptomatology. How to get turned in on the total family interaction system rather than focusing on individual members.

9. Problems of autonomy and responsibility of family members in family therapy.

10. Communication patterns of disturbed families and communication analysis as the method of family therapy.

11. The treatment of marriage problems in family therapy; the use of "well" or nonproblem siblings; the sibling relationship in family therapy.

12. Therapist-family relationships — transference and countertransference phenomena.

13. The therapeutic use of the co-therapist relationship in family therapy.

14. The handling of typical resistances in family therapy: Divesting the therapist of his professional role; passivity, denial, and silence; denying the family problem; family collusion to keep the therapist out of the picture, etc.

15. The neutral observer role of the therapist versus the active participant role.

16. Active supportive role of the therapist in assisting the family in problem solving versus interpretation analysis and development of insight.

17. Criteria for selecting from the myriad of family issues, and from the verbalizations and nonverbal interactions that occur in a session, for effective focusing and intervention.

18. The use of one's own affect to instigate constructive family affective expression in a suppressed family.

19. Acting as referee in family conflict: When to protect weaker from stronger members and when to "take sides" with a family member.

20. How to follow and understand and interpret the shifts in dyadic alliances and splits that occur among family members during a session.

21. Handling of destructive or provocative acting-out of a child or adolescent toward parents and therapists during a session; how long to wait for the parents to exercise their parental control function and when to demonstrate a proper parental function for the benefit of the parents.

22. Special problems in treatment: the acting-out family, the passive-dependent family, the chaotic family, the nonverbal family, the multi-problem family.

23. Preparing for the termination process in family therapy.

When we consider that the successful mastery of the challenging complexities of the role of the family therapist is at this time probably more of an art, involving personal spontaneity and creativity, than a science, it may appear somewhat pretentious and premature to offer a planned and structured training program. The trainee has learn to listen, perceive, understand, and respond to a whole family as it is interacting, to sense its underlying unstated problems and hidden messages, and to figure out where the family operational system is going wrong. He must be an observer and a participant at the same time and must, while maintaining objectivity and his own autonomous and guiding role, let the family take him in and use him as a substitute for weaknesses and deficits in their relationships. He must make decisions on the spot, decide which of many issues to pursue, and control the flow, direction, and purpose of the session. He not only has to be a representative and exponent of the values of the culture when the family distorts those values, but sometimes he has to represent to the parents the avant garde or cutting edge of cultural change as it is being developed by the youth of the society. (Some casework trainees tend to perceive their client, the family, as the passive recipient of service, and need to learn to permit the family to identify with the helping role and do active therapeutic work themselves.)

Obviously, all this cannot be achieved in a day or in a short training program of several weeks' duration. Our training program was planned to last one full calendar year, with an average of ten hours of activity planned per week for the trainee. We consider this to be the minimum time required for a training program in family therapy. Extensions of this minimum time required for training would depend on the individual trainee and the amount of training and experience he has had in his respective discipline and in psychotherapy.

The trainee needs to feel that the teaching and supervising staff support and have confidence in him, and that they do not expect him to learn the entire complex of skills at one time or to perform them perfectly the first few times he tries them. This encouragement by the teachers, together with the stimulation of the new idea of family therapy and the support of the agency and society in providing for the substantial cost of an intensive, time-consuming training program, enables the trainee to face the formidable challenge of doing family therapy and to tolerate his initial anxieties and mistakes. It is not unusual for individual therapists and social case workers, even when intrigued by the idea of family therapy, to accept the family initial anxiety about, and resistance to, coming for treatment together, as a way of rationalizing their own anxiety about facing the challenge. By observing an experienced family therapist, the trainee can learn to recommend the conjoint therapy approach in a matter-of-fact way and to listen to the family's initial anxiety and reassure them without allowing his own anxiety to determine the decision of whether to start. He learns that families will come and work together in spite of their members' understandable initial resistance to being confronted with each other.

Obviously, training for family therapy differs from training for individual therapy. Since family therapy is more difficult and complicated, it follows that there is some advantage to being a well-trained and experienced individual therapist before learning family therapy. But there is also a disadvantage (perhaps less serious than the disadvantage of lacking prior training and experience) in that certain ways of thinking about individual therapy have to be unlearned before one can conduct a truly family-oriented therapy or treat the family system rather than treating separate individuals in the presence of members of their family.

Family therapists and family counselors may be developed from a number of different professional disciplines. Whatever the core training, family therapy training should include courses in theory, concepts, problems, and techniques, together with continuous case seminars and controlled supervision of cases by an experienced teaching family therapist. Perhaps the best way to learn family therapy is to become sensitized to how a family experiences therapy by undergoing family treatment oneself. Very few practitioners thus far have had the courage to do this.

Ackerman pioneered in using films of family therapy sessions as an aid in teaching family therapy technique. Jackson et al, Ackerman, Haley, Paul, and others, including ourselves, have found that playing back tape-recordings of family therapy sessions, together with the therapist's explanation of why he intervened when he did and the way he did, is an effective training method.[1-4] Beeks and Ferber have utilized psychodrama as a training method, with some trainees playing the roles of members of a family coming for treatment and other trainees taking turns playing the role of the family therapist.[5] One who has not experienced or observed this procedure first-hand may find it hard to believe how sophisticated professionals could become as genuinely, affectively and intensely involved as they do in this interaction initiated by a simulated family situation. Because it seems so real, it affords an opportunity for the trainees to experience something of what it feels like to be in family therapy. At the same time, other trainees are given the real challenge of handling the responsibility of the therapist's role.

We made some use of these special training techniques (including Ackerman's films, video-tapes of other family therapy sessions, tape-recording of our own family therapy sessions, role-play of family therapy sessions, etc.), in the comprehensive training program reported in this books, but the method that constituted the mainstay of our training program was having the trainee work as an active co-therapist (together with his teaching family therapist) in the live ongoing treatment of families, with an opportunity for analysis of the therapy process immediately after each session.

Use of Family Therapy Sessions and Co-Therapy Method for Training

The family therapy sessions were used for training objectives and were integrated into the training practicum by the following specific methods:

1. Observation through a one-way screen of live family treatment sessions conducted by an experienced family therapist or by an experienced co-therapy team.
2. Analysis and discussion of films of live family therapy sessions.
3. The trainee conducting a family therapy session solo. This was observed through a one-way screen by the supervisor who subsequently reviewed the session with the trainee.
4. Using excerpts from tape recordings of live family sessions for purposes of analysis and to demonstrate principles of technique.
5. Planning by supervisor and trainee, immediately before a family session, of the specific approaches to be used in the session.
6. Review and critique of each family session by supervisor with trainee immediately following the session.

7. Getting familiar with the routine of going to the client's home to conduct a diagnostic family session or to conduct ongoing family treatment in this setting.

8. A continuing case conference, including observation at regular intervals of live therapy sessions of the family being discussed.

9. Using a completed case to review the total process of family therapy and to demonstrate phases of treatment and termination process.

Some trainees found that functioning as an observer and recorder in family sessions conducted by an experienced family therapist was a way to start learning in a less threatening situation before taking on the role of an active co-therapist or solo therapist. Actually, a trainee could observe and record the work of an experienced therapist for one or two years and still not feel ready to function independently. The trainee in such a situation would gain considerable understanding of family problems and family defensive operations, and of therapeutic technique from the observation and critique of another therapist in action. He would see how the experienced therapist side-stepped or neutralized family resistances, breathing fresh air into a stalemated or repressed family condition. He would have the opportunity to compare his own emotional reactions to specific family situations with those of the experienced therapist, and to vicariously play therapist by fantasizing what he would do in given situations a moment before he observes what the actual therapist does. He would thus learn from his reactions what some of his biases are, such as whether he tends to identify more with mothers' points of view than with fathers', etc. But learning in this passive way to understand all of the foregoing is still a crucial step away from learning to implement therapy actively and effectively by oneself and to actualize it with one's own personality; this calls for a good deal of trial and error practice in the actual role of therapist.

Thus, the heart of our training program was the participation of the trainee in live family therapy as a co-therapist with an experienced family therapist. Lectures, case presentations, films, video-tapes, tape-recordings of sessions, and discussions and dissections of the process of family therapy sessions were all secondary to the actual practice and supervision of the trainee in family therapy. We have used the one-way screen to permit the trainee to observe family therapy conducted by an experienced solo therapist or co-therapy team but we found that observing the "master" at a distance is not as good a training method as plunging in, getting one's feet wet, and actively participating in the therapy. The person who merely observes tends to become a pseudo-therapist in that he does not learn to use his own style and his own personality, but tends to imitate the teacher he is observing.

In the beginning of the co-therapy relationship with a senior teaching therapist the trainee may tend to contrast his performance with that of the more experienced, skillful therapist and may thereby feel more uncomfortable and awkward than if he were learning family therapy on his own. He also might prefer to avoid being observed and having his performance judged, and to learn whatever he can by his own mistakes. However, it is worth giving up the relative comfort and defensive self-protection of the isolated solo learning experience in order to participate in a live cooperative learning experience with a skilled therapist, to identify with selected aspects of this therapist's behavior, and to engage in an exercise of openness in discussing the questions and doubts one has concerning one's performance as a family therapist.

The question has been raised as to whether it is better for the trainee to have a long intensive experience with one teacher or to have shorter experiences with several teachers. Since we value the personal intimacy and the depth of relationship which develops over a period of time with one teacher, we provide each trainee with one rather long experience with a teacher. However, whenever a teacher reports that the relationship has become somewhat repetitive or frozen and that the trainee is not making much progress, we transfer the trainee to a shorter experience with a second teacher. An occasional "one-shot" consultation, arranged by having a teaching therapist sit in on a session with a trainee therapist and his family, may have some value in breaking an impasse or stalemate in the therapy process and may also be a learning experience for the trainee; it cannot, however, be expected to equal the learning effect of an ongoing teacher-trainee co-therapy relationship.

REFERENCES

1. Jackson, D. D., Riskin, J., and Saler, V. Method of Analysis of a Family Interview. *Arch Gen. Psychiat.* 5:321-339, 1961.
2. Ackerman, N. *Treating the Troubled Family.* New York: Basic Books, 1966.
3. Haley, J. and Hoffman, L. *Techniques of Family Therapy.* New York: Basic Books, 1967, pp. I-X.
4. Paul, N. Effects of Playback on Family Members of Their Own Previously Recorded Conjoint Therapy Material. *Psychiat. Res. Reports* 20:175-187, 1966.
5. Beels, C. C. and Ferber, A. Family Therapy: A View. *Family Process* 8(2): 280-318, September, 1969.

Answers to typical questions of the trainee therapist

Jerome E. Jungreis

In the course of three years of directing family therapy practicum seminars for senior social workers, we noticed that certain questions were asked in every seminar group. Some questions — usually concerning specific problems of technique — would be raised a number of times in a single seminar group. These questions have been collected and are presented here, with answers, in the hope that they will be of value to those undertaking family treatment. Since the answers which appear here are not given in response to questions about specific families, they will be broad in their implications. We have divided the questions into sections relating to the different phases of treatment and to the unfolding interests of beginning family therapists.

Pre-Clinical Phase

Question: There are frequent references to the patient about whom the family expresses concern and for whom it wants treatment as either "the designated patient," the "symptomatic patient," or some such term. Why do you keep referring to this person in that way?

Answer: One of the basic concepts of family therapy is that the family is the unit of treatment. A member of the family is seen both as an individual and as a part of a system in which every member plays a significant role in determining or stabilizing the family pattern or homeostasis at some level. The level may be a pathological one, and may require one member of the family, or more, to assist in accommodating this level by the expression of problems and symptoms. The prospect that the symptoms may disappear requires in turn a realignment of the balance of relationships in the family, and may be unsettling to the family concept. As we shall see, this has important therapeutic implications in terms of the therapists' awareness of the fact that to focus excessively on the designated patient because he is the one carrying the symptoms is to doom treatment of the entire family. What we then have is treatment of the patient with the rest of the family looking on. Further, this process of focusing on the symptomatic patient distracts attention from the family processes that are of primary significance in treatment. We consider the entire family to be a part of the pathological process expressed in the designated patient and that therefore the entire family, as a unit, needs treatment. To treat only or mainly the symptomatic patient would be the equivalent of treating the skin eruptions of a systemic infection while ignoring the infection itself.

Question: What differentiates the therapeutic approach to a family group from the one-to-one type of interview to which we have been accustomed?

Answer: There are a number of significant differences between seeing the family as a group and interviewing each member separately. To have the whole family meet with the therapist is in one sense an artificial contrivance. Nonetheless, the spontaneous family life transactions which are going on in the presence of the therapist give him a much closer view of the reality of the family life than he could obtain were he to see each member in the family individually. Seeing the family together poses a number of significant problems as well as opportunities for the therapist. On the personal level, he is confronted by a far greater intensity of subjective feelings. The patient is not talking about a mother who remains a shadowy figure; the mother is right there. The therapist's unresolved feelings about his own mother, father, or siblings are less amenable to suppression. Further, to observe a member of a family being scapegoated is a far different experience from having a patient tell you about it later, *tête à tête*, in the cozy quiet of your office. To witness the grossest kind of communication binds, the cold rejection by one family member of an appeal for help by another, generally arouses in the therapist anger, the strongest desire to intervene, the resurgence of rescue fantasies, etc. Sometimes such intervention is therapeutically indicated but sometimes it is not, and it is rather difficult to detach oneself sufficiently from one's own needs to employ what is in the best interest of the therapy. Finally, in connection with the need for self-awareness on the part of the therapist, we should mention the infinite possibilities for exasperation that a family can provide to prevent the therapist from attempting to be helpful. The family can work together, much like a smoothly working machine, to deny the therapist his useful role.

Considering the family as a unit of treatment, it is necessary to be aware of the nature of the multiple relationships that exist between all members of the family and between each member and the therapist, and of the fact that these relationships are changing from time to time. These multiple relationships can also be used for resistances, and can be destructive to the progress of the family therapy. Certainly we see resistance and attack in individual therapy as well, but when there is a ganging-up by a family on the therapist or co-therapist, the therapy of the family assumes further dimensions of strain and hazard.

Family therapy presents the therapist with an opportunity to observe and deal with a real ongoing life situation, to point out what is happening, possibly to explore together with the family why it is happening, and, finally, to help the family attempt new and healthier ways of coping with their problems. We shall mention only one more of the many advantages of family therapy at this point. In traditional therapy, all too frequently attempts at intervention are undermined by another member of the family during the rest of the week and, indeed, during the rest of the treatment. In family therapy, individual family members have much less of a chance to restore the homeostasis to its previous pathological level if the entire family works together on its problems.

Question: In what ways do I have to reorient myself when I become a family therapist?

Answer: The therapist does not have to reorganize himself in a totally different way. What he brings to the therapy from previous training and experience has a high value. He now adds to his orientation and style another orientation which needs to be integrated into his previous mode of operation. His previous orientation in some specific ways becomes reinforced. For example, depending upon the type of therapy and the casework that he has been doing, the focus in family therapy tends to be more on the interaction between the therapist and the family, and between one member of the family and another. There is a stronger need to listen to the underlying motives, to understand not only the conscious but also the unconscious communications, and to be aware of non-verbal cues and signals which must be made more explicit than in a one-to-one type relationship. In a family interview one can frequently be shut off from understanding many of these multiple messages. Concomitant with the need to tune in much more to the interaction of the family, its moods, its underlying motives, its basic mechanisms and means of maintaining itself, is the need to think of the family on two levels: as a family unit, and as separate units grouped together. This is one of the reasons why the word "transaction" has become more prominent than the old word "interaction." The word "transaction" connotes that something going on between two people affects both of them, and not that they just meet at some point, share an experience, and then return to their unified state as before. It is important to understand the homeostasis of the family, which implicitly and explicitly means the mechanisms that are used to ward off changes in the family system. The nature and feedback of the various homeostasis mechanisms are frequently very intricate and must be learned if one is to help the family to change on meaningful levels. A corollary to the need to be aware of the multiple relationships that are possible in a family is the danger of being used by them to maintain their homeostasis. One of these mechanisms is an attempt to get the therapist into a dyadic relationship with each member of the family. In effect, this would mean doing one-to-one therapy, one member at a time, rather than treating the family as a unit. It should be understood that treating the family as a unit does not mean that one does not deal with individual members at times. What it does mean is that one has to be aware constantly of the effect of this one-to-one interaction upon the rest of the family, its meaning to the family and its therapeutic potentials.

In sum, then, orienting oneself to family therapy means essentially to think in terms of the family as individuals and as a unit, regardless of what kind of interaction is taking place. To think of the family as a unit means to be aware of the general family patterns, of the nature of the family homeostatic balance and the feedback mechanisms which maintain themselves on a pathological level, of the role the family will try to assign the therapist in order to maintain its pathological stance, and of the family mechanisms of communication and affective exchange.

Early Phases in Clinical Training

Question: There is too much going on during the family therapy session; people in the family keep switching from one topic to another. I don't understand what they are trying to get at, and, in general, there seems to be too much distraction. How can I *possibly* understand what's going to be with so many different people talking at different times about different topics and meaning different things? A correlated question is: What do I pick up, what do I follow? The sessions go too fast, it's too confusing; and, finally, how am I supposed to remember all this for re-cording purposes?

Answer: One way of answering this question might be to ask you to pause for a moment and think back again to one-to-one therapy. If you recall the earliest training you had in clinical work, you may remember that learning almost any type of "therapy" is quite confusing to a beginner. Frequently, even an experienced one-to-one therapist finds it difficult to admit that an individual session can be *that* confusing. There is some internal need to feel "organized" — to feel that one should understand a lot more of what's going on than one does. However, if you think of yourself as a trainee and remember that there is no stigma attached to not understanding everything, it may be easier to relax. It is appropriate to assume that any kind of new therapy is going to be very difficult at the beginning, that it is going to sound confusing, and that the questions of what do I pick up, what's really going on, what is my focus, will always occur. There is no substitute for experience.

However, when you start to think in terms of "family" rather than to listen to what an individual is saying, and begin not to focus so much on the manifest content, the latent content will come more into prominence and an underlying unity may frequently be observed. For example, on the manifest level the family may talk about ten different subjects during the course of the therapy session. If one tunes in to the family as a unit it may become clear that its members are refusing to be aware of something that the therapist is trying to point out or that had been pointed out in the past. Also, depending upon the pathology of the family, it may well be that their confusion and their inability to focus on their non-problem-solving capacity is one of the problematic aspects of the family's problem. It should also be remembered that for many families meeting together as an entire family and talking things over is a totally new experience and that the confusion may stem from their attempt to grapple with this novel experience. Consideration must also be given to the need an anxious trainee may have to be in control of the session. However, one can observe, one can cross check with his co-therapist, or ask questions which will elicit family responses which will clarify what is happening. In the first session, you are also attempting to set some boundaries and a framework for the ensuing therapy. As the rhythms of the family tend to repeat themselves, you get to see the relative roles of the members of the family and get a sense of the family structure. You can observe, for example, that all communications in one particular family go through the mother, or that the mother encourages the father to take charge of the family but whenever he attempts to do so she cuts him off.

In summary, then, two things should be borne in mind:

1. You should not expect that family therapy will be similar to one-to-one or even group therapy. It is more complex, and therefore you should not demand total understanding from yourself.

2. You should become more attuned to what the family is trying to say, in a general sense, how the members view therapy, how they express these views, what roles are assumed by whom, and how they view the problems in the family, than to picking up the manifest content of each separate family member's communications. To a certain extent, the latter is important and necessary, but what we are talking about here is the relative degree of emphasis upon the individual and the family.

Question: What are the typical dynamics of the first interview?

Answer: One of the general tendencies on the part of the trainee just before the first interview is to want as much information as possible about the family, particularly if he comes from an agency that makes a strong point of getting as much collateral information as possible before seeing any member of a family. It might be important to differentiate between how much of this information is really necessary and how much of it is being used by the trainee in an attempt to deal with anxiety. We frequently find that it is not necessary to get as much specific information initially as we need in a one-to-one therapy session. Much pertinent information can be meaningfully elicited from the family as part of treatment, to be dovetailed with additional information from other agencies when needed. We are attempting here to caution the trainee not to go overboard on prior collection of information but to realize that it may be his way of handling anxiety in anticipating a new and unknown experience.

We are now ready for the first family session. What can we expect? What is typical?

It might be best to say that there is no typical structure for the first interview. Much depends upon what the family brings, how they view their problems, the nature of the service they are really seeking (e.g..

"Just get her to stop acting out"), and the degree of family agreement about what they want. However, we can talk about some typical ways in which families start. In some families one or another member will try to align himself with the therapist as a member of the helping team and to join him in treating other members. In other families, the focus will be upon the designated patient; family members will want to talk only about this person, their understanding of him, and their frustration with him. Some families handle extreme family tension by extreme family passivity. They act as though they don't know how to start or what to do, and wait for the therapist to ask questions. What could ensue, without an understanding of how to deal with this situation, is a straight question and answer period. On the other hand, the family may take over completely by wildly interacting from the very first moment, which can leave the therapist feeling very passive and ineffective himself. Since a family can present itself in the first session in any of these ways, it might be helpful to point out some techniques and attitudes the therapist may want to use during the first session.

It is important not to let the family overwhelm you or to let yourself be caught up in their mood, which may be one of anger, frustration, depression, or whatever. Some basic ground rules should be laid down for the family during the first one or two sessions. For example, it should be made clear to the parents that the children must be permitted to talk freely at the sessions without fear. Usually this is done by indicating to the parents that what goes on at home certainly is something that they should handle as they see fit, but that at the sessions themselves the children should feel free to express themselves without fear of reprisal either at the session or later on at home. This is a theme which will have to be replayed at other times during the therapy; however, one ground rule has thus been tentatively established. Another vital point to make in a variety of ways is that the focus of the therapy sessions is on the family problem and not only on the symptoms in the designated patient.

A technique that we have found to be very useful in the first session is to ask all members of the family what their individual problem is, after first discussing with them their view of the general *family* problem. Sometimes, this questioning of each individual may not be necessary. Much may depend on the responses to the question of what the family problem is. Thus, we structure the interview from the very beginning toward the problem of all the family members and/or the family as a whole, and not only toward the problems of the designated patient. We should not be discouraged if the answers come back in terms of the designated patient, i.e., that the only family problems are the ones raised by him. At least we are beginning to get the family to look at itself as a unit rather than to focus on scapegoating.

We have also found it very helpful to focus on the natural curiosity a family has about what is going on and to encourage this curiosity so that everyone feels he has a right to talk. Curiosity is also useful in bringing out a number of issues which may not otherwise come out until much later. It may be well to mention that if you start right off by relating to the sexual material, first about the daughter and then broadening the topic to the family as a whole, and do it in an off-hand manner that is designed simply to elicit the information as part of understanding the family, you establish from the first interview that this is a subject that can be discussed. Sometimes the family persists in talking about the designated patient. In that case, the interview can be structured so that, while you are discussing with the designated patient the meaning and nature of his or her experience, you are demonstrating to the family how one can communicate, how one can try to understand, and the kind of attitude that is so much more helpful in such a situation than a stalemate of angry condemnations and punitive remarks. It is a way of telling the family that sexual experience can be discussed in the family as a whole, a fact which will probably become very important later on in the therapy. Having established this point in the first interview, it is also easier to continue the discussion of sexual material rather than to open it at a later point in the therapy. At that time, strong resistance can be encountered, much of it based on some kind of lower- or middle-class reality sense of what is permissible to discuss in the family and what should be discussed only in private. As you involve yourself in some of the therapeutic tasks mentioned, you are building with the family an interest in relationships and meanings rather than techniques. This is to say, the family will tend to want specific answers from you to questions such as "What do I do when this happens?", or "What do I say under these conditions?" Seeing the therapist relating to individual family members during the session not in terms of technique but in terms of understanding them and the family in whole, and seeing him trying to appreciate the session's experiential meaning to the individual members of the family, provides the family with a model which will be of value to them as well as helpful in the therapy itself.

One of the initial problems in family therapy may be the question of the absent member. It is not at all unusual that at the first session the family either mentions directly, or the therapist finds out, that a rather significant member of the family is not present. This may be the father, which makes the problem very obvious, or a sibling, or a significant member of the family who lives at home but is not part of the family of procreation. It is very important that this question be dealt with immediately, be considered a meaningful family event, and be carefully examined in terms of its meaning; it should be made clear that family therapy cannot be continued indefinitely without the entire family being present. Specialists in the field differ as to the treatment of a family where a significant member absents himself. Some therapists refuse to see a family unless every member is present, and others will see the family to explore why the absent member did not show up. This question has been thoroughly explored elsewhere.[1]

All of these problems which we really only touch on in the first session become increasingly crucial as the intensity of family therapy increases. There is a natural tendency during intense moments for the family to regress to earlier levels of interaction. But if the therapist has from the start structured the therapeutic encounter and established models for family interaction, such regressions will become shorter and more avenues to satisfactory resolutions will be available.

In sum, then, your knowledge of your professional ability, the rules of family therapy, the open discussion of sexual material in the first session where this is opportune, and the use of family defenses for therapeutic purposes are all part of the general techniques which can be used in the initial sessions with the family.

Question: One of the typical questions, depending upon one's previous orientation, is how much of the first interview should be devoted to history taking.

Answer: Here again there is considerable variation in the techniques which experienced family therapists use. Some feel that the history taking should involve the whole family, should let them know about the parents' first encounter, their courtship pattern, their marriage, their ideas about raising children, and the problems encountered along the way. Other therapists sit back and see what the family is going to bring to the first session; they are more passive and observing although they will use opportunities to establish some of the ground rules we mentioned in the previous Question and Answer. It might be wise to remind you again that you do not shed your background in taking on this work. If you are made more comfortable by getting the family's history, and if you consider it significant both in planning the treatment and in understanding the family, go ahead; the question here is really a matter of emphasis. The emphasis in the history taking process should be on the total family; it should include significant events in the family's history, their conflict and resolution, and an indication of how the family has dealt with past crises, including that of the sexually acting-out daughter.

Question: This question is an elaboration of one of the points mentioned in an earlier answer: "How do you deal with the family when they all want to focus on the designated patient?"

Answer: As noted, you can utilize the family's need to focus on the designated patient in a positive way. Besides asking questions relating to the entire family, you can use the designated patient to get the family's reactions and feelings about him. This frequently leads to expressions of feelings about other members of the family. You will often find that it is almost impossible for other members of the family to talk about their feelings or fantasies in relation to the designated patient. They can only understand what they would want to do to him or how they would handle him; they cannot articulate their personal subjective reaction, i.e., how the designated patient makes them feel.

Get them to talk about their own feelings. Often the family insists that they had a happy family life until the designated patient got into difficulties, and they can do this in a very convincing manner. It is important that you not be taken in by this, because to accept this version without careful exploration means going along with the family defenses. When the family focuses on the designated patient, one of two things will happen. They will either try to ally themselves with you against the designated patient, or somehow the designated patient will use what's going on to ally himself with you and evoke your sympathy. Both are to be carefully avoided and understood as part of the family's coping mechanisms which they use in dealing with each other and with you. Such mechanisms indicate how the family makes use of outside help in general, and probably also indicate an internal structural arrangement in which various members of the family take sides. By resisting these traps, you are utilizing their concern and desire to talk about the designated patient and turning it into a therapeutic maneuver. The focus upon the designated patient has become so ingrained that it will be some time before the family will be able to reflect more upon the family as a whole and upon the members as individuals. This projection of all family problems onto the designated patient has to be understood as a warding off by the family of an awareness of intolerable personal feelings and fantasies. This means that you may have to deal with these underlying fears concomitant with the shedding of the designated patient's defenses. The suggestion to set aside an interview where there is no discussion of the designated patient at all can fruitfully evoke the family anxiety in other areas. But one should be careful not to let this question become a power struggle between the family and the therapist. Such a struggle frequently ends in a stalemate. Generally speaking, to focus on the delinquent girl as the problem is a technique which is being used by the family either to avoid treatment themselves, to change without outside help, or to demonstrate how they have used outside help in the past. Setting up a non-power-oriented, objective attitude in the first session will frequently help as treatment progresses. Nevertheless, it is important to be aware of this power struggle as a possible element in therapy and one which could easily sneak up on the therapist without his being aware of it. Sometimes, by not fighting the family and letting them talk the issue to death, they will drop the topic of the designated patient themselves. However, this is an extreme measure, to be used only when the tenacity of the family defenses precludes confrontation of such defenses. You should also remember that you are involved in a parallel series of therapeutic attempts of which direct confrontation about the issue of the designated patient is only one. To evoke a discussion of the problems of other family members in the family as a whole, to transform the static series of relationships, to investigate the nature of the communication system in the family, and to expose conflict-laden relationships in the family, are just some of the techniques which are an attempt to broaden the family issues.

Questions in the Middle Phase

Question: How active or passive does a family therapist have to be?
Answer: While the degree of the therapist's activity or passivity will depend upon the ego strength of the family and their ability to react reflectively to his comments, one may say that the therapist has actively to engage the family. This activity is made necessary by the need to intervene in the family life and system. Since the family is in the process of handling their conflicts and anxieties in their typical stereotyped fashion — a fashion which they have found to be the best for themselves (though ultimately unsatisfactory) — to ask them to reflect upon the therapist's interpretation, comments, and confrontations per se will not yield any results. The ego-syntonic satisfaction derived from the customary transaction patterns of a family is so great that the only way to make them aware of the pathology in their transactions is by not permitting them to continue in their customary patterns. This, therefore, calls for activity on the part of the therapist in a variety of ways. He may suggest that one member of the family stop talking and another begin to talk; he may engage one family member in some operation to the exclusion of the rest for a particular phase, or he may attempt to prevent continuance of certain communication patterns. A typical example is a case where all communication in the family tends to go through one person. To insist that the family not go through this one person is one way to help them become aware of what is going on, what is wrong with the present practice, of the reason for their need to handle their communication patterns in this way, and of the anxiety and concern entailed in changing it. To simply comment upon the practice will not change it. Again, a fairly healthy family might be able to use a reflective observation in an effective and therapeutic manner. But, in general, the more disturbed the family, the more active the therapist must be.

Question: One member in the family wants to talk only about himself. Is this progress?
Answer: At certain phases of treatment, when the family as a system in which no one is able to be aware of his identity without in some way relating to other members of the family has been broken up, talking about oneself can be a very effective therapeutic maneuver. However, in the early and middle phases of treatment, talking about oneself frequently masks a resistance against the environment of the entire family and is an attempt to set up a dyadic relationship with the therapist — an alliance of sorts, a competitive advantage — and to exclude other family members. This has to be carefully evaluated. If it seems as though a family member's discussion of himself is leading to some change, then it is part of the process of differentiation and should be encouraged. However, if his persistence in talking about himself does not lead to corresponding changes in the way he reacts to the rest of the family, then his behavior must be viewed as a

resistance. To elicit the responses of the other members, to insist that they react instead of the therapist, will frequently discourage this attempt at monopolizing. As a general rule, consistent attempts to get other members of the family to intervene, to react to, to reflect upon, and to involve themselves in some way with what one member of the family is attempting to do can effectively serve to diminish this dominance on the part of one family member in the therapy. One of the dangers is that the family member who dominates the therapy may blackmail the rest of the family by subtle or not-so-subtle hints at the possibility of acting out. For example, the daughter in one family, when stopped by her parents from dominating the session, immediately threatened to act out again.

Question: When do you make home visits and what are some of the differences between a therapeutic session at home and at the office?

Answer: Home visits are frequently helpful in the early phases of treatment as a diagnostic tool. Seeing the family in their own milieu, their own setting, often adds a dimension of understanding that cannot be obtained in the office. Usually the family feels more comfortable at home; its members are more apt to be themselves, and are less given to assume the public stance that they display outside the home. As people walk in and out of the room, the family attempts to play host and hostess; family pets can be observed in their interaction with the family, providing helpful cues which aid in understanding the family. A plateau of resistance encountered in the middle phase of family treatment frequently can be overcome by one or several home visits which add a dimension of exploration and thus prevent the family from denying the presence of certain kinds of problems. For example, a family that presents itself as reasonable and rational in the early phases of treatment will probably present the therapy team with an opportunity to see other things when they visit the home. The team may find at a home visit that the family's public front crumbles when they realize the therapists' awareness of a member of the extended family who lives in the home and whose presence has been denied; they may also find a strong reaction of the family to the therapy team's intrusion upon their privacy and may use this reaction to elicit family feelings about the therapy; they may discover an uncontrollable house pet in a seemingly well-controlled, "reasonable" family, or find that the father spends most of his time working by himself in the cellar, away from the family, although this has been denied in sessions at the office.

In a general way, we get a sense of the decor of the home, the physical layout of the rooms, the investment the woman of the family has put in the care and planning of the home, and of the degree of sophistication with which the family handles visitors and the intervention of relatives or neighbors. We also note who walks in and out during the session. All these observations can be very helpful to the therapy team in that they provide significant clues which can open up attempts at further exploration.

Question: Could you mention, in a general way, some of the actual working techniques most frequently used in a typical session?

Answer: You have already been apprised of some of the techniques that are used by the active family therapist, such as to guard against certain typical alignments and methods of communication which occur in the family. In addition, it is always important to clarify communications, to relate the observations you have about how things work in the family, to raise questions about why certain things are the way they are, to take sides and, when necessary, to change them in accordance with what seems to be the need at the moment. If there is one technique that can be said to be basic, it is to attempt, by a variety of imaginative means, to see the family and have them see themselves in a manner different from the way they typically view themselves. The other important element is that they be able to view their transactions in a framework of significantly evoked feelings and reactions. To confront a member of the family or an entire family prematurely is a waste of effort and may possibly lead to reinforced resistances. Timing and dosage, as in all therapy, are of great import, and skill in using them only comes with experience. The presence of the therapist is actually an intervening force which can be exploited for the benefit of the therapy if he is able to utilize his presence in such a way that the family cannot continue to maintain their pathological and active transactional patterns. Once they can no longer maintain these two similar transactional patterns, anxiety and discomfort will set in. They will then question, in a resistive way, and later, with the support of the therapist, in a helpful, positive way, the need for this change; they will also discuss their underlying fears of change, and will finally seek out healthy alternatives.

Question: The family seems extremely resistive to therapy. We go over the same issues again and again and nothing seems to change. What can we do?

Answer: When the family is very resistive to therapy, it is important that you consider two factors:

1. Is family therapy suitable for this family?
2. Is the therapy team engaged in a power struggle with the family?

There are several clues to a power struggle. Reports, for instance, that a father who is very passive in the session is very free-spoken in negative comments after the sessions are over, are indicative of such a struggle. It is important that the father's position as head of the family not be directly threatened. Other indications are: The family's position that the therapy team prove to them the effectiveness of therapy, or even the need for it; the family's success in being able to arouse angry and negative feelings in the therapist which block objectivity. Some families are very paranoid or become very paranoid about the therapist. It is important than the therapist be as above-board as possible with the family. Telling them of your credentials, or being open about any aspect of your personal life that bears directly upon the therapy, can be helpful if judiciously used.

The family may be trying to tell you something that is important to them that they either can't convey effectively or that you seem to be dismissing. One family, for example, mumbled at an early session only once that the father had difficulty keeping the regular appointment time, but they kept coming at that same time, and became very resistive. In checking over any possible misunderstanding, we learned of the great difficulty the father had, acknowledged it, and changed the appointment time as soon as practical. We also explored why the father or others could not impress us more with his needs. Another suggestion that may be helpful is to see subunits of the family with sessions geared to understanding the cause of the resistance. Seeing the parents only, the children only, or various other combinations of the family may well provide some leads to the source of the need to defeat the therapy.

In some families, this need to defeat the therapy and/or the therapist may be too great. Some members may sense very early, even at the first session, that therapy for all means change for all, and some, usually a parent, are made too anxious by this implication. To such a person, therapy means a change that for him is sterile and lacking in positive gains; it means giving something up without getting anything in return.

The general question of which families benefit by family therapy will be discussed below.

Question: How do I deal with the problem of a countertransference?

Answer: We have found the presence of a co-therapist to be extremely helpful with this problem as well as with a number of others. It would be unusual for two therapists to be hung up on the same countertransference problem. When one therapist is hung up, the other can be very helpful in pointing this out. Discussing the case with your supervisor or with your colleagues in a seminar are also useful adjuncts. The general need for self-awareness, regardless of the kind of therapy used, should be stressed in family therapy. We have already noted the particular importance of self-awareness because what we are working with is a vivid family experience with a real father, a real mother, real children interacting together, and any unresolved feelings the therapist may have from his own childhood with regard to his parents or siblings can easily be aroused by the family, sometimes in very subtle ways. We have found that to comment, in a frank way, upon our own reactions to what is going on in the family, asking the family to join us in understanding our reactions, is frequently not only helpful to us in terms of our own feelings but also assists the family in being more honest with each other.

Question: The particular resistance that the family indicates is one of deadly passivity. How do I deal with that?

Answer: It is typical that one member of the family, frequently the mother but sometimes the designated patient or the father, seems to be the energizing force around which the family can be expressive and can interact in a lively way. The absence of such a person will reveal an otherwise lifeless, passive family. However, there are times when the entire family manifests a deadly passivity. One of the problems in dealing with this passivity is that the therapists often find themselves forced into becoming the energizing person for the family, feeding them and lighting the fires upon which they will glow. When the therapist becomes passive himself, the glow seems to fade. Some therapists are rather successful in being able to outwait the family until they are finally forced to start dealing with their problems. However, there is a risk that the family will quit treatment. Several other possibilities are open. One is to start a discussion and then drop off as soon as the family is able to pick it up and continue to do this until they are able to go it on their own more and more. Another is to focus upon this passivity over and over again, talking about it exclusively, wondering why it goes on. Frequently, we find that what it means is that members of the family have very little sense of themselves as persons and only see themselves as reacting to someone else. When they are called upon to take the initiative, there is a fear and anxiety associated with expressiveness, and an inexperience with it that they find frightening. At other times such passivity may indicate considerable hostility to the therapist and again should be thought of in terms of family resistances, discussed in the previous Question and Answer. In the middle phases of therapy the gradually increasing passivity of the family should be viewed in the context of some of the elements of countertransference, particularly impatience with the family's progress. Finally, you should not overlook the possibility of restraint due to some family secret, some criminal activity, a secret family shame (real or imagined), or even a continued contact by family members with others in the helping profession, that for a variety of reasons they are not yet ready to share. Some of these possibilities occurred to me in treating families.

Question: We note that generally mothers seem to be the force for therapy, rather than the fathers. Why is that?

Answer: There are a number of reasons why this exists. One of them is cultural. Mothers, in most socioeconomic classes, are expected to be the ones more concerned and more involved in family life. Another reason is that the fathers in these families often have given very little time to the family. They either work an odd shift and are not at home with the family, or stay away from the family, or simply are not available when the family needs them even though they happen to be home. By having the father present at the session and attempting to involve the entire family in the therapy, we are working directly against the family system as it has existed until this point. The father is threatened. His role must be acknowledged by a recognition that change in his role also means changing the roles of others. The aggressiveness of the therapists also will be a factor, particularly with the passive type of father, and the competitive feelings of the father will be aroused by the "take charge" strength of the therapists. Finally, it should be noted that culturally, too, women are expected to be more dependent, to need help in solving problems, and to seek the nurturance and guidance of others. Many fathers view *any* indication to the family that they possess some weakness as totally threatening and destructive of their role in the family and of their self-image.

Question: Do we discuss sexual material with the family?

Answer: We have already alluded to the answer in our discussion of the early family sessions in which we pointed out that by discussing the question of the sexually acting-out daughter in the very first session, or at least in the early sessions of therapy, the ground was prepared for considerable future discussion during the middle and later phases. Much depends upon the therapists' own conviction that it is important to discuss sexual material. It is not infrequent for social workers to tune in much more readily to the family's dependency problems, to the neglect of the sexual problems in the family. The discussion of sex does not generally center on the specific techniques used in intercourse but relates more to the feelings of sexual partners for each other and their complementarity and satisfaction with each other. We have generally found, when we have explored sexual relations and sexual feelings in the family, that before long the subject spontaneously leaves the specifically sexual area and begins to discuss general feelings. These may include feelings of exploitation, anxiety, or reluctance to be emotionally close and intimate. In the course of these discussions you may find that the really close relationships in the family are not between husband and wife but between the mother and the other members of the family or the extended family. The same may obtain with the husband. We have found that where we were comfortable in the discussion of sexual material, introduced early in the therapy, the family was able to discuss it. Sometimes a parent will state that he doesn't feel it is appropriate for such discussion to take place in the extended family group but is willing to discuss it with just himself and the other parent present. It may be helpful to go along with this once or twice. You will frequently find that no such sexual discussion takes place even with only two of them present. If such discussion does take place, it can be made valuable by bringing it back to the family and relating the problem to terms of intimacy and closeness. Since the sexually acting-out delinquent's symptomatic behavior is a key issue in the family's coming for treatment, you will find that it is often a very dynamic component of the family's pathology and will have to be explored.

Question: What is the lower age range of children in family therapy?

Answer: In the early evaluative sessions it is important that the entire family be present, no matter how young the child. In sustained treatment, some therapists restrict the lower age range to about eight or nine, reasoning that, on a physical basis alone, a younger child cannot maintain a comfortable position in a chair and engage in a verbal interchange for an hour to an hour and a half. Other therapists encourage the children to remain present throughout all sessions, with the family bringing in some play materials for the young child. The mere presence of the very young child can be of great help, particularly as the therapist notes his play patterns, his interaction with family members, or senses in him the family mood. We ourselves feel comfortable with having a child as young as four or five years of age present at all the sessions, with either the family or us bringing in some play materials. Sometimes in a large family, or even in a small one, the youngest child seems to have the role of a family mascot. That is to say, the entire family can agree on one thing, if nothing else, and that is their fondness for the youngest child or for the family pet.

As the trainees we supervise move into later phases of therapy, certain questions of a general nature tend to come up which could easily have come up earlier but somehow only appeared at the later phases of their learning experiences with families.

Question: What are some of the criteria for determining whether or not a family can or should use family therapy?

Answer: There are some generalities that we can talk about and there are some specifics. In general, any family that can use individual treatment can profit from family therapy. Various people disagree with regard to other criteria. Some people view destructive activity in a family as precluding family therapy. Some therapists feel that initial strong resistance to family therapy precludes it as being the therapy of choice. We ourselves have found family therapy to be generally effective, provided it is accepted at some early point. We found it easier to get fathers and other members of the family to come into treatment when we suggested family therapy. When individual sessions were suggested to each member some always declined to come. There are families who agree to come because the help is for the entire family; individually, they would never all come. The designated patient, for instance, will come only when she is forced to by an authoritative referral source or when she is hurting badly. Frequently, the mothers will also come to therapy, but it is rare that an entire family will agree to get help for themselves. Socioeconomic class is also a factor, and for lower socioeconomic groups particularly, often the only way in which the family will come for treatment is together.

Our general orientation is that family therapy is a treatment that can be used with most families unless there are specific contraindications. Some of these contraindications have to do with such things as the physical inability of significant members of a family to attend either regularly or at all. Another possible deterrent is the influence of a peripheral member of the family who is very important in the family, who will not come to the therapy sessions but will consistently undermine and sabotage the therapy. Finally, the inability of the family itself to come on a regular basis for a variety of reasons would be a contraindication for therapy.

Question: What are the basic goals in family therapy?

Answer: Our general response to this kind of question is based on our operational concept of what a healthy family is. When members see themselves as a collective of autonomous units in which each one knows who he is and how he fits into the family, then the matrix is there for a satisfying life for each member. The degree to which people living in a family can individuate is a reflection of the dynamic quality of family life which includes the permissability of a series of multiple relationships, flexibility in dealing with changing roles and status in various family members, the ability to understand and be understood. We feel one of the basic problems we have observed in our clinic families is their inability to change their fixed patterns of operating when they are confronted with the inexorableness of change. Reaction to the stress of new accommodation can only be expressed in pathologic terms. Symptoms serve the purpose of helping to maintain the old balance despite such revolutionary changes as the children's growing up, their going to school, their making friendships and relationships outside the home, a change in the parents' social status and similar factors. Few members of a dysfunctional family can tolerate individuation without fear of disintegration of the family, or murder, incest or abandonment. We have significantly refrained from mentioning diminution of symptoms per se as the main goal of family therapy. The reason is that we have noted that very shortly after therapy begins, and singularly unrelated to transactional changes in the family, the sexual acting-out will disappear. This we relate more to a reactional phenomena to therapy than to significant alterations in family structure. We would regard significant changes in family roles and adaptive mechanisms, an ability to transact in a different way and in a different order and most important, the development of a sense of each individual member's own autonomy within the family constellation, as being evidences of successful movement in therapy.

Question: Could you say something about the termination phases in family therapy?

Answer: Assuming the goals of family therapy to be the kinds of changes that were mentioned in the previous question, the termination phase would emphasize the ability of the family to tolerate differences among themselves and changes in the way they relate to each other. As in individual therapy, one of the concerns must be to help the family dilute the intensity of the dependency relationships that have been established earlier. One of the reactions of the family as the termination phase approaches is regression to an earlier feeling: therapy is like a magic amulet, with it they can carry on; on their own, they cannot succeed. The increased passivity of the therapist in the sessions, with the family gradually taking over its own control and direction, will assist in diluting this fantasy. Lessening the frequency of visits also will assist in the final termination phase. We have found the family's increasingly productive use of its time without the necessary intervention of the therapist to be one of the significant clues as to the family's readiness to terminate. As the therapist becomes more and more passive and the family tends to take over his activities more and more, its members will raise the question of stopping on their own. Sometimes the therapist has to raise the question himself and have the family struggle with this in the termination phase. What should also be mentioned at the end of therapy is that if any member of the family should need help in the future, the therapy team will be interested only in discussing help for the entire family. Neither therapist should be available for individual help. We consider it necessary to make this point as it solidifies the unifying experience of individuals in a family in perceiving their problems within the family context. As an individual member sorts out his own problems with the awareness that the solution rests with him, he should not be referred to a therapist who is identified with the family, but rather to one who will reinforce the individuating experience.

You may have noted that your background and experience offers you considerable help in working with whole families. Some of our replies probably don't sound too different from what you would have said. Few of our points would seem foreign to an experienced member of the helping profession.

You may also have noted that our answers were direct, specific responses, mostly on technique. We have necessarily limited ourselves to brief practical applications of complex concepts and ideas, many of which have been or will be thoroughly discussed in the burgeoning literature on family therapy. Much has yet to be understood, digested, and used to help families in trouble. Our answers should not be construed as final. We hope that you will join those of us who have found family group treatment interesting and rewarding, perhaps to make your own contribution in an area that is as yet only partially explored.

REFERENCE

1. Sonne, J., Speck, R., and Jungreis, J. The Absent Member Maneuver as a Resistance in Family Therapy of Schizophrenia. *Family Process* 1:44-62, 1962.

Dos and don'ts of family therapy

John C. Sonne

Chapter
7

The task of writing out instructions for the conduct of family psychotherapy is a puzzling one, alien to the goal of psychotherapy itself, a goal which includes the value that no personal act has meaning unless it contains within it something peculiarly personal, timely, and pertinent to the unique situation in which one finds oneself. Generally, when one reads books on techniques, one finds oneself reading about theory, dynamics, concepts, and observations, but not much about the technique which he was hoping to learn and which perhaps the title of the book or article suggested he might find. Perhaps this is as it should be, since if one has knowledge he may use it in a very personal way, as he sees fit. To tell a therapist what to do may, at its worst, create an act somewhat reminiscent of a perversion, since the insecure therapist may seek to by-pass his personal role in the situation by automatically following advice, i.e., borrowing or using the instructor's executive power instead of his own. Reciprocally, the instructor may blindly be ignoring the therapist's observing, creative, and executive powers. This can be particularly true in written instructions of "dos and don'ts." Perhaps this is not such a problem in mechanical matters, such as how to assemble a piece of machinery, but it is a serious matter in an activity as personal and creative as psychotherapy. Psychotherapy done by rote may well create "rote patients."

Most instruction in the actual practice of psychotherapy takes place in seminars or precepting sessions which are very alive. In addition, one learns a great deal without formal instruction in the actual field experience of one's everyday psychotherapeutic work with patients. The values here are the personal, the momentary, and the situational. One often finds oneself saying in a seminar, "In this situation, I would forget the principle I have emphasized so often, and do such and so." The dread fear of the instructor is that his suggestion will be blindly followed at a novel and crucial moment in a therapeutic situation.

Without many reservations, and with the plea that the reader not do anything unless *he does it himself*, with integrity and authenticity, I shall begin my chat and express my thoughts on some "dos and don'ts" of family therapy. *Caveat emptor!* I shall probably live to regret this paper.

1. My first advice has to do with an over-all general attitude. I would suggest that the therapist approach family therapy with a sense of humor and a sense of adventure, that he pay close attention and think a lot.

2. Don't get depressed. It's the family's problem, not yours, and if you get depressed, you've joined the gang, so how can you help them or yourself?

3. Work with a co-therapist, preferably one of the opposite sex. This not only increases the observing power, but it also gives the therapist someone to talk with and to blow off steam to. It also helps one maintain hope and cheer and provides the family with a model of communication. If the team is a heterosexual one, so much the better, for the model stands for so much that is creative, hopeful, and fun.

4. Don't compromise on your contract to work with the family as a total family, with all members being viewed as involved in a system of socially shared psychopathology.

5. Beware of a phone call from a single family member, and, if possible, state in advance that you will not take such a call, since you are afraid it would greatly complicate treatment. If caught on the phone unawares, say, "Before you say anything, I would like to say that I feel that whatever you have on your mind would best be brought up in our next family therapy session with everyone present. Would you please hold it, and I'll see you all then. Good-bye." If necessary, to make this stick, say, "I'm not going to listen to what you're about to say. I'm going to hang up. Good-bye." And hang up.

6. Don't hold any meetings in the absence of a family member or your co-therapist.

7. Don't countenance sex or anatomy being treated as hush-hush topics not to be discussed in front of the children. Remember that this is a sick family situation in which the parents are as sick, or sicker than, the children, and that to avoid sexual discussions or to exclude the children from them does not protect the already confused and over-stimulated children or help the adults, but, on the contrary, helps maintain the children's confusion, and fails to see them as seekers after truth who may help the confused parents.

8. Don't worry too much about facts and descriptions. Families are often so occupied with attacking and counter-attacking, describing, documenting, and indicting, that one might think one were in a courtroom. Far more important than the facts are the feelings. For example, daughter may say, "Mother, you don't buy me enough clothes," and mother may respond, "Yes, I do." Underneath this, both feel hurt and unloved. Get them to say so, to make the experience personal, alive, and moving.

9. Elicit evidence to illustrate the transmission of irrational modes

of relating from generation to generation, showing that imitation, sado-masochism, denial, and projection have crippled the parents' matura-tion, and are now crippling their mate's and their children's maturation. For example, if the father's father was sadistic, instead of rejecting his father's sadism in anger and becoming a better father to his son, the father will laugh at his hurt from his father and dish out sadism to his son in the name of "father should be boss." If it is possible to get the father to recognize his hurt and anger toward his own father, or to get the son to recognize his hurt and anger toward the father, one is on the way toward the development of a healthy father-son experience rather than a generational repetition of history going no-where. Sometimes a way to reverse a parent-child, sado-masochistic interaction through insight from the preceding generation is by asking the mother something like this when, for example, she is hounding her daughter about staying out late: "How did you and your mother get along about this?" The mother is likely then to reveal not only her hurt and hostility toward her own mother, but also her confusion as a parent in imitating her harsh, condemning mother while simul-taneously encouraging her rebellious daughter to act out her unex-pressed, lifetime resentment toward her own mother. When the mother sees this, she not only feels more accepting of the "child" within her-self, but is able to be more loving toward her daughter and more accepting of love from her daughter. The need to encourage imitation and acting out abates, and healthy, affective relationships can develop.

10. Work more with the father early in treatment than with the mother. Generally speaking, a sick family is somewhat matriarchal and primitive in its organization, but before this level of pathology can be dealt with, it is necessary for some degree of increased reality sense to be developed in the father. The fathers are often so terrified of their wives, and so utterly dependent on them, that they will stop the therapy rather than have the "little lady" mistreated. By contrast, the mothers do not seem to feel so extremely threatened if the fathers are subjected to a critical analysis early in treatment. Hence, one is not only able to work with the father early in treatment, and unable to work with the mother, but it is necessary to work with the father if eventually one is to successfully treat the mother and the mother problem in the family.

11. Don't threaten the mother too early in treatment. Work with her extensively when everyone else in the family is strong enough to hear her and to help her. At this point, one is able to deal with the mother's deep sense of worthlessness and failure. If she is approached too soon she will reinforce her stance as a phallic, masochistic, paranoid mother and one will have gotten nowhere.

12. Encourage direct, appropriate physical contact between fam-ily members and don't block the translation of an insight into action in this unusual situation where real love objects are present. Poignant moments are realizable in family therapy which are perhaps unusual, and are unique to family therapy. Sharing such intimacy to such a

degree is not experienced in one-to-one treatment and is probably rarely experienced in life.

13. Don't be afraid to deal with hopelessness. If one can't talk about hopelessness, one can't talk about desire. If one can't talk about hopelessness in one's own family, this is hopelessness itself. For the therapist not to deal with hopelessness is to identify with the family and validate despair.

14. Don't expect suicide. Put your weight on the family and encourage interaction. Many possibilities are open to the suicidal person in family therapy: he can fight his love objects instead of his harsh superego; he can be loved and encouraged to fight his harsh superego; his superego can be ameliorated. And even if the forces are inclined to reinforce his harsh superego, this in itself represents such an involvement that the suicidal risk is slim. For the therapist to pussy-foot shows little faith.

15. If a significant peripheral person appears to be involved with the family in such a way that he is reinforcing the family pathology, bring the person into the group, or in some imaginative way explore this relationship and weaken it. If this is impossible, stop treatment before you get hurt.

16. Don't let splits occur in the co-therapy unity. Make sure that there is adequate communication and that the family does not succeed in incorporating one or the other or both therapists into psychopathological dyadic alliances. Many of the stresses and processes in the co-therapy experience are induced by the family as part of their family therapy experience, and it is helpful to bear this in mind at times of seeming disunity.

Bon voyage! Have fun!!!

The supervision of the trainee family therapist

Oscar R. Weiner

The purpose of supervision is to provide the trainee family therapist with an opportunity to acquire, from an experienced family therapist, the knowledge that will help him to function more skillfully in the therapeutic situation. In this respect, the supervision is very similar to the supervision which forms such an integral part in the training of an individual psychotherapist or a social case worker. It is different, however, in that it exposes the trainee to a kind of "patient" (a whole family) which is far more complex than any previously encountered. For the most part, the therapist who ventures into the field of family therapy has had a very limited experience with the families of his patients. In the past, traditional psychotherapy has generally recommended that the family be avoided so as to preserve the one-to-one relationship in an uncontaminated state. Even social workers who work in family agencies avoid seeing the family together, and usually see either one member or some subgroup, i.e., one parent and the designated patient, the parents alone, or the patient alone. The same is true in child guidance clinics. It is important, therefore, that the trainee familiarize himself with the large body of knowledge that has been recorded in the last decade by the pioneers in this new therapeutic medium. It is absolutely essential that he understand the basic nature of family psychopathology before he proceeds to the difficult task of dealing with the family as the "patient." While the theoretical background that trainees have developed in their previous training provides them with important information, it is simply not relevant enough to help them in this new work, and this is also true of therapists who have had extensive experience with peer group psychotherapy. While group therapy may appear to be similar, since it and family therapy both encompass a multi-individual setting, the actual dynamics are completely different. A family has a structured system of interrelationships and a shared pathology which has developed in a day-to-day experience of living together over a long period of time, while the therapy group is artificially created and the contact of its members in the group makes up only a small portion of its members' total ongoing life experience.

With this as an introduction I should like to proceed with the main objective of this chapter. I will attempt to convey some of my experiences in supervising therapists from different disciplines and from three different settings (psychiatric clinics and hospitals, child guidance clinics, and family service agencies). I will attempt to describe the merits and disadvantages of each and to explore some of the problems encountered by the trainees and the supervisor. It will become apparent to the reader that there is a bias toward the co-therapy arrangement; this undoubtedly stems from the fact that I was first introduced to family therapy through this particular therapy approach.

The first method I want to discuss is the one conventionally encountered in the training of any psychotherapist. The trainee sees the family alone and brings to the supervisor a summary of the session or sessions for discussion, criticism, etc. One practical advantage of this method is that it can take place at the convenience of the supervisor and entails a minimum amount of time and effort. However, this places a heavy burden on the supervisor (unless the sessions are taped) to elicit carefully the multiple interactions that occur between the members of the family as well as between them and the therapist, in addition to whatever additional material is relevant. So much happens in the average family therapy session that the beginning therapist is apt to fail to perceive one or more significant aspects of the dynamic interaction. For instance, he may fail to perceive and detail all the nonverbal communications that make up an important aspect of how the family patterns and pathology manifest themselves — the seating arrangements, the looks that pass between the members, their postures, facial expressions, and so forth. The supervisor, faced with the task of helping the trainee understand the family, knows that, even when what has transpired has been recorded on tape, there will be large areas that cannot be fully transmitted. Also, it is quite difficult to deal with the transference-countertransference problem when so many people are involved. The supervisor must depend on the trainee's impressions, and it is difficult at times to convince the latter that he may be overreacting in a situation. As an example of this, one of our trainees reported to his supervisor that he had told "his" family that the treatment was about to terminate because the father refused, despite the pleadings of his wife and two children, to take part in it. It was pointed out that terminating the treatment on these grounds did not seem realistic, since it was the father's phone call that had initiated the therapy, and since he had at first seemed quite willing to come. He had taken part in the two sessions that had already taken place, and his sudden refusal to participate seemed inconsistent. On closer questioning, the supervisor learned that the father had been objectionably noisy in the sessions and had later been severely criticized for this by the rest of the family. This possibility had been overlooked by the trainee, who had, unconsciously, also reacted strongly to the father's behavior. When the trainee recognized his own feelings, he pointed out to the family that there was to be no criticism of the father after the sessions, and the therapy proceeded. In this case, the trainee had let himself be influenced, and perhaps overwhelmed, by a powerful coalition between the mother and the children, all of whom wanted to portray the father as an ogre.

Another method of supervision is to observe a therapy session from behind a one-way mirror. The family is told that they are being observed and the session is put on tape. The initial problem in this method is the anxiety created in both the family and the trainee by the fact that everything that transpires in the session is under the scrutiny of another person. In my experience, the families usually adjust to this more easily than the trainee; they know that they will not be held "accountable" for what they say and do. The anxiety in the trainee-therapist may persist throughout the sessions to the point where he is completely inhibited and is preoccupied only with doing the right thing; he anticipates being criticized, and feels unable to defend or justify his therapeutic maneuvers. There is some justification for this anxiety, since being observed by colleagues can be a trying experience initially even for an experienced family therapist. There is a tendency for the observer to compete with the trainee and, in effect, to tell him that he (the observer) could do it better. This may result in unjustified criticism and diminish the therapeutic efforts of the trainee.

The observation room also provides a distortion that must be recognized and taken into account: the mirror, while affording the observer a visual and auditory impression of what is going on, creates an experience that is different from that being experienced by the therapist who is participating in, and empathizing with, the family interaction. I became acutely aware of this one day when I was observed by a group of medical students. I had been treating a family for a period of four months and felt that the session had gone particularly well. The mother, who had been psychotic, was under good control, and while she was still hostile toward her daughter, there was a marked change in affect. The daughter looked better, was better dressed, and could deal more effectively with her mother. Following this session, the students reacted strongly, feeling that I had allowed the mother to attack the daughter and that she had appeared crushed. I realized that part of this reaction was due to their inexperience, but the main reason was that, while they had heard the words and viewed the scene, they had not been able to experience the positive affect between mother and daughter which had been so apparent to me, sitting in the same room with the family.

The one-way-mirror method is more time consuming, for it entails observing the therapy session and following it by a longer discussion period than is required in the co-therapy method. It also requires coordination of schedules between supervisor and trainee. The advantages, however, are great, since the preliminaries can be dispensed with and supervision can proceed at a more dynamic level.

The third method, which was the one used on our project, consists of having the trainee join the supervisor as a co-therapist in treating the family. This method affords the trainee the opportunity of working with an experienced therapist. This, I feel, approximates more closely the teaching situation that generally exists throughout the field of medicine. A resident in surgery, for example, learns his skills by assisting an experienced surgeon, and only after sufficient time has elapsed is he allowed to perform surgery himself. Even then he works under the direct supervision of an experienced man. It is only in recent years that this method has been introduced to psychotherapy. It is also used as a training method in group therapy, but there it differs in that the trainee usually acts as a recorder and observer instead of as a participator. Perhaps it was the difficulties that solo therapists experienced when treating some of the more disturbed families that helped to bring in the trainee as an actively participating part of the co-therapy team.

The trainees on our project for treating families with sexually acting-out girls were experienced social case workers of both sexes who had worked in family agencies for many years. Most of them held supervisory positions, which was a factor in their selection. The supervisors were mostly psychiatrists, but included a clinical psychologist and a psychiatric social worker who had worked almost exclusively as partners of co-therapy teams in the treatment of families. This meant that in the course of their own development as family therapists they had come to the conclusion that co-therapy was the preferred therapeutic arrangement in the difficult task of coping with family pathology. Their previous experiences had been mainly with families having one or more schizophrenic offspring.

Most of my subsequent remarks (see Chapter 10) regarding the trainee co-therapist will concern the senior social case worker group mentioned above. However, I have used the co-therapy approach in supervising trainees (psychiatrists, psychologists, nurses, etc.) from other disciplines. These will be mentioned only in passing, since the problems encountered with them, while in some respects seemingly different, are strikingly similar in regard to the essential issues.

It was decided that in the first phase of the co-therapy relationship the trainee would act as reporter and submit written observations to the supervisor on the aspects of the therapy session that he considered significant. The writing requirement helped him to formulate his own concepts and questions. The family therapy sessions were one and a half hours long, which meant that the supervisor and trainee would spend approximately two and a half hours together each week (including an hour for discussion after the session). The trainees had already attended a number of lectures and seminars dealing with the theory of family pathology and its dynamics, with special emphasis on the sexually promiscuous girl and her family.

The majority of the trainees had worked with families before, although generally with selected dyads, such as mother and child or mother and father. Siblings were rarely seen and members of the extended family, such as grandparents, aunts, and uncles, were never seen. Some of the trainess had even seen entire families before, but in a different framework — that is, there was always a clearly defined problem with a designated patient. History taking played a large part in the initial sessions, which generally meant collecting evidence for the indictment of the child about whom the complaints were made. It was easy, depending upon the circumstances, to become identified with the child against the bad parents, or with the parents against the bad child.

Because most of the trainees had never worked with an entire family (including all of the siblings, whether married or not, and all other relations living in the same house), some of them regarded doing so as a rather frightening prospect. There was much questioning concerning the advisability of including younger siblings because it was feared that they would either be traumatized or would get nothing out of the meetings. The idea of including other siblings living away from home (i.e., married, away at college, etc.) was met with some negative feelings. In one family with many siblings, the question was raised of whether it might be better to exclude them since they tended to be noisy and fidgety, causing the parents to spend a great deal of the time correcting them. It was pointed out to the trainee that this was part of the family resistance and that the children provided the parents with a means of breaking off discussions which had become too penetrating and revealing. Another family at first refused to exert any control over the children, and the whole situation became chaotic. The father finally became angry and scapegoated one of the children by beating him with a belt, while at another time he reduced his oldest son to tears by humiliating him in front of everyone. The trainee over-identified with the children and became very angry at what he regarded as the father's brutality. He was angry, too, with the co-therapist for not intervening to rescue the children. It was necessary to point out that doing this would only have intensified the scapegoating and that perhaps the father's anger was even a sign of progress for the family, since this father had always been distant and remote; even beating was perhaps preferable to completely ignoring his children. It was also clear that the sons had to learn what it was that provoked this response in order to avoid it by relating to their father at some other level.

Also disturbing to the trainees was the open statement to the family that there would be no privileged communication between individual members and therapists outside the sessions (i.e., telephone calls, written notes, private sessions) and that all secrets would have to be brought into the open once their presence was detected. Also, that despite the family's designation of who the patient was (in many cases this designation was supported by social agencies, courts, or other community authorities), we would consider the *family* as the *patient*, which meant that there would be no overt or covert alliances. This attitude seemed to overwhelm the trainees, who felt it would not only create chaos and be destructive to the family's image, but that it would tend to obliterate the separation between the generations rather than encourage separation and individuation.

As far as the trainees' attitudes to the family were concerned, the most disturbing area generally centered around the discussion of sexual material, despite the fact that sexual acting out was the initial reason for therapy. Discussion of sex, to some trainees, seemed to be a violation of all that was sacred in the family, and was seen as intensifying the problem rather than alleviating it. The discussions on sex were handled differently by different therapists. Generally. even when the parents were seen alone, it was with the clear understanding that, if deemed necessary, the material would be used by the therapists, in the presence of the whole family. One trainee was never able to fully adjust to this and during the entire treatment chose to focus on hostility and aggression rather than on the sexual problems which the family struggled with.

In the course of treatment many of the trainees found themselves reacting strongly to different members of the family at different times. Generally, they would begin by being particularly sympathetic to the primary patient but would react negatively as soon as they were rebuffed. The male trainees would often feel angry and negativistic toward the mothers, while the female trainees more often disliked the fathers. Their attitudes were frequently determined by how they were treated by different members of the family. This became very apparent with one trainee whose ethical, cultural, educational, and social background was far removed from that of the family he was helping to treat. Their style of living and functioning was foreign to anything he had ever experienced, and his alienation was intensified by the family's maneuvers to reject him by being politely silent whenever he spoke. He felt out of the family and out of the treatment; his anger was so intense that he wanted to terminate. Only after it was pointed out that his need to impose his own value system was the cause of this impasse was he able to deal with them in a more relaxed manner. This led to his acceptance by the family and a complete reversal of the previous pattern.

Because of the trainees' preconceived ideas and attitudes as to the ways in which they expected families to behave and accept help, they would frequently find themselves furiously angry when their expecta tions weren't met. This would usually manifest itself by strongly sympathetic feelings toward the member who was seen as the scapegoat, and only after they were made aware of the intricate system of alliances, dyads, and collusions within the family were they able to deal with its members more successfully. They were then able to avoid the temptation of being the good, giving parent and could tolerate being seen as the bad parent when they refused to comply with a family's demands.

Problems arising from the co-therapy relationships

This was the first time that most of the trainees had worked with a co-therapist. The majority of them were performing in their agencies in a supervisory capacity; now they found themselves reduced to the position of students. There was a difference in the professional status within the co-therapist teams, since the supervisors were psychiatrists. The trainees were to be co-therapists in treatment situations which they had never encountered before.

In the early phase of their work as co-therapists they were silent for the most part. The questions they asked were usually neutral, aimed at eliciting some historical data. If the family was well behaved, they were able to participate somewhat — if not verbally, at least non-verbally. The violent or repressive families were generally completely overwhelming to the trainees, who would later confess that they emotionally withdrew.

It was important to establish an early feeling of trust and confidence between the supervisor and trainee so that a real co-therapy team would become a fact. This involved learning about each other in terms of family, life experiences, philosophy of life, etc. The trainee was encouraged to talk freely about his feelings toward the family he was helping to treat and toward the supervision, and the supervisor did the same. This enabled the co-therapy team to know each other as persons and created a milieu in which the trainee could begin to function more effectively in the sessions.

Part of the trainee's silence at the beginning of his work as a co-therapist was a reflection of his disapproval of the supervisor's approach to the family and of his need to see the family differently. As understanding developed and the co-therapy relationship was established, the trainee was able to become more active.

The next phase was one of increased activity, usually in direct support of the senior therapist. Frequently, however, there would be disagreements which were reflections of problems in the co-therapy relationship. These would occur for a number of reasons, one of which was the need a male trainee might have to compete with the supervisor. This sometimes manifested itself by the trainee tuning out what the senior therapist was saying and following his own line of questioning, thus blocking therapy. Or a trainee might have a need to hold on to what he felt was his own identity by denying that family therapy offered anything different from what he had been doing for years. Or a trainee might be seduced by one of the family members to the point where this dyad was used to exclude the senior therapist and the rest of the family.

Many of the trainees expressed mixed feelings regarding the techniques employed by the senior therapists. When discussions suddenly developed at the primary process level, they sometimes felt anxious and overwhelmed. The activity of engaging the family, which would range from small talk with the children to open flirting with members of the opposite sex, often gave them feelings of isolation and anger. This was frequently attributed to their not knowing beforehand what the strategy was to be and feeling betrayed that they hadn't been told. As they came to recognize that it was not always possible to fully prepare strategy before a session, they were better able to tolerate the abrupt changes in direction and even join in.

Problems stemming from intrapsychic factors

Some of this has already been discussed with regard to trainees' attitudes toward the families since much of their feelings could be seen as projections of their unconscious feelings toward their own families (father, mother, sister, etc.). Since the aim here is supervision and not therapy, much of this was left untouched. However, in the hours spent discussing the families, and in establishing a good co-therapy relationship, some of this inevitably came to the surface. This is to be expected when two people work together in the stimulating and frightening arena of family dynamics and pathology. The trainees were constantly bombarded with situations and conflicts which touched off deep and painful areas in their own lives, past and present. By open discussion, it became possible for the trainees to recognize what was happening and at times to work it through. If this was not possible, at least the recognition and acceptance of the problem on the part of both trainee and supervisor helped the trainee to control the countertransference effects of these situations and to avoid projecting onto the family being treated.

The next two chapters illustrate how family therapy is taught and how family treatment is conducted by a supervisor-trainee co-therapy team.

The process of the therapy of a family
(As seen by the trainee therapist)

Jean P. Barr

Chapter 9

In this chapter, I wish to give my selected impressions of a family with whom I worked as a co-therapist for about a year. Because I wish to share the impact that the new method of co-therapy had on me, most of the impressions relate to the initial sessions with the family. To provide a frame of reference for my reactions and "insights" as a trainee in a family therapy program, it seems essential to describe the family as it came to us. Prior to being referred for family therapy, the family had been frequently diagnosed and had had the attention of caseworkers and psychiatrists. They presented themselves frequently and regularly at one or another community clinic or agency where they literally chewed up thousands of hours of professional time. They "reached out" but, to the best of my knowledge, were never touched.

Mother, who was not the primary patient, was the fulcrum of the family pathology. Everything radiated from or was mediated through her. Before our contact, mother had had eight years of psychotherapy for obesity and depression. At 35, she was markedly obese (over 250 pounds) and had multiple somatic illnesses for which she was regularly admitted to a local hospital. In her years of therapy, she had acquired much intellectual insight but no understanding.

Father, age 37, was small, wiry, and wary. From previous information we had learned that he had "raped" the oldest daughter three years earlier. This was the reason for the referral and mother was most eager to get the sessions focused on this horror. Father had actually been railroaded into a psychiatric hospital following this "rape," had served three months' time there, and then had follow-up outpatient psychiatric treatment. Clearly, father was the villain and we were supposed to give him an overhauling. He had many paranoid qualities and played the tough-guy role so well that it was tempting to pursue that line of action. However, under the tough-guy, "I-don't-need-nobody" exterior was a wistful, lonely guy who hungered for contact with his family.

Gladys, age 15, was the supposed victim. With her Nordic build, her good intellectual resources, and her seven-year stint as "mother" in the home, the idea of rape somehow didn't fit. Gladys had been in a body cast for scoliosis the better part of the preceding year and had reigned as queen from the dining room, where her bed had been

78

set up. During the previous five years Gladys had had three referrals to child guidance clinics for stealing, lying, and difficulty with peers. The third referral was for the "rape" and led her to us.

Doris, age 10, was not next in age but was so closely aligned with Gladys that it was difficult to separate them. Doris sat next to Gladys and for months seemed pulled by invisible strings emanating from Gladys. Doris continued for months to seem most unreal.

Peter, age 13, was the "dirty, smelly, delinquent" adolescent. He had a full year's head start on us with a chronic truancy record, running away, and stealing, for which he had been referred to a child guidance clinic. He was repeating seventh grade.

Hans, age 11, was the smiling, neat, "good" boy. He had managed to stay out of the open conflict by being as neutral as possible. He had a severe reading disability, and had had extensive remedial work in that subject.

Richard, age 7, was the "baby." He was unruly, undisciplined, and was clearly acting out all kinds of infantile feelings for the family. He was repeating first grade.

The remarks that follow are largely subjective ones, but I think that these personal reactions may be helpful to other beginning family therapists.

A formidable family? I thought so. As I looked at the array of problems, agency contacts, etc., I thought that if family treatment could solve all this, I was sold on it as a form of therapy. I probably should have felt that at least we could not fail more miserably than had the previous therapists, but I remember no such reassuring thoughts.

My co-therapist, Oscar Weiner, was someone I knew and liked. I had worked with him briefly some five years earlier but had had little interim contact. He had had considerable experience in family therapy in the meantime, but that fact was lost on me at that moment. In my eagerness I arrived early for my first session. The family, also early, arrived shortly after I did. They were not easy to overlook or misidentify. I urged them to be seated in the waiting room and disappeared until my co-therapist came. We had a few moments for a brief exchange of greetings and I am sure he offered some comforting words, but my anxiety was unallayed. Despite several years of psychiatric nursing experience with very disturbed patients, teaching experience, and considerable casework experience in family and psychiatric settings, plus seminars in family therapy, I felt totally unprepared for this encounter.

I have often thought that therapists should periodically put themselves in a completely new learning situation, not only for the perspective gained but for the opportunity to re-experience the initial anxiety of a new situation. For me it serves as a reminder of what the client or patient experiences when he enters therapy.

In retrospect, I think the intense anxiety I felt in this situation was not only appropriate but normal. Part of it relates to the fact that for most of us this is an entirely different frame of reference and we have come to count on our "frames" for security. We are used to groups, but in a social, interactional way. We are used to problems and the problem-solving situation, but in a one-to-one frame of reference. We are used to learning and supervision, but not in such a direct and unrehearsed form. We are used to focusing on a problem, but here I saw seven live problems and had, at least in my thinking, a clear dictum to relate to none of these. To mix up or reverse all one's usual operational references has a disorienting effect which only increases the anxiety of an already difficult and new situation. I sensed that the family, however pathological, was at least partly within their usual frame of reference, which only increased my tension. They knew each other and had well-established means of communicating.

What happened was that, rather than attempt to interact, I fell back on my observational powers. I have long been a proponent of non-verbal communication and with my co-therapist carrying the verbal and interactional load, I was able to observe the non-verbal interaction long enough to get my bearings. In a family the non-verbal messages are multiple and fly fast.

In one-to-one therapy this non-verbal communication is often dismissed under the heading of intuition and is usually not considered to be of the same order of factual value as oral communication. One of many things I have not so much learned as found confirmed in family therapy is that the non-verbal has a very high level of communicability and factual content. Repeatedly, when my co-therapist and I checked notes on something we sensed in a session, we found that our impressions were highly consistent. This consensual validation was often later verified with verbal material from the family. The co-therapy relationship has a great deal to offer in spelling out more clearly how and what we communicate with words. Getting my clues and my reassurance from sizing up the opposition, as well as from my co-therapist, helped me regain my perspective. I was consciously aware of thinking, "How can I convey what I feel and see going on?" Thinking of how to describe this helped me begin to objectify my observations and feelings. In working with individuals, I jot down immediately my initial impression of the individual. This initial observation is probably my most accurate impression of how she or he appears to the world at large. Later that impression is contaminated by the relationship, transference, countertransference, and an understanding of *why* the person behaves as he does. Also, change often begins early in the contact and this initial impression is an important reference point.

Time has borne out the accuracy of my initial impressions. A year later, my original impressions of Gladys have changed. I realize that she is probably not as huge as I then saw her, although she is still mighty imposing. Peter is no longer dirty or smelly, but that has to do with changes in Peter, due, I think, to an adolescent crush on me and an identification with Dr. Weiner. Doris, whose name I could not remember for three sessions, is still the most elusive member. I remembered the three boys' names but was not certain who was who for the first session. This, I think, relates to the problems of identity in the males and the fact that everyone shares even his name with someone else. Hans' three roles of good boy, butler, and clown bear out my initial suspicion of an identity problem. Richard is more clearly the "id-kid."

Mother's intellectual approach and position as co-therapist were transparent even in the beginning. Only the why's are clearer now. Father's tough-guy role and his alienation from himself and his family have been spelled out more clearly, but the core of the problem was there in the first session. The alienation, projection, faulty communication, disorganization, dishonesty, and merging ego boundaries were evident from the beginning.

It is a far jump from descriptions of the individuals and some of their individual reactions to each other to the family itself, and the how, what, and why of this family.

At the first session, an attack was initiated within five minutes by mother against all four males, whom she saw as having the problems. In child guidance clinics the child is frequently brought as a projection of the problem, so this was not new. In the case of this family, however, the handling of this was much more direct and was attempted much earlier in the treatment because there was more evidence and because confirmation was more readily accessible. In the sixth session Peter spelled out the issue clearly and poetically. "In our family, it's like a tug of war. There are three girls on one end and four boys on the other. One boy (father) lets loose and we all get pulled over to the girls' side. I'm not a girl and I don't want to be on the girls' side." We spent a year trying to get father to hold on to his end of the rope.

This gave me a clue which may not have been necessary but was reaffirming. Throughout the year, not only in relation to my co-therapist but in very active interaction with Peter and father, I conveyed that not all women pull against men. I repeatedly showed my honest liking and respect for both Peter and father. Peter responded quickly and found opportunities to sit next to me, to bring in school work or drawings to show me, to touch me in the guise of examining a ring or seeing the time. By the sixth session he had cleaned up, settled into school, and brought up his grades. By midyear he was promoted to eighth grade. There was no further truancy. He took extra work in the summer so he could start ninth grade the following fall.

Much of my support of Peter was done through support of father. I repeatedly indicated my acceptance of father as a responsible, likable man whose opinions I respected. I was also able to demonstrate to Peter that father was a sensitive, feeling person who knew a great deal and used to write poetry. We noted subsequently a much improved relationship between father and Peter and the fact that Peter defended father against mother's attacks.

In the beginning, much of this support of the males was an intuitive, natural response. Later, during the discussion of the rape and our refusal to set up another kangaroo court, it was more planned. It was very helpful to Peter and to father to see that we neither considered father "crazy" nor approved of mother's machinations. Our refusal to accept mother's projections probably did not help her accept them as pathological but it did help the males see them as less valid.

Projection and transference responses were multiple and intense. From a therapist's point of view, though, the intensity of the counter-transference was even more impressive. There were many episodes, but the most difficult time for me was the seventeenth session when father, in his attempts to discipline Peter, made him stand in the session until the tears were flowing. Peter was hurt and humiliated in front of us, and I felt a tremendous empathy and wish to help him. It was brutal to watch, but, it followed a session in which Dr. Weiner had tried to get father to take responsibility for handling the children. Father, in his usual immature way, went too far, but at least was trying to be a father and needed our support. I empathized with Peter's humiliation and hated father for inflicting it, but knew it was too important to interfere at that point. Later we could pick up on father's hurt at Peter's not communicating with him.

This procedure of discussing family secrets openly felt natural and right, although it was very different from the usual tactic of getting permission to discuss *this* piece of information with *that* person, as is done when several family members are being seen separately and individually.

In the third session, when mother's promiscuity and the festering question of Peter's paternity arose, the reasonable thing to do was to pursue the subject. I honestly felt that the discussion might have clarified a few minor details for the children but the fact did not come as a surprise to me. This was true of all the so-called family secrets, including the parents' sexual activities. The real family secret, which was elicited in the fourth session, was that there were no parents. Mother did not cook, clean, or set limits for the children. When hurt, each child ran to his or her own room — no one felt mother or father could help. In her eight years of therapy, mother had never gotten beyond projecting all problems on father. She had never discussed her part in the family's difficulty, i.e., her delinquency and inability to be a mother.

Father's concept of fathering was somewhat more real but fell far short of the ideal. He worked and supported the family and when angered, meted out severe beatings. His standards were somewhat better than mother's, but he was arbitrary in his application of them. Much of the time he played a game of being the hurt, left-out one in the family, refusing to participate in activities. There were constant battles between mother and father.

This is where the treatment began. We laid down some ground rules for parenting and throughout the year held mother to her responsibility.

The process of the therapy of a family
(As seen by the teaching therapist)

Oscar R. Weiner

The Boulder family differed from other families seen by us in that there was no indicated primary patient. About eight years before we saw the family, Mrs. Boulder had sought help because of marital difficulties that finally resulted in her husband leaving her for approximately 13 months. When he returned, she had asked him to go to therapy with her but, since he refused, she continued to go alone until the time we began to see the family.

Gladys, the oldest child, has also had previous psychiatric exposure because of a number of problems — enuresis, stealing money from mother, and telephone calls to sailors at the nearby Navy Yard at the age of twelve. About two years before we saw the family, the father had been accused of attempting to rape her, which resulted in his being sent to a VA hospital where he was kept for three months and then discharged to outpatient treatment. After the reported rape attempt, there had been no psychiatric follow-up as far as Gladys was concerned, and while this was a factor in bringing the family to treatment, it was not considered of paramount importance. A year after the "rape," she was operated on for scoliosis, so that for most of the preceding year she had been in a body cast and confined to the home.

Father had been discharged from the Navy because of emotional problems; for these he had had some treatment, but had otherwise not been involved in any therapy until that following the episode with his daughter two years ago. Of the four remaining children (three boys and one girl), the three boys were considered by the parents to be the primary reason for seeking help. The oldest son, Peter, 13, was a frequent truant from school and had failed to be promoted at the end of the past school year. The middle boy, Hans, 11, had a reading problem for which he was receiving special attention. The youngest child, Richard, 7, was a behavior problem and had been suspended many times for fighting with other children and for disobedience in the classroom. The only child free of problems as far as the family and the community were concerned was Doris, 10.

The initial referral had been made about a year prior to our first

meeting, but the family had decided to wait until Gladys' back operations were nearly healed before they began therapy. Even though the
back operations were a reality factor, putting off the therapy was indicative of the family's style of functioning. As we shall see later on,
this family functioned in a manner that seemed so chaotic and yet so
gratifying to them, that there were many times when we wondered
why they had come to therapy on their own initiative in the first place
and what made them continue.

The co-therapy team consisted of a psychiatrist (myself) and a female social worker. We had known each other for a number of years
and we felt a mutual respect which enhanced our team relationship.

Initial Interview

The mother opened the session by relating the impelling reasons for
family treatment, namely, the problems with the three boys. As she
continued, it became clear that she was actually referring to *all* the males
in the home, including her husband. Mr. and Mrs. Boulder had been
married for 18 years and had never gotten along. There had been
constant fighting and bickering. Father wanted the children to be clean
and to pick up "like any family." He felt that they defied him and that
mother let them do just as they pleased. No matter how good he felt
when he came home, according to him, things were soon made very
unpleasant. For example, mother would greet him with a list of complaints about the children and expect him to administer punishment.
She felt unable to punish the children herself. When pressed for an
explanation, she said she was afraid of losing their love.

Another problem was money. Mother had always handled the finances
and had done a poor job. She liked to go places but said that Mr.
Boulder refused to take her. Until four years ago when her father was
killed, he would come regularly on weekends and take her and the
children for a ride or to the movies, thus providing them with recreation
and entertainment. Mr. Boulder never went because his father-in-law
always insisted on picking up the check, which made him feel like a
freeloader.

Mother was an only child. She had spent her entire life in two homes
that were around the corner from each other. The house the Boulders
lived in had formerly belonged to Mrs. Boulder's maternal grandparents,
and she said she had spent most of her childhood there, although the
reason for this was not made clear. Mrs. Boulder described her mother
as a very proper and very religious lady who she felt had never really
loved her. Mrs. Boulder was still subject to much criticism from her,
particularly with regard to the children, and had never been able to
defend herself in a real argument with her. She described her father
as a hard-working man who drank a lot but who was always very kind
to her. Both Mr. and Mrs. Boulder agreed that Mrs. Boulder's mother
would always side with her son-in-law against her daughter in any

argument. Neither husband nor wife could cite any specific instances of Mrs. Boulder's mother's failing to love her daughter, but when Gladys was born, the older woman had said, "Now you will have someone to love you." Mrs. Boulder attempted to portray the family from which she came as being highly respected members of the community; she became very angry when Mr. Boulder pointed out that he had lived across the street and that everyone knew that her father beat up her mother whenever he was drunk.

Mr. Boulder discussed his family with a great deal of reluctance; one of the few things he could say was that his wife had always deprecated them because they were poor. He was the youngest of four children, with a half-sister from his mother's previous marriage and two full brothers. His father had married following his retirement from the Navy, and Mr. Boulder remembered very little about him except that he sat a great deal in a rocker, collected his pension checks, and meted out punishment Navy style. His mother now lived with his younger brother and the Boulders saw her occasionally. His older brother was considered odd and was generally shunned by the other siblings, although Mr. Boulder felt he understood him and was on good terms with him.

Throughout most of the first session, Mrs. Boulder was the spokesman for the family. She focused on the problems and faults of her husband, who made very little effort to contradict her other than to mutter cryptic remarks that he refused to clarify. She said he removed himself from the rest of the family, refusing to participate in family activities. For instance, he would sit in the kitchen while a birthday party for one of the children was going on in the next room. Mrs. Boulder felt that she and her husband could never agree on anything, a feeling her husband said he shared. Although she faulted herself to some extent for the family's problems, it was obvious that she did this to show that she was only a minor factor in causing the family's difficulties. At times she assumed the role of a therapist and seemed quite perturbed when we made it clear that, despite her previous experiences in therapy, we considered her a patient like the other members of the family. It became apparent that in her past therapy she had avoided getting involved in her own problems and the part they played in creating the difficulties at home by spending most of the time talking about her husband and children. It was suggested to her that perhaps this was the first time she was really ready to deal with her own problems and that this was the reason they had sought family therapy. She responded by saying that she was really surprised that her husband had agreed to come after having refused to do so before.

Our concern in this first session was how to involve the entire family. Since the children had been quiet, we suggested that they each state what changes they would like to see in the family and in themselves. The oldest child, Gladys, responded by saying she expected nothing and wanted nothing; that she was biding her time until she was old enough to leave. Peter gave the most support by saying he would like things to be better at home. The other children were unable to respond;

this inability was only reinforced by the proddings of the mother, who wanted them to answer the doctor.

We made a special effort to involve Mr. Boulder, both because he so willingly played the scapegoat and because we felt he would be the key to the continuance of therapy and its ultimate outcome. He received a great deal of encouragement, both verbally and nonverbally, from the female therapist, to whom he described his background and his struggles to make something of himself. We attempted to neutralize mother from the very beginning by questioning her picture of the family's problems and by relegating her to the role of a patient equal to the other members of the family. This was a way of supporting father, who did not seem to have much of a position in his family — although most of this was probably his own doing. When he stated that he wasn't sure he wanted to continue therapy, we asked him if he thought he was hopeless. This evoked a stormy emotional response and he replied that he had a lot of fight left — that he had fought all his life for his family and kids, and now he was ready to fight for himself. There were tears in his eyes, and as he left the session he shook hands with the male therapist, which seemed to signify the signing of a contract for therapy.

It was our impression following this initial interview, that the positive attention given to father, despite his lack of open cooperation, and our challenging of mother had been very effective in countering the family system in which father was the scapegoat and mother had all the power. Although we still were not sure that this would result in a firm commitment to treatment, we did feel that there had been a dramatic momentary reversal of a pattern that had existed for many years. (There was substantiation of this at the start of the next session when Mr. Boulder offered us money in payment for the first two sessions.) There was still some question about the family's motivation, for it was not clear to us, despite the problems that had been discussed, what the impetus for treatment was at this time.

Phase I: Uncovering the Secrets

The following sessions were spent in eliciting more information about the family and getting a more complete and detailed description of how they all functioned. We also laid down the ground rules that the children were to be encouraged to talk and that there were to be no reprisals following the sessions.

Father discussed his own childhood and his lack of relationship with his father, a lack that was apparently connected with his inability to be a father to his own children. When asked whether he ever took his boys to a ball game, he said they always had to go by themselves. At this juncture, Peter came in to defend his father by saying that he had taken the children fishing; this was the first positive statement about the father from anyone in the family.

The problem of Peter's truancy was forced into the limelight by the family and by calls from the school authorities. Mother stated that Peter had told her he wanted to leave school. He was now repeating seventh grade, having flunked two majors and a minor, and had not attended summer school. We wondered what Peter might be responding to and felt that, whatever it was, it probably went back a number of years and was not only connected to the present family situation. Mother then said that her husband had left her for about 13 months when Peter was 5 and that Peter had felt responsible for this; he had cried constantly and said that father had left because he, Peter, was bad.

Each of the parents blamed the other for the separation. Mr. Boulder hinted that the real reason he had left had to do with a man whose son truanted with Peter. Upon direct questioning he finally acknowledged that the man had been a boyfriend of his wife's before the marriage. There was a feeling of secrecy in the air and the parents resisted all efforts to get them to talk about this. In an attempt to open up the secret, after Mr. Boulder said it was his wife's story to tell, it was suggested that there was some question about Mr. Boulder being Peter's father. Father responded by saying that he had always accepted Peter as his own and mother became defensive, saying that she could not see what could be gained by discussing this in front of the children. When Peter was asked if this was new to him, he said he was aware that the man in question liked him while his wife was openly antagonistic. He had overheard some arguments between his parents in which his father had been accused of not accepting Peter as his own.

It seemed to us that we had touched on something very crucial in this family which everyone was aware of at some level, but which was not to be discussed openly. Peter felt himself to be on the spot and, as he described it, to be the "cannonball" that was shot off between his parents in their war with each other. This was the third session, and we thought we should concentrate on opening up the family secrets, which seemed to be hardly secrets at all except as far as the therapists were concerned.

In the following session, Richard was absent and mother said that Hans had been telling the neighbors that he didn't want to come any more. She then went on to state that since the last session Peter had been a different child and had returned to school without the constant battles she always had with him in the morning. The silence was intense and father seemed to be belligerent. He refused to talk, saying first that he had said enough and then that we really hadn't scratched the surface. He refused to say more, remarking that he had been over all of this at the VA hospital and that he wanted nothing for himself, just a fair shake for his kids. Mother again raised the question of whether this could be helpful to the children, since she didn't want to "destroy their illusion about their parents." (This was a phrase which was to be used again and again throughout the therapy as a focus of the resistance to change and as a hostile retort to the therapists for uncovering the family secrets.) It was pointed out to her that this was considered part of family therapy and that the success of the treatment depended upon the family's being open and candid. Mr. Boulder felt it would be too painful to discuss certain things in front of the children. The silence continued, with the parents and the two older children smoking up a storm. We had come to an impasse and as a way of dealing with it we decided to see the parents alone for approximately twenty minutes; the children would then be invited back when we were finished. We informed the parents that although we agreed to see them alone, this did not mean we would keep anything they might say confidential; rather, we hoped that they would be able to talk about it afterward with the children present. In addition, we stated that we would feel free to use this material as we saw fit should the occasion arise when the entire family was present.

The discussion then started about Peter's paternity, with the father insisting he accepted Peter as his own but that he didn't acknowledge Richard as his (Richard was born after father returned to the family). We asked if there was a question about any of the other children. This was denied. Mother then began by saying she had been promiscuous since she was 14, had had an illegitimate child at 16, and was married about six months later. Following the birth of Gladys she had started to have an affair with a former boyfriend, and this continued until about a month before Peter was conceived. However, she was "about certain" that Peter was really her husband's child. During or after the pregnancy with Peter, she became involved with another man and later there was a third affair.

Mr. Boulder was working nights at that time and a female cousin who lived with the family stayed with the children while Mrs. Boulder went out. During this period she would often withhold sex from her husband, because, she said, she had asked him to stop working nights but he wouldn't. This was offered as a partial explanation and defense for her own behavior. When Mr. Boulder left his wife he had begun living with her best friend, which made Mrs. Boulder highly indignant and hurt her deeply. He only returned because her girl friend put him out (according to Mrs. Boulder). However, this stopped her acting out, which never recurred.

Mrs. Boulder claimed that her mother knew nothing about these affairs, but would have done nothing about them if she had, since her mother had told her at 14½ that she was uncontrollable. There was no expression of guilt or remorse about her acting out and she was at a loss to explain it. At some level she knew that this wasn't exactly the right thing to do and she felt her mother had always been a moral person and set a good example. However, she described with a great deal of feeling how angry and upset she was when her mother had become involved, within a year after her father's death, with a man thirteen years her junior who was considered a worthless bum. She had been living with him in a seashore town and had called on Mr. and Mrs.

Boulder to bail her out after both were jailed for disturbing the peace (she got into a fight with him and the police were called). It was difficult for Mrs. Boulder to reconcile her mother's behavior with the picture she had of her as an active church member and a highly moral person. However, this was not the first evidence that her mother had acted out sexually, for Mrs. Boulder had discovered that her mother had been pregnant with her before she married her father.

We then asked about "the boarder uncle" who had lived with Mrs. Boulder's grandparents, and who now lived with Mrs. Boulder's mother in a trailer. Mrs. Boulder seemed shocked and wanted to know how we knew "this." "This" turned out to be the fact that Mrs. Boulder's mother had actually been fathered by the "uncle," who had been Mrs. Boulder's grandfather's best friend. The three of them — Mrs. Boulder's grandparents and the "uncle" — had lived together for most of their lives. Mrs. Boulder's mother had been told the truth only a few years ago after *her* mother's death.

At this point Mrs. Boulder felt put on the spot in having to recite these details about her family, whom she had always held up to Mr. Boulder as being superior to his. She retaliated by talking about her husband's "running around," which she deduced from the fact that he had not been sleeping with her for the last nine months. This was something entirely new in their sexual relationship, for there had been none of this even when her husband had been aware that she was having affairs. There had also been no interruption in their sexual relations when he returned home from the hospitalization that followed the attempted "rape" of Gladys. With this revelation, mother's willingness to get involved in family therapy was finally made explicit. Her fantasy now was that we would in some way get her husband to comply with her sexual wishes, which would return things to the way they were before. She was furious at his persistence in withholding sex, which, coupled with his taking over the finances, had divested her of the power she had wielded for many years without questioning from anyone. The question of his refusing sex was to come up repeatedly throughout the therapy (it was never resolved), with Mrs. Boulder showing intense anger at not being able to get her husband to submit. He countered at one point by saying his wife didn't recognize the difference between sex and love and he felt that he didn't want one without the other.

When the children returned there was some discussion about their feelings about grandmother's behavior with her lover, and they all took the position that this was her concern, and they would not be willing to judge her. In response to how they felt about the parents sleeping separately (mother on the couch near Gladys, who slept downstairs because of her back, and father upstairs with the boys), they were hesitant to say much, although they agreed it would be nice if their parents slept together.

Following this interchange, the female therapist asked about the organization of the home, since we had been told that mother would frequently stay up all night with a girlfriend (not the same one father had an affair with), drinking cokes and talking. This brought an instant response from father, who said, "You hit the jackpot — I was wondering when you would get around to it." This delinquency on the part of mother had been a bone of contention for years, but father had been reluctant to bring it up. Mrs. Boulder reacted defensively, stating that she had been able to function well until four years ago when her father died. (He was killed by a stray shot from a gun while riding in a car with Mrs. Boulder and Richard.) The home was described by Mrs. Boulder's mother as dirty and completely disorganized. The children made their own breakfasts and got themselves off to school while mother stayed in bed. Dinner wasn't ready until 8 or 9 o'clock and mother was never home when the children returned from school. They were frequently left alone at night while mother stayed out until 3 or 4 A.M. at the girlfriend's house. Mother was frequently ill, taking to her bed and even going to the hospital repeatedly as a way of getting a "vacation" from the children. Gladys had openly taken over the running of the home. The children constantly turned to her for their needs. Even grandmother's comment on the condition of the home had no effect. Mother seemed to get support from her girlfriend, who apparantly functioned in a similar fashion, but with the added advantage that she was a divorcee.

This became the biggest bomb of the evening, revealing as it did Mrs. Boulders delinquent behavior, which was far more damaging to her as a mother than was the private recitation of her sexual acting out. She immediately retaliated by asking if there was enough time to bring up another problem which she felt was the reason they had come originally, and which had sent father to the VA hospital, namely, the attempted rape. Father said, "I knew you'd get even with me!" We felt that there wouldn't be any benefit in exploring this, that we needed to deal with what had already been uncovered, and therefore postponed the discussion until the next week. We also felt that there was a need at this point to intervene actively, and thus we gave mother an assignment, i.e., to get up in the morning, cook the meals, and clean the house. The family left in a somewhat depressed mood, although father seemed more alive despite his complaint about a cold.

This revelation about mother's complete dereliction of her role as mother and (as we learned subsequently) her mishandling of the family finances made clear what father's interest was in the therapy. In a later session, while mother was in the hospital (the first of three times during the course of therapy), he came alone with the children and talked about how his wife had squandered the family's money so that they were in debt to doctors and department stores. She had stolen his income-tax refund check as well as the check from Blue Shield for Gladys' surgery, and cashed them both. No one seemed to know what she did with the money, including Mrs. Boulder. Some of it was used in "bribing" the children, some of it was spent on food in a childish way, i. e., to buy sodas, candy, cokes, etc. for herself. Mr. Boulder had finally taken over complete responsibility for the family's financial affairs and was looking to us to support him. The children had all been aware of this delinquent behavior on mother's part, but had remained silent for the most part since she would reward them with gifts, etc. However, in this particular session they seemed ready to support their father in his attempt to displace mother as the head of the home. Although Mrs. Boulder's mother and father had been aware of much of her delinquent behavior, they had made no effort to deal with it either before or after her marriage. Mr. Boulder had been ineffectual in dealing with her and his needs were so great that he had capitulated each time he had made some effort to rebel. In addition, he had further weakened his position (to the point of slavery) by sexually approaching his daughter, and it was only during the last year that he had felt strong enough to take a stand against his wife. The first step was to withhold sex, and the next was to assume control of the money. His fantasy about what would be accomplished by family therapy had to do with finding someone who would support his position and make it easier for him to withstand the onslaughts of his enraged wife.

The following sessions proved to be as tense as expected, with Peter acting out as a way of dealing with all the tension that had been generated in the family. Peter described the family as a struggle – a tug-of-war between the four boys and the three girls. However, he felt that his father too frequently "let loose" and they were all pulled over to the girls' side. He followed this by saying, "I'm not a girl and I don't want to be on the girls' side." This attitude was jeered at by mother and Gladys, who both agreed that all men were jackasses. At this point the female therapist became more active and involved father in a number of conversations about things he was interested in. Under her empathetic approach he revealed himself to be a person with broad interests. He had written poetry and once had had a large collection of classical records which had been destroyed by the two older children with the not so unconscious complicity of his wife. He had also been very interested in tropical fish and had become quite an expert in the field. The female therapist also encouraged Peter, who began to appear at sessions with books he was reading for school, a fact that she noticed each week and commented on. There was direct encouragement of his school work and he announced one week that if he did well, he would be able to enter his proper grade at midyear and thus rejoin his own class.

Following our directive to mother that she function as a mother with the children, and with the establishment of more room for the males in this house, the problem of Peter's truancy disappeared completely. Mother retaliated by getting herself hospitalized, but to no avail. We also insisted that the family save fighting for the therapy sessions, even though we knew that this might be an impossible request. However, the family members were able to report that there was a general decline in family tension. Although mother appeared to be quite angry with us, she was unable to verbalize it. We did have a passing anxiety that she might have a coronary, since she was tremendously obese and had a chronic hypertension problem. But despite this fact, we confronted her with her delinquency problem and helped diminish her power position in the home, and we also gave her a great deal in terms of control, which she had never experienced before. She was able to say that she had thought of not coming to the sessions but that she recognized that she was getting a lot more out of them than from her previous therapy experience. There she had been able to hide her own pathology behind endless complaints about her husband and children.

In the next month the situation at home changed markedly in that the family moved into Mrs. Boulder's mother's home, which was completely furnished and unoccupied. The children seemed quite elated about this, but mother expressed some ambivalent feelings. The move presented her with a new challenge since she could no longer use the excuse that the house was in poor condition to cover up her failure as a housekeeper. There was also the question of how this would affect her relationship with her own mother, who had always been critical of her and who would be coming up periodically "to check up on her." The family also worked out interesting sleeping arrangements, with the three females occupying the three bedrooms while the four males had what they called bachelor's quarters in the basement, with two double-decker beds. At this time, also, Gladys had her cast removed and was allowed to return to school. This meant she would no longer be ensconced in the middle of the living room, serving as a substitute mother to both her siblings and her mother. She admitted to being quite anxious, since she had not been out of doors for approximately two years, and also to being worried about catching up with the other children, scholastically as well as emotionally. There had been some attempt by Gladys and her mother to delay her return to school by not going to the doctor for a final examination. However, under our direct urging, and by our helping Gladys to explore some of her feelings, it was finally accomplished.

Approximately two sessions after the move, the last big secret was finally revealed. What led to this revelation seemed to be the children's awareness of some of the material we had previously obtained from the parents in private, material concerned with the illegitimacy which had involved three generations. Mother began quite abruptly by acknowledging that she had probably been molested by her father. She had been "aware" of this since the episode between her husband and Gladys three years ago. Although she denied certainty of this as a specific memory, she felt it accounted for her mother's behavior toward her. Her mother had told her a few years ago, "It's a shame we're both in love with the same man." She felt that her father was the only one who had really loved her and her world fell apart when he died. In a subsequent session she returned to this discussion and said she was much clearer about it now, and there no longer was any question in her mind that she had been molested. This was said despite Mr. Boulder's efforts to silence her and his statement that he could never believe this of his father-in-law. (This was the beginning of a pattern which persisted to the end of treatment, i.e., Mr. Boulder attempting to silence his wife's discussion of her family.) She told of a dream where she was lying in her parents' bed and her father was tickling her stomach when her mother walked in. Although there had been times in her previous therapies when she had gotten close to talking about this, she had always terminated instead. She said that, as her father was leading her down the aisle to the altar, he had urged her not to marry Mr. Boulder. Until the time of his death, he had maintained a husband-like role with her.

The stimulus for the revelation of this material appeared to be the return to the "scene of the crime." Mrs. Boulder was now living in her parents' home, sleeping in their bedroom, and in their bed. We also felt that the previous sessions in which she was able freely to admit her delinquent behavior and still get acceptance from the therapists made it possible for her to finally face this. The revelation was also related to Gladys' re-entering the world and returning to school. (This will be elaborated on later.) With the uncovering of this material we were able to show the children that mother's delinquency did not come out of the blue, but was the result of her disturbed relationship with her parents. Father was the only one who resisted, accusing her of making it up. In spite of this, there seemed to be a more genuine communication between the two parents and they were able to have a more meaningful conversation.

At the following session mother spoke about her conflicts with her own mother since the start of family therapy. There had been a growing tension, which seemed to increase when the family moved to their new home. Mrs. Boulder had never spoken negatively about her mother before — she was literally afraid that death would be her punishment if she did. Lately she had been acutely aware of her angry feelings toward her mother, but was fearful that her own children would respect her less if she were to criticize her mother. She said that she felt like a nobody and that if she lost her mother it would be a catastrophe. She could not remember having ever felt this way before. She had always respected her mother by never talking back, although now she had begun to wonder why such respect was really necessary. In a sense, she equated her husband with her mother, for she said that they both considered themselves always right. Mr. Boulder responded by saying that he was never given the opportunity to backtrack or admit errors since his wife was always jumping to conclusions. Both therapists tried to help Mrs. Boulder to see that the angry feelings she was now aware of were not new, but had been there for years and had always been projected on to her husband, who had lent himself to this role. She confirmed this with a dream she had had in which she was fighting her husband, who suddenly turned into her mother, and was pushing him into the bathtub. We finally suggested to Mrs. Boulder that she might invite her mother to join the family sessions. The children were directly sympathetic to their mother, saying that she had been doing a pretty good job in the new home. They also encouraged her to stand up to grandmother, even though this meant a sacrifice to them, since grandmother usually came to the home like Lady Bountiful, with presents, money, and invitations to the seashore.

Grandmother sent us a poem in which she ridiculed her daughter's efforts to keep the home clean. We interpreted this as a request for an invitation and the family brought her to the next session. She was a striking contrast to her daughter, looking younger, sexier, and full of life. She confirmed most of the information regarding her own parentage and the premarital conception of her daughter. There was some guilt about this and she had been quite resentful of her daughter when she was an infant. There were no other children because she was "selfish." She denied resentment of her husband's attention to her daughter and we did not question her as to any knowledge of the incest. There was an interesting slip when she referred to her husband as "my father" and "her (daughter's) husband." Her philosophy of life was to gain gratification from group and social relations. Even though she does feel depressed at times, she is able to throw it off by prayer and churchgoing. Mother sat through the session in a quiet, somewhat anxious mood with only an occasional comment. Father seemed annoyed and resentful, accusing us of trying to get our "psychological fingernails" into his mother-in-law. Actually, grandmother seemed calmer than either of the parents, and seemed to enjoy the conversation, especially with the male therapist.

In the following session both parents said they felt we had been rough on mother's mother, although Mrs. Boulder expected (wished?) us to be rougher. There had been no follow-up discussions between Mrs. Boulder and her mother about the session. Instead, grandmother had cornered Gladys, pumped her, and thus heard about the incest between her daughter and husband. She responded by saying that grandfather had been a good provider throughout their marriage, without attempting to deny that the incident was true. She also felt that the treatment was not helpful and that the children should not hear such filth. Father attacked Gladys for talking, but Gladys received support from the therapists and mother for having the guts to stand up to her grandmother and for being loyal to her family. Mother felt her mother's presence had been helpful to her in that she was now able to recognize her mother's weakness and see her more as a person, which was also frightening, since she had always seen her mother as infallible. Her comment was "Gods fall slowly!"

The result of this session, as reported, was the improvement of Mrs. Boulder's relationship with her mother to the extent that she was no longer interfering in the Boulder house, which helped diminish tension. (An interesting aside was grandmother's question as to whether the male therapist had wanted her to return.) Mother, however, was not able to handle this change easily, and reverting to form, got herself hospitalized for back pain.

Richard now began to emerge as the new problem. Since January he had been having serious school problems and had been expelled three times. Although Mrs. Boulder expressed anxiety about this and wanted to know what to do, we felt that there was no real concern on her part and refused to be directive. Other than this, this the family seemed to be functioning fairly well, and father began to talk about moving up to a higher job which would entail trips out of town, greater responsibility, and a large increase in pay.

After seven months of treatment, we felt that we were ready to deal with what had originally been the chief complaint, namely, the attempted rape. We were told that a brick wall existed between Mr. and Mrs. Boulder with regard to this subject: they had never discussed it before or after his hospitalization. Mother related what had been told to her by Gladys and confirmed by Doris, who was there. While the words Mr. Boulder had used had implied a sexual proposal, there had actually been no rape. This had all taken place at about 3 A. M. Mother said she believed it because she had been expecting it all her life and had always felt that she had to stand between her husband and her daughters. After coming home that morning and hearing the girls' story, she immediately called her girlfriend for help. She did not confront her husband or give him a chance to defend himself. The two women arranged with the local magistrate to get him arrested on a charge of attacking Gladys. After receiving a hearing, he was remanded to a VA hospital because of his previous Navy neuropsychiatric history and discharge.

Mr. Boulder described with great feeling the guilt he had for what he might have done, but denied any memory of that night. He went on to tell how he had been arrested by the police the next day when he returned from work, and placed in a cell without shoes or belt. During the three months in the hospital he was never able to remember what happened. When we asked Gladys to give her version of the episode, she refused to talk, saying that she could not see how it could help. Mother interjected that she felt Gladys was so angry at both of them that she would do nothing to clarify the situation. Although we encouraged Gladys to talk, pointing out that this would be helpful, she refused. We felt that if anyone was being protected here it was mother; father had nothing to lose by what his daughter would say, but it was mother's position, and in time her daughter's, which would suffer if she were to repudiate the story. There was a connection here with the family's power structure and the way the females in the home, in alliance with grandmother and the helpful girlfriend, ruled the roost. This also explained why mother was only able to talk about her incestuous relationship with her father when Gladys had returned to school; there seemed to be a very hostile, blackmailing, and intimidating relationship between Gladys and mother (Doris was only slightly involved). Mother was able to say that she had some regrets about the way she handled the situation, and that she would do it differently if she had to do it all over again.

Despite Gladys' refusal to cooperate in breaking down the barrier, we felt that the open discussion had been useful. Both mother and Gladys were able to talk about the rape attempt in terms of a culmination of events that had started when Gladys was eleven. At that time, following her father's death, mother had begun to take to her bed and neglect the house. She had encouraged her daughter to assume the role of the woman of the home, and had become concerned about it only when Gladys began to telephone sailors and to demand clothes which were too old and sexy for her. The family was helped to see that the attempted rape was the result of a collusion between all three participants. We were never able to explore further the role of mother's girlfriend, who had helped to arrange father's arrest on another charge so that it would never appear on the record. We noted, however, that this prevented the court trial which would have resulted if the charge had been rape, and where Gladys would have been forced to testify. Such a trial might also have exposed mother's delinquency in not being home at 3 A.M., and her questionable relationship with the girlfriend.

In discussing the girlfriend, it was revealed that she seemed to have the run of the home, and to act as a parent to the children. She would stay there until late at night and was a confidant to Gladys as well as to mother. When she was told by the family that we had been discussing her she became furious and threatened to sue us for libel. We suggested she be invited to one of the sessions, but she replied that she would meet us only in her home with a lawyer and a psychologist present. Mother admitted that this was an unhealthy relationship, and stated that her mother had frequently accused her of being homosexually involved with this woman. It was clear that the children were also quite ambivalent about her since, although she provided them with attention and excitement, at the same time she was quite destructive in encouraging mother's delinquency and in getting mother to take punitive action toward them.

Phase II: Resistance to Change

After the intense, emotionally packed sessions which had occurred, the treament settled down to a rather monotonous level. The family seemed to be functioning fairly well, including mother. She had started to wear her wedding band again and seemed to pay more attention to her physical appearance. Peter had made up his school work and the prospects were good that he would be able to complete two years in one. Gladys was functioning fairly well in school, after making some changes in her roster. She looked attractive and acted more like a young adolescent than she had at the start of treatment. Doris, who had seemed withdrawn and almost schizoid at the start of treatment, was more alive and participated actively in the sessions. Hans was also able to participate, although he did not speak much. Father, however, was unable to follow through on his aspirations to get a better job and finally withdrew his applications. Part of this seemed to be due to mother's anxiety that he wouldn't come back, coupled with his own apprehension about leaving his home to work in a strange city for two or three weeks at a time.

The main carrier of the family's pathology was now Richard, whose problems in school became more serious. He was attending school less than one or two days a week, due to repeated suspensions. His teachers complained that he was a constant disruptive force and that they couldn't cope with him. Since the school authorities were aware that the family was in treatment, they were anxious to consult us, hoping we would be helpful to them. We were only able to indicate that the major problem was Richard's relationship with his parents and their reluctance to deal with him directly.

We decided that it might be useful at this point to see the family in their home, hoping that this might increase our understanding of what seemed to be a school phobia in Richard. The family responded positively, and when we arrived they were perfect hosts; the female therapist was offered iced tea (which we learned the family drank by the gallon), and father made a special trip to get beer for himself and the male therapist. The family seemed fairly relaxed and the session proceeded smoothly.

The major topic was Richard's school phobia. Its onset was traced to Gladys' return to school, which was felt as a great loss by mother, who had been very dependent on her. Her girlfriend had gone away for a few months and she now lacked all outside interests and rarely left the home except to go to the doctor. Her husband did all the shopping. It had been difficult for her to make this adjustment, and she acknowledged that it was much more pleasant with Richard at home, since he was very helpful and wonderful company. We also learned about Richard's fears concerning mother's health, and his anxiety that she might not be there when he got home. He expressed a great deal of anxiety about her repeated hospitalizations, and verbalized fears that she might die. (This reminded Gladys that she had to contend with the same feelings at age eleven when she was forced to run the house.) Another aspect of Richard's problem with school was mother's habit of asking him to do something for her just before he was ready to leave in the morning. Usually it was something that was unimportant and could have waited until he returned from school. The situation was similar to the one that existed during the time that Peter was truanting.

We continued to see the family at home and were interested in the difference in interaction that this made. Father seemed much friendlier and the males generally extended themselves by offering us food and drink. Richard in particular seemed to latch on to us, walking us out to the car and referring to the male therapist as "Daddy." However,

we seemed to make very little headway as far as Richard's problem
was concerned. Since summer was approaching, the school decided
to let the matter rest until the fall. Peter and Gladys made plans to
attend summer school while Hans was to attend a special reading clinic.
A big hassle developed between Mrs. Boulder and Gladys on one
side, and Mr. Boulder on the other. Gladys had wanted to stay down
at the shore with grandmother and "Uncle John" in order to work.
Father objected and said he felt this was not a healthy environment
for her. It was interesting that when this was fully discussed it became obvious that, although mother had supported Gladys in her plan,
she was not really willing to have her go, since she was so dependent
on her. However, by appearing to support her daughter's desire to get
a job and live at the shore, she involved her husband in a fight with
the result that Gladys was not allowed to go. This pattern was seen
repeatedly and was true of her dealings with the other children also,
especially Richard.

Phase III: Dependency Resolution Through Dissolution of the Family

There was a one-month hiatus in treatment during August because
of the therapists' vacation. When sessions resumed we found that the
family had generally regressed, with Mrs. Boulder appearing very
depressed. She had stopped taking care of the household, and again
Gladys had taken over these duties. Mother was also spending a great
deal of time in bed and was always fighting with the children, especially the boys. Peter and Hans seemed to be the only ones who were
able to continue functioning. They had completed their summer school
sessions and had done well in them. Father announced that he was
definitely giving up the idea of a better job and seemed more distant
than he had been prior to the vacation.

Mother attributed her depression to the break in treatment. She
recalled a dream she had had in which both therapists were present.
This was the first such dream, and in it she was glad to see us and
talk to us. This forced her to recognize how dependent she felt, something she had always denied before. She also missed her girlfriend,
who was still away. There were no direct complaints about her husband
and their relationship continued in much the same way as before, with
the slight improvement that there was less open conflict. The impending
hospitalization of Mr. Boulder for minor surgery was discussed. He
would be out of work for three weeks without pay, but since he had
some insurance as well as hospital coverage, they felt they could
manage.

We announced to the family that treatment would be terminated
in three-and-a-half months, and suggested that the intervening time
be used in attempting to solve the problems that they felt were still
present. It seemed somewhat cruel to announce this while they were
still struggling with their feelings about the summer separation, but

we felt that this would also be helpful in revealing some of their dependency problems.

The following sessions revolved around mother's depression, and an apathy seemed to pervade the entire family. She was still not functioning and Richard's problems again became acute as soon as school started.

After Mr. Boulder entered the hospital we decided to hold a session there, with just the parents present. This decision was partly motivated by the limited number of sessions remaining, and partly by the feeling that father needed our support. The sessions were very revealing in that we were able to observe the presence of a deep and meaningful relationship which had never been demonstrated in the presence of the children. We had only seen glimpses of this from time to time when father defended mother positively, or acknowledged something she had done. However, in the hospital there was an open display of warmth and closeness. We remarked about this and wondered why the children were permitted to come between them, and suggested that perhaps this was something they could alter by spending more time together. Mrs. Boulder talked about her husband's failure to respond, although she did admit that he had always been there, and she had not tried too hard. She also talked about her difficulties at home now that her husband was not there and of her recognition of how important he really was to her. The main problems apparently were with the boys. She found herself fighting with Peter again; she also recognized that she was more aware of his physical development, and admitted to having had some fantasies about him. In addition, Richard was sleeping in her bed again. Despite the fact that she knew it was wrong, she felt disinclined to do anything about it.

The following session was held in the home, after Mr. Boulder had been discharged from the hospital. This session marked father's exit from treatment. He left the house as soon as we got there, and didn't return until we left. The session was extremely tense, with the whole family appearing ready to explode. We were almost completely ignored and felt like intruders. All attempts to start a discussion were met with hostile, sullen, or abrupt answers. We retaliated with annoyance and confronted the family with their behavior. The following weeks' sessions were resumed at the clinic, with father bringing the family without attending himself. The ease with which his absence was accepted by the entire family made us feel that this had been anticipated and was even welcome. Mrs. Boulder offered the explanation that her husband felt the meetings had done more harm than good. He also seemed particularly angry at the uncovering of the "secrets," even though this had happened six months ago. In addition, he felt that the family image had been destroyed and the children would no longer have respect for their parents. (This coincided with what the maternal grandmother and mother's girlfriend had said, and it was interesting to see the alliance between father and these two women.) Mrs. Boulder admitted that she had entertained similar thoughts, but she didn't believe that these were the real reasons for her husband's leaving. She felt that the real reason was that her husband was jealous of her feelings toward the male therapist, especially since she had always openly verbalized her distrust of all men. Another factor was her admission that in a way she was pleased that he was absent since she could now get more time for herself. We also connected this with Richard's school problem and his repeated suspensions that enabled him to stay home and be with her. We then suggested that she make a determined effort to bring him in, particularly since she recognized this ambivalence in herself. There was some thought about our making an effort to bring Mr. Boulder in, with the female therapist taking the lead. But in view of the little time remaining, and since we felt that we had extended ourselves enough, we decided to let it ride. Whenever we saw him in the hall, we invited him in, but he declined each time. Perhaps it would have been better if we had informed the family that we would terminate if he failed to attend, as this would have forced them to deal with him if they really wanted to continue. On the other hand, this might have given them an excuse to terminate before we were ready to do so. We were also interested in exploring this particular family in order to understand them better. Mother reported back that she tried to have father join the family, but to no avail. However, he continued to bring the family each week. The final factor in our decision was our concern for the children and the feeling that, despite the antitherapeutic effect of father's absence, we could still give them something.

The total effect was less than satisfactory, since the boys in particular became very disruptive in the sessions, and mother once appeared with just the two girls, saying the boys were staying in the car with their father. We pointed out that this was her attempt to extrude all the males and made her bring the boys in.

The situation with Richard deteriorated so that he was permanently expelled from school until he reached the age of eight. In addition, mother was forced to deal with his hostility in the sessions and had to use physical restraint. Hans also became more obstreperous and at times seemed very disturbed. Even though mother seemed to be trying to establish a more adult role for herself in the family, it was obvious that only Peter and the therapists were willing to support her in this endeavor. The other children, plus father, and Mrs. Boulder's mother, were more interested in blocking these efforts. The role of adult would be a very hard one for mother, for it would mean giving up all the gratifications derived from acting as a child in her relations with her mother, her husband, and her children. She had been very successful at this all her life, and only with the death of her father about four years ago did the first break occur in a pattern that had existed unbroken since childhood. She showed her anxiety at the impending termination by asking what would happen after the last session. We offered to help her find a therapy resource if she still felt the need after our therapy had stopped.

Results of Treatment

Evaluating the therapy in this family is difficult because of our lack of experience with this type of family. In addition, there is the bias that therapists bring because of their own middle-class morality and standards. It is easy to talk of what, ideally, we would have liked to achieve with this family in terms of creating a real marriage between mother and father so that they could then function as parents. In connection with this theme would be a dissolution of the unhealthy alliance between the females against the males, and a return to mother acting as a mother, father acting as a father, and the children being children. However, it became obvious that we were not able to reach this family as far as these goals were concerned. It seemed to us that usually they didn't really understand what we were talking about. It was as if there were a language barrier. In addition, there was the active support of a number of peripheral persons, and social and community forces, that acted in a way to encourage and maintain their particular way of life. To this extent they proved to be much stronger than we were in the end.

What did we accomplish that was of any value? Ironically enough, it was through the exposure of the very things that the family seemed to object to the most, the family secrets, that we achieved a measure of success. The frank and open discussion by the family of mother's sexual delinquency, the confrontation of the family with the facts about the attempted rape, the incestuous relationship between mother and her father, and all the other sexual acting out involving mother's mother and grandparents were positive accomplishments. Mother's frank admission of her feelings with regard to men, of her homosexual tendencies, and of her regressive behavior, and the open discussion of father's pathology were the most therapeutic avenues in the whole treatment. They dispelled the threat of incest and murder that had been prevalent in this family from the very beginning and had ensnared the other members of the family as mother herself had been trapped since she was a little girl.

Engaging the family and developing a family treatment orientation: The initial phase of treatment

Geraldine Spark

Geraldine Spark

INTRODUCTION

Chapter

11

One of the major tasks that confronts a family at the beginning and throughout treatment is examining all problems as family problems. Even though the presenting symptom for treatment is located in a designated "patient," all the other members are directly involved and often all are suffering. As soon as feasible, therefore, and usually in the first treatment session, the focus is shifted from a manifest symptom in an individual to the family.

In this chapter I will present and discuss the first three family therapy sessions of a case because they illustrate the major techniques of helping the family understand and accept family-oriented treatment and of shifting the focus from the manifest symptom to the individual's involvement in the family system. Following the case discussion, we will examine the implications of this approach for the organization of practice in family service and case-work counseling agencies.

CASE ILLUSTRATION

Mr. and Mrs. Rivers had been seen at a family agency concerning their daughter Lucy's sexual delinquency. After several months, when it became evident that they were also concerned about the behavior of several other siblings, they were referred to us for family treatment. Individual casework with the parents and Lucy had not brought about any reduction of anxiety or tension in the family, nor had there been any modification of behavior. When the family's resistance to continuing casework at the family agency mounted, a referral for family therapy was suggested to the family because of the multiplicity of their problems. It was also felt that because of the "inadequate ego strength" of the parents and their "poor impulse control," they could not effectively tolerate or use the individual approach.

102

Family History

The family was white and Catholic and consisted of Mr. Rivers, 51, Mrs. Rivers, 46, and their seven children. The couple had been married for 24 years. The oldest son was married and lived away from the home; the second son was in the service. The primary patient was Lucy, 16; the other siblings were Kathy, 13, Agnes, 11, John, 9, and Bill, 7. The family had recently moved to a new neighborhood to escape "bad elements" in the old neighborhood.

The referral source indicated that the family problems were of long duration. The precipitating events were Lucy's staying out late, drinking, associating with acting-out teen-agers, and threatening to run away. She had been placed in a girls' institution where her behavior was described as a "cyclic pattern of good resolutions and failure." Before she returned to her parents' custody a referral was made to the family agency because it was felt she had been "caught and used as a pawn in the Rivers' marital conflicts."

Mrs. Rivers was described by the family agency as a very anxious woman with many somatic complaints: ulcers, low blood pressure, and other frequent illnesses minor and major. While growing up, Mrs. Rivers had been given great responsibility by her crippled mother. When she reached high school age she went to live in the home of an aunt and uncle, preferring this to her own home. At 16 she returned home "because her mother wanted her to come." After brief attendances at two high schools, she had to leave to go to work as a salesgirl. Her earliest memory of her father, whom she described as "cruel, mean, and unaffectionate," was "when he beat me so bad for defending my mother I couldn't go to school for a week." One of the earliest things that she remembers about her mother, whom she described as "cold, distant, and soft," was that "I used to tell her not to fight with my father when he came home drunk. I always felt like running away."

Though Mrs. Rivers complained of her many burdens, she was the one who ran things and assumed most of the responsibility for the children and the household. She considered herself a good manager who could live on a tight budget. Three years previously she had been hospitalized for bronchitis and pneumonia, and she dated Lucy's misbehavior from that time. Mrs. Rivers was quite religious and attended church regularly, and resented that her husband was not a church-goer and did not "live by his religion."

Mr. Rivers presented himself as a competent parent, lenient but a participant in the discipline of the children. He stated that, although he was easygoing with the five younger children, he had been firm with his two oldest sons. As long as he could remember, he had had a nervous stomach and difficulty in sleeping. An ulcer condition had developed and a few years previously a complege gastrectomy had been performed. He always worked long hours, leaving most of the care of the home and children to his wife. At the time of the sessions he worked from 6 P.M. to 4 A.M. as a waiter in a taproom. At work and in the neighborhood it was of the utmost importance to him to be liked. Outside of the home he acted forcefully and assertively. The family caseworker summarized Mrs. Rivers' view of her husband as "passive, dependent, wanting to be left alone in the evenings while he drinks and watches TV. At times he drinks excessively and stays out late or remains away from home; also runs around with women."

Mr. and Mrs. Rivers both had had alcoholic fathers. While Mr. Rivers had been "babied" as a child, Mrs. Rivers had had to play the role of mother substitute to her siblings. There had been stress and tension between Mr. and Mrs. Rivers from the beginning. Mrs. Rivers had sought legal advice regarding separation but had never followed through; instead, the couple steadily withdrew from verbal and physical contact until an emotional divorce existed. What they shared jointly was a poor image of, and lack of an identification with, a strong, protective father. According to Bowen,[1] "Clinical experience suggests that people tend to choose spouses who have achieved an equivalent level of immaturity, but who have opposite defense mechanisms. The phenomenon of emotional divorce is an important factor in family dysfunctioning and one that is closely related to the pattern of over-adequate-inadequate reciprocity."

First Session with the Rivers Family

All the children except the two oldest sons accompanied the parents to the first session. Although the younger children giggled a little and smiled back and forth, they were fairly attentive: Mr. and Mrs. Rivers felt fairly free to speak, as did Lucy, but the latter readily became impulsive and explosive and cut herself off when her mother disagreed with her. While Lucy openly disagreed with her mother, Mrs. Rivers never handled things with her directly. Kathy talked when encouraged to do so, and even though she differed with Lucy, she apparently aligned herself with her against her mother. The younger children, Agnes, John, and Bill, were too shy at first to express themselves. The boys were not aligned with anyone yet, but Agnes, who rarely spoke, was mother's favorite. Mr. Rivers was more active than we expected, but it remained to be seen how much he really wanted to become involved.

The parents started off the interview by complaining about Lucy sneaking off at night and dating Burt, a negro boy. Lucy almost sounded as though she might marry the boy if her mother didn't stop nagging her. Father began to say that there was more to the problem, but he never got around to exploring it further.

Lucy didn't think there were any problems when she was not at home. She feared that her parents wanted to put her in jail, an institution, or a hospital. She believed that that is what would happen to her at the next court hearing. Although both parents denied this, we found, when we questioned the parents' motivation for using our help, that Lucy's hunch was close to the truth. Lucy was quite outspoken and strongly expressed her differences with both parents. She felt that her father put on a front — it seemed that the children had learned that he was not very consistent or firm and that he differed with his wife as to how to cope with the children. All the children, including little John, attempted to protect Lucy when father got angry at her. Everyone — especially Mrs. Rivers — agreed that Lucy was her father's favorite, but for the past year father had been less protective. Although he believed that Lucy wouldn't get away with as much if he were home more often, when he *was* home, it didn't seem to make that much difference.

Mrs. Rivers attempted to present a calm, understanding exterior, but her anger and hostility were obvious. She openly admitted that she didn't trust Lucy and that she was afraid Kathy was learning from her. (Mrs. Rivers' mother had never trusted her — Mrs. Rivers — either.)

We offered the family the possibility of help through weekly sessions, wondering how far they were willing to go. Mrs. Rivers practically asked us for a guarantee of a complete cure, which we couldn't give her, and then acted as if she expected to have all her problems solved after one interview. When actually pinned down, she said she was afraid she couldn't take it, that she was close to a breakdown and was, besides, tired of running back and forth to the family agency. We told them we didn't think it would be necessary for them to continue with the agency. Mr. Rivers made quite an issue of not being able to take time off from work to keep our weekly interviews. He said he couldn't afford to lose the money and asked if we wanted him to lose his job by taking time off. I suggested that he arrange to alternate with someone. Dr. Wiener felt that his attitude was a repetition of his never being around very much and of wanting to keep it that way, especially now when we offered him an opportunity *to get back into the family in order to help stabilize it.* Mr. Rivers said he would discuss it with his boss and let us know, but he was not ready to commit himself even as far as next week's interview. We suggested a home visit if the family would like it. At this point, the parents turned to the children to ask what *they* wanted. The children were noncommittal but said they would come if their parents brought them. Lucy was the only one who could really say she wanted our help, but she was indirectly reflecting her own uneasiness about the fact that her parents weren't ready to commit themselves yet. At this point, Mrs. Rivers said she would like to try, and Mr. Rivers said he would talk to his boss.

Summary of the First Session

In this initial evaluation session, all the family members who were still living at home were seen. The technique of the co-therapists was to focus primarily on the manifest symptom of the daughter who had been sexually delinquent. The mother had used "nagging" as a way of coping with Lucy's behavior and the father had projected all responsibility and blame onto the mother. Lucy accepted the scapegoat role for the entire family. As Johnson and her co-workers stated, "Through identification with the unconscious wishes of the parent the child acts out the parent's unconscious emotional conflict. The acting out serves as a 'defense' for the parent, making it unnecessary for him to face his own conflicts."[2]

When motivation was explored, the parents denied their own need for help. Their resistance became apparent when the mother said she could not attend because she was near the 'breaking point' and the father stated that he could not take time off from work. The reality of this was reviewed by the co-therapists with the family in the light of the family's pattern of avoidance and denial, and the father was handed the responsibility for the treatment by being told that he "was being offered an opportunity to get back into the family in order to stabilize it." This challenge turned out to be very effective. Haley has discussed the importance of who assigns and who accepts the assignment of the responsibility for the treatment: "A therapist takes charge by placing the family in charge of what is to happen, emphasizing how the initiative for solving problems must come from the family."[3]

Although Mr. Rivers denied any marital problems, he revealed later that he not only was out of the home a great deal, but that even when he was home it didn't make much difference because his wife was so occupied with the children that, as a couple, they had little time for themselves. Six years previously, after a hysterectomy, Mrs. Rivers had moved into the bedroom of the son who was away in the service and marital relations had ceased.

The history elicited in this session provided a dynamic implication for the current situation. Mrs. Rivers described her self-concept and role in the past as well as in the present family. As the oldest daughter in her original nuclear family she had substituted for a crippled mother and was made responsible for her siblings. She described her mother's distrust of her and how she, in turn, mistrusted Lucy. The agency had stated that Mr. Rivers drank and ran around with other women. Mrs. Rivers said that her father drank too, and this led diagnostically to a consideration of current marital disharmonies as a repetition of the kind of marital and family friction that had existed in their families of origin.

Psychoanalytic theory had made us cognizant of the repetition compulsion in the individual, i.e., the unconscious need to re-enact painful experiences in words or acts. There is a similar mechanism in the family system: Parents will repeatedly state that they want to create a family life different from the one to which they had been exposed as children. Yet, as happened in the case of the Rivers, families are bound and trapped in a pattern similar to that of the parents' families of origin. A number of concepts derived from work with pathological and immature familes, and which have been described in the literature, were clearly seen in this family. There was a tendency to parentify the children; there was an emotional divorce between the parents; there was a breeching of the generational boundaries with dyadic alliances where two family members formed an inappropriate coalition against other family members. Scapegoating, whereby one individual was elected to be the troublemaker or problem bearer, was also present.

Spiegel comments on such disorders and discontinuities in family life as follows: "Much of what occurs in the way of behavior is not under the control of any one person or even a set of persons, but is rather the upshot of complicated processes beyond the ken of anyone involved. Something in the group process itself takes over as a steering mechanism and brings about results which no one anticipated or wanted, whether consciously or unconsciously."[4]

The first session with the Rivers family delineated their life style. There was a lack of trust; feelings and impulses were stimulated and acted out by parents and children; there was a lack of adequate impulse control in the family; parental care and responsibility rested with a single parent rather than being mutually shared – or, as illustrated in this session, the parents turned to the children as decision makers and asked them for their opinions. Thus, the executive guiding function of the parents was nonexistent, and the necessary limits and boundaries were not clear. Such conditions permit unconscious wishes and phantasies to be lived out and such family disorganization often leads to a kind of crisis which no one really wants, e.g., an illegitimate pregnancy or a delinquent act. Individual and family tensions are relieved by acting out outside the home, as illustrated in the Rivers family by both father and daughter. In this way, solutions are often unconsciously sought through the use of external authorities such as jails or other social institutions. The co-therapists offered this family an opportunity to find different mechanisms for coping with their tensions, alternative solutions to their current problems, and an opportunity for better understanding of family and individual feelings.

Second Session (The Following Week)

The night before the court hearing, Mr. Rivers was still uncertain about being able to keep our appointment, and Lucy ran away. When she returned the next day, the court was asked to suspend the bench warrant provided that the whole family continued in therapy, and that Lucy keep out of trouble and stop running away. As a safeguard, the court requested that the family have an interview with the social worker in case hospitalization was required.

At the second session, at which Mr. Rivers did, after all, appear, all the children were uneasy and giddy, and Dr. Weiner felt it had to do with the father not being ready to definitely commit himself to coming to the third session next week, despite the possibility of Lucy being sent to jail. When Mr. Rivers still wouldn't commit himself, Lucy volunteered to come by herself, but since we didn't consider the situation as her problem only, we told them that we expected the participation of the whole family. Lucy smiled when Dr. Weiner asked whether her offer to come alone was to help out her father. We gathered that, although she was concerned about how her father felt about her and wouldn't risk incurring his anger, at the same time she didn't really feel close to either parent, nor even to the other children. When Lucy said it would be easier for her mother to have her out of the way, Dr. Weiner asked whether Lucy really wanted to help her mother in this way or whether she was afraid that her parents could not control her. Mr. Rivers tried to make us yield on the time and to let next week go by, but we could not change the time and, besides, we felt matters were too serious at this point to let a week go by.

Lucy denied that, when told by her mother that her father wasn't going to keep this week's appointment, she had replied that she didn't care about doing anything further with the family. (Mr. Rivers denied that he had said he wouldn't come, but Mrs. Rivers insisted that he had.) We were finally able to get Lucy to admit that she was deeply concerned about her father's coming to the session. She now revealed that she told her mother that she had run away with her boy friend, Burt, the night before the court hearing in order to get married, but that she couldn't tell this to her father. When we reminded her that she had told us last week she had no plans to marry Burt, she angrily denied that she had ever said such a thing. Mr. Rivers said he had wondered whether Lucy was getting back at him by running away, for she was well aware that he was more concerned about her going with Burt than was her mother. Although she denied that she had run off with Burt because she was angry at her father, she admitted that she sometimes got angry with her father but couldn't express it, and didn't know what to do with it. (She was not aware that she was taking out some of her hostility by slapping John whenever he laughed during tonight's session, until father had to stop it.)

When Mrs. Rivers was asked how she felt about what was happening, she couldn't even say that she was angry and merely said, "It would be a shame for this boy to marry my confused and disturbed daughter." Lucy now lashed out at her mother for wanting to put her in a hospital so that she would give up Burt, and said that she'd rather go to jail. With encouragement from us, Lucy could say that father wanted this too and that he had even threatened to put her in jail if she didn't stop seeing Burt. Kathy corroborated having heard this from her father (which was about the only thing that she had to contribute to today's session). Lucy wasn't sure whether she could trust us and was afraid she might be picked up by the police on the street. Apparently she felt we were connected with the court and would cooperate with her parents to force her to give Burt up. Dr. Weiner stated that we were not associated with the court and would keep family confidences. If Lucy chose to continue with us, he said, our only expectation would be that she stay out of trouble and not run away. However, if she felt she was unable to control herself, the facilities of the hospital were at our disposal — she could go there and we could still continue with our family sessions. Lucy assured us that she would have no reason to run away if she knew she would not be put in jail. Dr. Weiner said that he didn't feel that she needed to be hospitalized at this point.

When Lucy said that all her problems were the ·esult of going with Burt, we reminded her that she had gotten into difficulty prior to this. She then was able to admit that the family relationships weren't good even before she met the boy.

Comment: In this second session, Mr. Rivers and the family continued to reveal their anxiety, ambivalence, and fear about committing themselves to therapy. More important diagnostically, it was revealed that Lucy, long her father's favorite, might be reluctant to have change occur because of the gratification both she and her father derived from this relationship. "Lucy ironed her father's shirts but did nothing for her mother." Spiegel conceptualizes this type of family alignment as follows: "A source of disequilibrium between the parents reveals, first, that mother defines the father's role as non-valid. In her eyes he acts like a lover to his daughter, and this is doubly inappropriate. It is not a part of his ascribed role as father, or of his achieved role as a husband. The denial is implicit — that is, they (the accusations) are only hinted at, not directly verbalized."[4]

Lucy's delinquency was a defense against her incestuous wishes toward her father, and so was experienced by her mother as rivalry. However, Lucy's overt anger toward her mother could also be viewed as an expression of her wish to be more adequately nurtured, as an attempt to defend herself against being rejected and abandoned, and then finally, against being unconsciously pushed to take the place of a wife. Lucy acted out the family's distorted roles and their confusion about sexuality. She was perceived by them as the "bad object" and the family problem. They ignored the fact that she had been pushed too early into the parentlike role.

Mrs. Rivers' dependency needs had never been adequately met in the past, since she had had to take responsibility for her crippled mother and siblings. Mrs. Rivers now turned to her oldest daughter for affection and closeness. Both Mr. and Mrs. Rivers, disappointed in each other, steadily withdrew from their relationship and turned to the children as substitutes. According to Boszormenyi-Nagy, "Pathologic need complementarity may have the value of overcoming feelings of loneliness, helplessness, or isolation. Parents who have been deprived of their own parents through loss or separation may seek unconsciously to recover the lost parent through a relationship with a child, especially if the marital partner fails to gratify this need. The child is then transformed into a parentlike figure."[5]

Lucy's behavior was seen not only as stormy adolescent rebellion, and as attempts to cope with her instinctual drives. In a broader and deeper context, her symptoms were an expression and manifestation of a dysfunctioning family system where parents need to parentify children as a way of obtaining their own gratifications. Thus, role distortions interfere with the children moving through their own processes of separation and individuation. Mr. and Mrs. Rivers' parents had been deprivers of dependency needs and gratifications, so that, unconsciously, Mr. and Mrs. Rivers sought this gratification from their children. Their own parents had been unable to help them control, postpone, or channel their instinctual feelings, and they therefore couldn't provide a model for Lucy and their other children.

The therapists aligned themselves clearly with the healthy components in this family, and maintained that jail or hospitalization was not a solution. Friedman, in reporting on the results of family therapy conducted in homes, concluded that "There may often be an advantage in maintaining the responsibility for the patient and his illness within the family, and not permitting the family to deny or exorcise what it considers to be the sick or bad part of itself by sending the patient to the hospital."[6]

Of even greater psychological import was the mutual recognition that the parents and Lucy had not effectively controlled behavior. Hope was expressed that there could be provided needed support and opportunity to find more constructive resolutions of conflicts. The therapists' confidence was based on their experiences with families who had changed or grown. If only segments of a family are worked with, some of the inherent assets in the family remains untapped.

Third Session (A Week Later)

The parents felt that Lucy was doing better and that things had been quiet since the last session. Since Lucy was embarrassed and was unable to ask what she had previously said she wanted to ask the therapist, Mrs. Rivers volunteered to ask "why Lucy bites." We learned that this was a way of showing affection but that she also did this when she got angry. We wondered whether Lucy was the only problem in this family. Mrs. Rivers was concerned about her husband's drinking so much, and both Lucy and Kathy spoke about the constant bickering between their parents; also, all the children wondered why their parents never went anywhere and reported that mother acted the martyr.

Mrs. Rivers was pushed to talk about how upset she became when Mabel, Mr. Rivers' oldest sister, called her. Mr. Rivers, who could tell his sister off, was aware of how domineering she could be — she had been critical even when they were children. Mabel had called to say that she had heard about Lucy's running away and volunteered the opinion that Lucy was no good and should be "put away." Although upset by this, Mrs. Rivers, who had never been able to stand up to her sister-in-law, couldn't tell Mabel to mind her own business, and instead asked her to "pray for Lucy." We learned that Mrs. Rivers needed people to like her and that she felt that Mabel liked her even more than she liked Mr. Rivers. We wondered how Mrs. Rivers regarded herself since apparently she would take anything from others as long as they liked her. The children openly expressed their hatred of this controlling aunt who seemed to feel she was above everybody, and Lucy burned with anger when she recalled how badly the aunt's children had turned out and that nobody dared to mention this. Kathy was the only child who, although not feeling positive about this aunt, was reluctant to express anything negative in front of her mother. Even Mr. Rivers could say that he didn't like his sister poking her nose in his affairs, but he did correct Lucy when she said that her aunt never did anything for the family. When Mrs. Rivers was sick, he said, his sister had volunteered to help, although it seemed to the family as if she expected everybody to bow down to her for this. Mabel was better off financially than the Rivers, but there was some question about the emotional stability of her family.

Although Sunday was the only day that the Rivers had to spend together, everyone took it for granted that they never went anywhere and that they could be dropped in on unannounced. Mr. Rivers' family did not visit, and it was usually Mrs. Rivers' family who came (it looked as though she couldn't tell them she might be busy). The children couldn't understand why Mrs. Rivers never wanted to do anything with her husband. Mrs. Rivers complained that her husband sat and drank all day and never asked her to go out, but the children did not agree — they said that there were often times when their father asked their mother to go some place and that she always refused. We deduced that, acting on the assumption that her husband didn't care for her, Mrs. Rivers never asserted herself to ask for anything. She said that she didn't trust men in general and had little interest in them. We wondered how *they* could have an interest in her when she carried around such an attitude toward them.

As a child, she had never received love from her own alcoholic father or her distant mother; she didn't feel angry towards her parents, but had just assumed this was her lot and had made the best of it. She was now concerned because, not only did her husband drink too much, but when her son came home from the service, he drank with his father. At this point Mrs. Rivers began to cry because, she said, her husband called her "skinny." We tried to help her bring out more of her feelings and she was able to say that she was not sure how her husband felt toward her and often wondered whether he loved her, since he never took her to the movies, had no time for her, and didn't visit her too often when she was in the hospital, whereas, when *he* was hospitalized, she used to sit by him steadfastly. He didn't fix anything around the house — it was always her brother who did this. Mr. Rivers jumped in to say that he did love his wife and guessed he ought to be more careful about how he talked about her since she was so sensitive to whatever he said. He had never realized this before. He had always sensed that his wife felt unloved, and he had also been aware that she had felt unable to cope with the children. This was certainly opening up a large area for him to give his wife more support personally and with the children. At this point, Mr. Rivers sounded as though he planned to woo his wife as if for a second honeymoon. In fact, it meant a lot to her that he volunteered to take her to the ball game with the two younger children.

Mrs. Rivers' impression of how her husband felt about her was expressed when she said that it was as though all the children stood in line to be kissed and that she was at the end of the line and got kissed just like another child. All the children laughed when they heard this and, when asked about it, spontaneously said that it would be "neat" for them to see their parents hugging one another. When Mrs. Rivers spoke of her husband giving her the same kind of kiss as he gave the children, John spoke up to say that his mother ought to "kiss better." When Mrs. Rivers saw that all the children were rooting for mother to be more romantic with father, her sad face lit up and for the first time we saw her smile.

Agnes was seated between Kathy and Lucy on one side of the table. Mother and father and Bill sat opposite. At the extreme end was John, who was watching a dead insect near his chair. Bill was trying to pull out two loose teeth in the front of his mouth and no one made him stop.

Lucy and Kathy both spoke about Mother letting Agnes get away with doing very few chores around the house. They did not think *they* could get away with this and wanted to know why Agnes did. However, they did not reject Agnes, and laughed and smiled when talking about this. Father said that Agnes was very slow, and he tended to support his wife in not expecting much from her. It was pointed out that being slow was one way for Agnes to handle her feelings and that it looked as if no one really held Agnes responsible for anything.

Lucy was beginning to wonder whether she should return to school or begin a beauty culture course, a question to which we agreed to devote some time next week. Both parents felt that either one would keep her busy and out of trouble. They were also thinking, of course, that if she went to school she might spend less time with her boyfriend. Lucy started to become angry with Dr. Weiner when she thought he said that she had to return to work. It was as though she thought that we also were trying to keep her busy so that she should give up her boyfriend. We quickly sensed her feelings about this and made it clear that this was not the situation.

Comment: In this third session, the splits, alignments, and family patterns were more clearly delineated. An important peripheral person, a paternal aunt, was described. She was perceived as a harsh, critical, superego figure whose support and approval had to be sought. Some members of the family described her as feeding into the destructive components of the pathological family system. By referring to the aunt, the children seemed to plead with their parents to take responsibility for their family and its behavior rather than turn to her. Meissner points out, "The influence of the extended family does not stop at the formation of parental personalities. Both husband and wife function concurrently not only in mutual interaction, but also in a continuing engagement and involvement with their respective families of origin. Consequently current patterns of interaction within the structure of the nuclear family cannot be adequately understood without reference to the extended family."[7]

As the session developed, the therapists brought out the potential strength that existed in the family. When Mrs. Rivers was helped to express openly her need for affection, approval, and acceptance, Mr. Rivers responded by stating that he *did* love his wife. The children supported their parents' need to give new and different consideration to the marital relationship. Only as the parental marriage was strengthened could they receive sufficient support from their parents and be permitted to function in their roles as children. Sibling rivalry was more readily expressed and tolerated after the children perceived the mood change in the parents. Humor relieved the family tension as the adults expressed more hopeful feelings toward each other. This was in marked contrast to Mrs. Rivers' previous hurt and critical attitude toward her husband and to Mr. Rivers' previous response of passive withdrawal from his wife and from responsibility for the children. Naturally, this was only a beginning, but it gave rise to the hope that the warlike situation in the family could be modified or changed. The family thus set its own goal for improvement.

This case illustrates how family therapists can bring into the open many of the problems existing in a family system. The problems of the Rivers had not been revealed to this extent and depth before. When three members were seen individually, Lucy was the presenting symptom, but the rest of the children were anxious, angry, and verging on delinquency. There was an emotional divorce between the parents. Mrs. Rivers appeared over-adequate and responsible, while Mr. Rivers was passively acquiescent and sought gratification outside of the home. The family sessions provided the family members with an opportunity to become aware that they were suffering, and that their current ways of resolving conflicts and tensions resulted in pain to the children as well as the parents. The previous methods of coping had been by acting out, denial, and avoidance, with the result that all felt hurt, angry, rejected, and isolated.

Family therapy attempts to help the family replace destructive, non-maturational patterns with a deepened awareness of self and each other. The co-therapists, via the therapeutic process, enable the family to use its inherent strength to deal more effectively with feelings and to find more constructive solutions to its problems. In the case of the Rivers, instead of scapegoating Lucy and "extruding" her from the family into a jail or hospital as a means of controlling her behavior, the parents were able to move into more parentlike roles and help this daughter (as well as the other children) through the turbulent adolescent phase.

IMPLICATIONS FOR FAMILY AGENCY PRACTICE

This case was initially seen by a family agency who handled it in the traditional one-to-one worker-client relationship, focusing primarily on the manifest symptoms of the designated patient. Since little was resolved or accomplished and more and more resistance was encountered, a referral was made for family treatment.

This kind of problem family is seen frequently in family agencies and child psychiatry clinics. Some individuals do respond to the individual, psychoanalytically oriented approach as that is generally offered in social agencies and psychiatric settings. But, as illustrated by this case, a symptomatic family member may be sent by his family to an institution for brief or prolonged periods of time if he does not respond to the traditional approach.

Through the years, progressive family agencies and psychiatric clinics have successfully adapted psychoanalytic and other principles to increase their knowledge, understanding, and skills, and this has enabled them to be helpful to many clients and patients. But when families evidence a multiplicity and complexity of problems which are not touched or changed by the traditional approach, consideration should be given to the different, newer and, from our experience, more effective therapeutic approach of family therapy. In other words, agencies should add family therapy concepts to their general knowledge and thus integrate and broaden their skills. By returning to the total family as the focus, they then can deepen their own insights and ultimately the family's. Splitting the family by assigning individual family members to separate caseworkers or therapists tends to reinforce splits and isolation in the family. Individual sessions cannot provide the opportunities afforded by conjoint family sessions. These enable the therapists as well as the family to observe directly the interactional problems and the extent of their ramifications.

In many child psychiatry clinics today, parents are still treated as adjuncts to the individual therapy of a particular child. His manifest symptoms are accepted as indicative of problems of his intrapsychic, individual system rather than as symptomatic of a dysfunctioning family system. And his "well" siblings are ignored.

If the family agency in the Rivers case had a family therapy consultant, or if its caseworkers were trained in family therapy, this case and others of a similar nature need not have been referred elsewhere. Thus, more families would benefit, and more people would be serviced and treated. Finally, when one caseworker or therapist sees a total family, professional time is more effectively used.

Many social agencies and psychiatric clinics throughout the country have recognized the validity of the family therapy approach and are achieving good results from this method, which may be described as being in a pioneering stage, with further training and experience being needed by all. It is of interest to note that the Family Service Association of America has recently published a book, *Casebook on Family Diagnosis and Treatment* (1965), and also has set up a Committee in Family Diagnosis and Treatment to encourage family agencies throughout the country to participate in this new approach.

Such activity stimulates and challenges the social work profession and other professions to re-examine existing concepts and techniques, which have been based primarily on psychoanalytic and similar concepts. It means an incorporation of these concepts into a new body of knowledge, and requires integration and acquisition of new skills. The learning and developing of modified psychoanalytic techniques has made demands on the professions of social work and psychiatry, and so will the learning of family therapy concepts and practices. However, the results of those already engaged in family therapy in both psychiatric and social agency settings seem to warrant such expenditures of time and effort. Encouragement also comes from the allied fields of psychiatry and psychology, as well as from progressive individuals and groups within the field of social work. The author herself, a former caseworker in a family agency and in child guidance clinics, has personally experienced the difficult but stimulating process, described above, of transfering from the traditional individual orientation to the newer family system orientation.

The newer method has helped to answer some of the baffling experiences with which all caseworkers and psychiatrists have at times been confronted: namely, why do so many troubled individuals terminate so soon? Why are appointments so frequently broken by an individual? Why, when the symptomatic child has improved, does the parent either mention or later return with another symptomatic child? Why is it so difficult to sustain change and keep crises patterns in families from recurring? One could add to this list, but the conclusion would be the same — the help given or received was not sufficient to bring about the benefits that these individuals and their families needed.

SUMMARY

In summing up the values of family therapy, its techniques, and practices, these points seem to be worth making:

1. Family therapy provides an opportunity to study the family system as a whole rather than separate parts of a family — e.g., the parents and the designated patient.

2. Cries for help are considered an expression of a dysfunctioning family system. An attempt can be made to search for underlying causes in the family system rather than to accept the manifest symptoms and complaints of one individual as the problem.

3. The entire family is enabled to gain a new homeostatic level. To reach this goal all family members have to be included, since the absence of even one person, regardless of age, may prevent the full evaluation of the resistances.

4. The absence of one person from the family sessions will interfere with the observation and study of all the alliances and splits that may exist in the family.

5. The conjoint session provides the family with an experience which may clarify:

   a. family roles and how the various family members function in these roles;

   b. dyads which are overtly hostile and aggressive and their forms of expression, and dyads which may be stimulating such responses;

   c. verbal communications and their interpretations or misinterpretations by the family;

   d. how warmth, approval, and acceptance are verbalized or denied;

   e. how the family arrives at decisions and supports or undermines them;

   f. how values and standards are perceived within the appropriate cultural context of this family.

6. Change in an individual may create a shift in the total balance. In family treatment the symptomatic individual may be relieved from carrying the excessive burden of change for all family members. Changes are more readily supported if they are familiar to all, even when temporary imbalances occur.

7. Flexibility in technique may provide opportunities to explore marital tensions as well as child-parent conflicts. In other treatment modes the changes that need to take place in a marriage may not be effected through the treatment of the child. In family treatment, the adults are enabled to work toward a solution of their individual and marital problems.

8. The individual may gain insight not only about himself, but also about the relationships and interaction of the family members.

CONCLUSION

Practitioners of family therapy in all settings will have to share their experiences more fully to increase learning and knowledge. There has not been sufficient time to learn all that needs to be known and understood. Clinicians in both types of settings who may be working with families whose presenting symptoms are different, may gain additional understanding and insights since they have a unique vantage point. As all these efforts are explored and combined, the field of family therapy will continue to grow until it reaches its full potential.

REFERENCES

1. Bowen, M. Family concept of schizophrenia. In *Etiology of Schizophrenia*, D. Jackson, ed. New York: Basic Books, 1960, pp. 346-372.
2. Johnson, A. and Szurek, S. A. The Genesis of Anti-Social Acting Out in Children

and Adults. *Psychoanal. Quart. 21*:323-343, 1952. Johnson, Adelaide M. Factors in the Etiology of Fixations and Symptom Choice. *Psychoanal. Quart. 22*: 475-496, 1953.
3. Haley, J. Whither Family Therapy? *Family Process 1*:69-100, 1962.
4. Spiegel, J. P. The Resolution of Role Conflict Within the Family. *Psychiatry 20*:1, 16, 1957.
5. Boszormenyi-Nagy, I. The Concept of Schizophrenia from the Perspective of Family Treatment. *Family Process 1*:103-113, 1962.
6. Friedman, A. S. Family Therapy as Conducted in the Home. *Family Process 1*:132-140, 1962.
7. Meissner, W. W. Thinking about the Family — Psychiatric Aspects. *Family Process 3*:16, 1964.

Some techniques useful with acting-out families

Ross V. Speck

Chapter
12

An attractive mother was loudly arguing with her teen-age daughter, who seemed to take delight in baiting the mother. So intense was the mother in her attack that she seemed scarcely aware that her husband and a younger daughter, as well as two therapists whom she had met for the first time a few moments before, were present. As the atmosphere became more charged, the father, who was sitting passively, responded to a challenge from the mother by threatening to beat up the daughter. The daughter scoffed in his face and muttered, "You wouldn't have the guts." The younger daughter looked at this scene in a disinterested way and asked if she might do her homework. She was just entering her middle teens and was still a dutiful daughter (a good clinical guess would be that she would not remain so for long). Obviously, the mother and the older daughter each expected that the therapists would come to their rescue; instead, the therapists elected to try to separate the combatants by pointing out the intense dyadic involvement. It was apparent that these two women only had eyes for each other. An impression of the father as an ineffectual, dominated, and henpecked male came across. Before the first session was over, the therapists had attempted, on at least 20 occasions, to shift the focus from the mother-older daughter relationship to the other members of the family and other problems, but this was only minimally successful.

Shifting the Dyads

When dyadic involvement is intense, therapists may have to proscribe arguments and fights between members of the particular dyad because the battle never ends and no one ever changes a position. Should the therapist take sides, and this is often difficult to avoid, the battle usually shifts from the original dyad to one involving the therapist. This can sometimes be helpful, but more often it leads to a stalemate reminiscent of the way the earlier arguments between the parent and the acting-out child became stalemated. The therapist shifts the dyads by

118

directing attention to relationships between other pairs in the family unit. One important such pair is the marital couple. If the therapist can get the parents to work on their marriage and improve their communication, less energy will be available for a binding relationship with an adolescent child, and maturation and individuation of each family member can take place.

Marital Metamorphosis

One repeatedly observes in the therapy of the acting-out family that, under a veneer of superficial conservatism, the deeper psychological strivings of the parents are aptly mirrored in the behavior of the acting-out daughter. This observation was first made by Johnson and Szurek in their well-known paper in which the concept of parental superego lacunae was developed.[1] For instance, a frigid, inhibited, and overly conventional mother has repeated dreams involving rape and promiscuity. At the same time she manifests disgust and revulsion at the acting-out behavior of her daughter. The mother and daughter are at least vaguely aware that the repressed impulses of the one are acted out by the other.

If the family therapy is to succeed, the therapist must be able to redirect the attention to the marital dyad. This is accomplished by repeatedly focusing upon the interaction between the husband and wife. Since the great majority of the fathers of the sexually acting-out girls whom we observed have abdicated their male role, it is up to the therapist to supply a male role which the father may then identify with or begin to emulate. Failing this, a sufficiently positive relationship must evolve between the therapist and the father so that the latter is willing to follow detailed instructions that are calculated to enhance his role as a man. The therapists may have to challenge the father to be a man. They may alternately challenge him, and support or encourage him to assume his masculine role. The therapists may also help him to uncover the anxieties and guilts that block his self-assertion. This method is generally more time-consuming and less effective than the more active techniques. For instance, the father may be actively encouraged to quarrel with his wife — a quarrel in which he must win. The majority of the fathers with whom we have worked have had a very passive orientation toward life, and very few are willing to switch to a fighting role in the family. These family therapy sessions supply a rehearsal for more continuing engagements in the home. When the fathers have been willing to stand up to their spouses, we have found routinely that the marital relationship and the authority pattern in the family have switched to one of mutual respect. There is much less anxiety in the family and the acting-out behavior tends to diminish. When the father takes charge in the family there is coincidentally an improvement in the marital sexual relationships.

Fortifying the Father

In general we have used two types of techniques in our attempts to strengthen the role of the father. In the first type the male therapist has supplied himself as an identification model for the father. This technique has been used when the father's passivity has been a primary problem in his abdication of the father role. In one case, for example, the father used emotional distance to conceal his passive-dependent relationship with his wife and adolescent daughters. The male therapist thereupon interacted with the women in a friendly, intimate way, without, however, getting caught up in their manipulations. He showed his enjoyment of the women and even exchanged gifts and embraced them at the end of sessions, but he refused their requests for additional private sessions and, in general, set limits on their behavior. The father followed suit after a few months, and invited the therapist to go fishing with him.

In cases where the father has never had a significant identification with a father figure, and simply does not know how a father should behave, the therapists have attempted detailed training by discussing with the father a position a male might take in any given family situation. Both these techniques require an ongoing relationship between the father and the therapists before they can become effective.

Combating Parentification of the Child

Sexual acting out by an adolescent female member of the family is often the outstanding sign of life in a family's otherwise dreary existence. It is as if a husband and wife, in their quiet desperation, have suddenly been galvanized into rapt attention. The whole circus of family life now revolves around incessant questioning, demands for information, vitriolic accusations, and intense interest. The parents tend to behave as if they are learning about sex for the first time and by their intimate questioning reveal their desire to learn about the facts of life from their adolescent daughter. The tables have been turned. The child possesses the marital rights while the parents are inquisitive children. While at one level it seems that the parents are superficially united in their disapproval of the girl's behavior, it turns out that they are actually working against each other in their attitudes. Also, on a more covert level, they are alternately inciting acting out.

The therapist's role is to encourage the parents to be parents. The parents' tendency to focus upon the intimate details of the adolescent's sexual life has to be thwarted. We have found that the best solution to this problem is to get the parents to concentrate upon their own sexual relationship. While many professionals and lay persons may object to this on moral or ethical grounds, we would like to remind them that sexual acting out in the adolescent daughter is a problem that exists before we get to see the family; and when we do get to know the family, we usually discover problems in the marriage. In some cases it is indicated to see the parents alone for this purpose. In others, where it is evident that the adolescent is already aware of the problems in the parental sexual relationship, it is an advantage to have the feelings about sex discussed openly in the family.

In some cases it is necessary for the therapist to reinforce weak parental objections to an adolescent family member's chaotic behavior. In one family with an annual income of $10,000, the adolescent daughter had, by threats and cajoling, obtained permission to acquire a horse and a car of her own. She had threatened to hate her parents forever if her wishes were not acceded to. The therapists were outspoken in their charge to the parents to take control of the situation. Female adolescents frequently complained that their parents gave in too readily and had set no limits on their dating or sexual patterns since early childhood. In one case, a seven-year old daughter insisted that she be allowed to observe the parents' sexual intercourse. In such instances the therapist will have to present the view of the larger community for setting limits on the impulses of the children.

Some of the parents appeared quite willing to turn over the parent role to the therapists, a willingness which worked as a resistance to resolving the marital impasse. In one family, the passive and ineffectual father had failed in two prior marriages, and his latest business (one of many failures) had gone bankrupt. His current wife asked the therapists to decide whether their 15-year-old daughter should marry a schizophrenic boy who was still in the hospital. If she did, the family would then have one less mouth to feed, and one less problem. When the therapists forced the parents to work on this problem themselves, the mother had to face her unrealistic evaluation of her husband's strength, and she began to battle for reality, communication, and role definition in the marriage. One marital partner can often force the other partner into therapy by shifting the homeostatic balance in the marriage (forming a new basis of relationship with the spouse).

Neutralizing Parental Superego Attitudes

As a group, the parents in our project had an overconventional, inhibited, and harsh view concerning sexual relations in general. Their own marriages tended to be conflicted and filled with inhibitions. They were apt to suspect any interest the daughter had in the opposite sex. When one daughter wished to stay out until 10:00 at night, her father quietly suggested that she not take her boyfriend to the golf course. She replied that she had never had such an idea, but that maybe he was suggesting it. The therapists found that frequently they had to interject their own values concerning female adolescent behavior because, while the parents tended to be overly strict, at the same time, by their rapt interest and attention, they showed an excessive response to their daughter's sexual concerns. It was not uncommon for both parents to expect a blow-by-blow account of their daughter's necking and petting behavior on dates. The therapists repeatedly had to shift the discussion from the daughter's behavior to the relationship between the parents. The parents usually made only limited and uninspiring comments about their own sexual activities but entered into a discussion of their daughter's sexual activities with much passion. The parents' ability to pay attention to each other and to withdraw the focus of attention from the acting-out daughter was usually the first sign of improved family function.

Therapists' Use of the Overpermissive Bind

A constant demand upon the therapist is to identify with either the parental dyad or the acting-out daughter. Whichever side the therapist takes, the other side will attempt to convince him that the alternative position is more valid. Early in our work we found that taking sides was apt to result in a stalemate. The strict position presented by the parents on the surface was completely at odds with their underlying permissive attitude. The permissive attitude of the acting-out daughter was at odds with her often-stated wish for controls. As a result of clinical experience, some therapists found that the best way to demonstrate to the parents that their strictness merely provoked the daughter was by recommending to them the use of ludicrously strict precautions in all aspects of their lives. Similarly, the therapists would suggest to the acting-out daughters that they had not lived enough, that they should try every type of sexual acting out possible. The purpose of these suggestions was to make both parents and daughters acutely uncomfortable in their characteristic attitudes — the therapists preempted the pathological positions which the family members had adopted by outdoing them in assuming these positions. These techniques were highly effective with some of the families. The use of the overpermissive bind by the therapists, furthermore, minimized some of the dangers and relieved the burden of substitute parenting by the therapists.

Definition of Male-Female Role

An advantage of male-female co-therapy teams is that the family is supplied with levels of interaction between the sexes. A successful working relationship presupposes that the co-therapists have explored their own relationship adequately. Most of our acting-out families had had weak, passive fathers and dominant, aggressive mothers, but our male-female co-therapy teams have sufficiently worked out their own agreements and disagreements about male and female roles so that they are not split by the family sex role reversal.

Exploring the Oedipus Complex in the Family

Overt family behavior is a convincing demonstration of the Oedipus complex in everyday life. We usually learn more about its role within the first three sessions of family therapy than we do in the first six months of individual therapy. Take, for example, the Arturo family. In the first family therapy session the mother told of her jealousy of the older daughter, Connie, who was promiscuous and who also had a homosexual love affair. The mother felt bitter and unloved because, since the older daughter's birth, her husband had ignored her and spent all his available time with Connie. Connie and her father held hands during the session and exchanged frequent looks of love. Because of the parent's poor marital relationship, Connie and her father were thinking of getting an apartment together. The father took Connie out while the mother stayed home. When the mother became depressed and angry because her husband gave all his attention to Connie, the father arranged for the mother to have electroshock treatments. The mother retaliated some time later by getting electroshock treatments for Connie while the father was out of town.

In the first family session, the therapists pointed out the not-so-latent incestuous involvement between the father and Connie, and they continued to work on this. Although each family member was defensive and tended to deny the latent incest, the father began to withdraw his intense libidinal attachment from Connie, and Connie rapidly gave up her promiscuous behavior and got a job for the first time in her life.

Although it is unusual for a family to admit incestuous feelings or fantasies, it is not rare for the various family members to listen to the therapists' interpretations and, though clouded by a cloak of denial, to make conscious attempts to alter their interactions in the family unit. In the case just cited, both father and daughter insisted that they were merely closely attached to each other and that the therapists' statements were bordering on the obscene. Both Connie and Mr. Arturo laughed when the latter was advised against such activities as unzipping Connie's dress, going into the bathroom when she was there, talking about getting an apartment with her, kissing her in a certain manner, flirting with her, etc. However, both seemed relieved by these injunctions and rapid behavioral changes occurred in Connie as well as in Mr. and Mrs. Arturo. It was as if Connie no longer had to be promiscuous in order to separate herself from her father; and Mr. Arturo began to pay more attention to Mrs. Arturo, who no longer was so jealous of Connie.

REFERENCE

1. Johnson, A. and Szurek, S. The Genesis of Anti-Social Acting Out in Children and Adults. *Psychoanal. Quart.* 21:322-343, 1952.

The Narro family

Geraldine Lincoln and Ross V. Speck

Chapter

13

Unconsummated marriages are more frequent than is generally realized. When Mr. Narro met Mrs. Narro she was in love with someone whose sexuality frightened her. Her fear of men made Mrs. Narro highly desirable to Mr. Narro. He had always been an insecure fat boy, with a high-pitched voice. Mrs. Narro tolerated his courtship because he never got fresh as the other boys did. Each convinced the other that they wanted no sex before marriage.

Mr. Narro was equally understanding when, on their honeymoon, Mrs. Narro did not want to have intercourse because she was frightened of it. Her tears overcame his passion. Mr. Narro was a study of consideration over the next two years whenever they made any attempts at sexual intercourse. Mrs. Narro would cry and Mr. Narro would comfort and reassure her. They comforted each other with stories of other married couples who had never had intercourse. The more she cried, the more he comforted, and the more he comforted the more Mrs. Narro wished to have children. Mr. Narro preferred not to have children.

After about two years, in order to satisfy Mrs. Narro's desire to have a child, they visited a family physician who performed a manual defloration in his office and caustically admonished them to begin a sexual life.

Neither Mr. Narro or Mrs. Narro enjoyed sex very much, and as the years went by Mrs. Narro became increasingly disturbed about not having a child. After years of childless marriage, Mr. Narro acceded to his wife's wishes by arranging privately to adopt a child through a lawyer in Chicago, and he and Mrs. Narro took a plane there to pick up their daughter.

Marilyn was described as a live wire by both parents. Mrs. Narro hovered anxiously over her, reading all available books on child care. By the age of two Marilyn was already giving Mr. and Mrs. Narro orders, and they were obeying. Marilyn was tiny but a tyrant. She took an early interest in sexual matters, and by the age of seven was demanding that her parents have intercourse so she could watch them and see how it was done. This shocked the parents.

By the time Mrs. Narro felt that the family would be happier with another child, she had already had a hysterectomy; another private deal was therefore made, this time in Florida, and Jane joined the family.

But now we are getting ahead of the narrative account of our therapy experience with the Narro family. Let us begin with the first meeting. The reader will be informed of the facts of this family history in the same order and manner that the therapists learned them.

The first meeting was of the multiple-impact type in which a team of four therapists would meet with the family members for about a half hour to get a combined picture of family problems; they would then break up into small groups of either twos or fours for about three quarters of an hour, and subsequently reconvene. The therapists and family would then further explore family patterns, family dynamics, and family motivation. This family, if accepted, would be seen weekly by a team of two: a male psychiatrist and a female psychologist.

The Narro family consisted of Mr. Narro, age fifty, a fat, pompous, well-dressed little man who was usually seen smoking an expensive cigar and behaving in a "hale-fellow-well-met" manner; Mrs. Narro, age fifty, also short and well groomed, a rather pretty woman until she smiled, at which point she looked as though she were ready to bite; Marilyn, their elder adopted daughter, age twenty, a thin, small, brittle girl with streaked blonde hair who appeared much younger than her years; and Jane, age sixteen, their younger adopted daughter, a youngster with a pretty face atop a heavy, stocky body. The family had been referred to the project by a social agency where they had been seen primarily to help Marilyn, whose sexual promiscuity had culminated in three illegal abortions. Marilyn had not related well on a one-to-one basis and it was hoped that she would do better in family therapy.

At the outset of our first multiple-impact interview with the Narro family, Marilyn challenged the team's authority just as she had challenged her parents' authority from the time she was two years old. She did this by directing her father to tell us that she would refuse to continue in therapy if her younger sister Jane were to learn that she had had three abortions. He complied with her wishes by relating the message to the social-worker trainee with whom he had had previous contact and who had referred the family to the project. The trainee, in turn, gave the three other team members the message. The team agreed that treatment would not and could not proceed along these lines dictated by Marilyn. Not only would she be controlling them just as she controlled her family, but it would be violating their principle that only through free discussion and honest exploration of all areas can family problems be resolved. To counter Marilyn's "game," they reversed their multiple-impact procedure by preceding the group meeting with individual interviews. It had been the group experience that there really were no family secrets but rather a tacit agreement on the part of all members to keep silent on certain subjects. Thus, the team thought that in an individual interview Jane would reveal that she either suspected or knew that Marilyn had been pregnant, and if so, Marilyn's objections to open discussion would be neutralized.

The female psychologist interviewed Jane, the younger, "innocent" sister. Although initially she stated that she had not wanted to come and would not talk for fear of hurting either her mother or Marilyn, she was so hungry for a sympathetic listener that in a very few minutes she was pouring out all her troubles. She complained at first that her parents were bigoted where a person's religious background was concerned, and would not allow her to date non-Jewish boys. Since both she and Marilyn were adopted, she felt that probably they were not of Jewish background and, consequently, when her adopted parents were critical of non-Jews, they were being critical of her. Furthermore, they differentiated between Marilyn and herself, not only by having allowed Marilyn to date non-Jewish boys but by having been far more lenient with her than they had been with Jane. Recently, she said, they had tried to restrict Marilyn, but she felt it was too late because Marilyn was already out of control. When asked to explain this, she said she suspected that Marilyn had been sexually active and possibly pregnant. The secret was out; the interview was terminated, having accomplished its purpose. It served another purpose, however, one not anticipated and perhaps somewhat detrimental to family treatment — it established a special relationship between the female psychologist and Jane. The two of them joined Mr. and Mrs. Narro, the project director, and the social-worker trainee. That interview had been used mainly for the purpose of imparting to the Narros the staff's point of view regarding the need for free and open discussion which would necessitate the revelation of all secrets. The Narros continued to justify their position on the grounds that such a revelation would disturb the relationship between the girls and also that Jane was too young to become aware of sexual relationships. This latter rationalization was negated when Jane told her parents that she was aware of the situation and she didn't like it that everyone was treating her as though she were stupid.

In another room, the male psychiatrist was interviewing Marilyn and also, at the same time, establishing a special relationship with her which was to continue throughout the treatment. The following are quotes from his notes: "Marilyn is a very petite, thin young girl, who looks about thirteen rather than twenty, and is not particularly attractive. She is quite blasé, flip, and tends to be controlling. She complained immediately that her parents are too strict with her, that she cannot stand Jewish guys, and that she does not see why the whole family has to be involved in her therapy. She stated that she started to date at eleven because she wanted to and that her problem is that she is very nasty. She talked freely about her three abortions, the last one occurring three or four weeks ago, and she was quite pleased to tell me that although confined to home by her parents, she had managed to sneak out and make love with an Italian fellow this afternoon. She volunteered how much she enjoyed sex and stated she could not live without it. . . . She insisted that her younger sister did not know about her pregnancies and abortions, and she would never allow this to be revealed. . . . She said that she could wrap her father around her little finger and that he gives her modern discipline by banishing her to her room where she has a radio, TV, record player, telephone, lots of good books, etc. Several times during the interview she said that I could not tell a certain thing to the family because it was confidential. *I refused to go along with this. . . .*"

At the end of this interview the four therapists conferred and related their findings. Following this, therapists and family members met together and summarized to some extent the individual interviews, emphasizing again that there were to be no secrets. Family history and problems were further discussed and many themes were touched on which were to be greatly expanded in the following twenty-seven months of therapy. Mr. Narro told us of his and his wife's great desire to have children and their disappointment at not being able to have their own. Mrs. Narro amplified the subject by stating that the gynecologist had told them there were no physical reasons for their inability to have children. In spite of her husband's objections, Mrs. Narro had been eager to adopt a child and prior to the adoption had been so unhappy that they did not have one that she had frequently cried herself to sleep. Both children were newborn when adopted. When Marilyn was six years old Mrs. Narro had a hysterectomy and one and a half years after that she became severely depressed and anxious. At that time she sought and received psychiatric help for a two-year period three times per week. Through this help she gained some insight into the fact that she had so greatly resented her mother's strict authoritarian approach with her when she was a child that she had leaned over backwards to reason things out with Marilyn. This had resulted in prolonged explanations and discussions between Mrs. Narro and Marilyn. When Marilyn, at age three, questioned the birth process, Mrs. Narro told her that the seed from which she was born had been in another woman's body but that she, Mrs. Narro, was her mother since she had raised her. Marilyn responded to this by saying she would stop eating, and become so small that she could re-enter her present mother's body as a seed and grow from her body. She actually stopped eating at the time, and has had an eating problem ever since. Jane complained that although her mother had talked a great deal with Marilyn about the adoption, it was Marilyn, not her mother, who had told Jane that they had been adopted. She pursued with her parents the complaints she had raised in her individual session pertaining to their bigoted attitudes on religion and the effect this had of restricting her social life. Mr. Narro expounded his view in a manner which seemed calculated to prove to the staff that he really wasn't so bigoted, and a few weeks later gave Jane permission to date non-Jewish boys. Mrs. Narro, as was her wont, disregarded Jane and focused on her complaints about Marilyn. She felt bitter that Marilyn disregarded her advice, and angry toward her husband for his inability to control Marilyn. At the end of the interview the family was asked if they wished to continue therapy. Mr. and Mrs. Narro enthusiastically said they did. Marilyn and Jane

also agreed, but Jane expressed some fear that her parents might retaliate against her for having expressed her feelings and differences.
They reassured her that this would not be so.

The staff members felt that the Narro family seemed fairly well
motivated for treatment, and decided to use this family to demonstrate
family treatment to a group of social-worker trainees. The meetings
were to be held weekly with all family members and the two therapists present. Both therapists were members of the Family Treatment
Project, and had had considerable experience in family treatment. In
the first regular family session, the family was informed that the sessions were to be tape-recorded and observed by a professional group.
From time to time a colleague might also sit in on one of the sessions.
The family raised no objections to these terms.

From the very beginning of therapy, the patterns of the family were
quite obvious and it was a major therapeutic task to make the family
aware of these patterns and get them to shift to healthier ones. This
was extremely difficult in that the family members not only frequently
interrupted each other and the team, but when someone was fortunate
enough to finish a thought, another family member would most likely
go off on a tangent rather than relate to what was pertinent. They did
not really listen to each other nor did they pay attention to the therapists.

Most of the energy in the family flowed between Mrs. Narro and
Marilyn. They were caught in a negative, homosexual bind that was
so intense and absorbing that the other two members of the family
were virtually ignored. Mr. Narro handled this by assuming the role
of peacemaker, soothing the injured feelings of first one and then the
other of his women. Jane's solution was to withdraw from the family
both at home and in the meetings. Frequently she would have a far-away
look in her eyes and, when questioned, would admit that she had not
been listening. When we attempted to draw her out, either Mr. or Mrs.
Narro would interrupt in an effort to bring the focus back to Marilyn.
They continued to do this despite the fact that the therapists informed
them that the psychological tests had revealed Jane to be severely
disturbed. Jane admitted she was very disturbed, saying that she was
very worried that she was flunking in school because she tended to
daydream there, just as she did in the sessions. At home, she retired
to her room because she received no pleasure or comfort from her
family, and in her room she spent much of her time touching the
various objects and pieces of furniture. She considered the inanimate
objects as being animate, and if she bumped against her desk, she was
as concerned about having hurt it as she would be if it were a person.

The therapists continuously pointed out to the family the destructive
nature of their poor communication patterns and family structure.
They repeatedly brought the focus back to Jane when the family
attempted to take it away from her. Jane responded with some warmth,
particularly to the female therapist, and complained that her mother
constantly served rich foods in order to fatten Marilyn, ignoring the
fact that both she and her father had a weight problem.

The therapists also pointed out to Mrs. Narro that Marilyn would bait her by using "dirty words" to refer to sexual encounters, and by stating that she preferred non-Jewish boys to Jewish boys. Mrs. Narro would react to the bait by becoming very judgmental and moralistic. Mr. Narro would then support his wife and Jane would support Marilyn in a superego vs. id battle. All family members made an effort to put the therapists into judge-like roles. The therapy, at this point, involved a consistent refusal on the part of the therapists to accept such roles and a refocusing on the family relationship patterns.

After about ten weeks of therapy Mrs. Narro responded less to Marilyn's baiting and the family reported that life was somewhat more peaceful at home. With this encouragement, the therapists turned to Mr. and Mrs. Narro to try to explore why their relationship was symbolized by flowers, candy, and politeness, but had no real depth and was completely lacking in sexual excitement. About two-thirds of the way through the session, Marilyn cut in to say, "What would happen if I were to become pregnant again?" The therapists pointed out that she was using this threat as a means of intervening between her parents, and that Mr. and Mrs. Narro were only too willing to let her do so.

In the weeks following this incident, the sessions tended to be quite factual, with family discussions centering around such topics as how much money they should spend on a vacation. For the therapists' benefit, they dispassionately reviewed the history of their financial situation, revealing that Mr. Narro had once been in a very prosperous business with his father-in-law. This business failed after the war; Mr. Narro's in-laws had managed to save a great deal of money and thus continued to live well, but Mr. and Mrs. Narro found themselves in greatly reduced circumstances. Since that time, in order to pay back past bills and maintain a moderate standard of living, it had become necessary for both of them to have jobs. Mrs. Narro said she had taken all this quite matter of factly — that it didn't disturb her nearly as much as one hot argument with Marilyn. Mr. Narro revealed none of his feelings. Both girls said they resented not being given more in the way of material things. Despite the fact that many arguments between parents and children centered about the handling of money, neither Mr. or Mrs. Narro would express any feelings on this subject.

Since it was summer time, there were some disruptions of treatment because of vacations. Mr. and Mrs. Narro and Jane went away for a week. Marilyn stayed at their home with a friend and planned to go away by herself later in the summer. When the Narros came back from vacation, the therapists planned to go to their home for a visit. The family attempted to be cordial and sociable, but Marilyn refused to be involved, spending much of the time on the phone and then telling the therapists that she was planning to move to New York. One of the reasons for this, she said, was that when her mother returned from vacation she checked her own bed and then accused Marilyn of being "bad" by saying, "Someone has slept in my bed." Mrs. Narro complained that, although she had kept Marilyn's promiscuous behavior a secret from her family, Marilyn had, in her absence, betrayed her by expressing her bohemian views about sex quite vehemently to Mrs. Narro's mother and sister.

The following week the male therapist was away and the female therapist saw the family alone. The week after that Mrs. Narro reported that the family had been doing better. Jane had been dating and Marilyn had expressed some interest in interior decorating. The male therapist noticed that Marilyn didn't look well. She said she didn't feel well, but couldn't discuss it. He asked her if there was any connection with her menstrual period. She said "Yes" but was extremely angry at him for asking the question and insisted he had no right to needle her by asking her questions pertaining to her physical condition.

In contrast to the family's factual method of dealing with Marilyn (their main emphasis was always on money, manners, morals and facts as illustrated by their asking such questions as "What did you do?" "How much did you spend?" "What did you tell your aunt?" "Is your friend a whore?" "What will it cost to live in New York?"), the male therapist became involved on a feeling level with Marilyn and then both therapists helped her to analyze her angry feelings. They felt this was extremely profitable. Marilyn was able to see a connection between her irrational anger toward her family when they returned from vacation, her irrational anger toward the male therapist when he returned from vacation, and her having been abandoned by her real parents. Mrs. Narro recalled that when Marilyn was four years old she had been entered in nursery school and that, on the advice of the teacher, she had slipped away without telling Marilyn, who became extremely panicky. When her mother told this story during the session Marilyn cried. The atmosphere had changed in an hour and a half from an extremely hostile one to one of warmth. Both girls stated that they never would desert an illegitimate child and Jane said she would never have an abortion. Marilyn said she was always very miserable when she broke up with a boyfriend but yet she liked boys who were indifferent to her. The therapists pointed out that her natural parents had been indifferent to her.

The male therapist told Marilyn at the end of the meeting that she was not ready to go to New York, that she was hostile toward men, that she didn't know who she was or what she wanted, that she was apt to hurt herself, and that even though she loved babies and wanted one "more than a husband," she wasn't ready to have one for she was apt to smother a child just as her mother had smothered her. This statement was a strong one and reflected an involvement and interest far greater than her father had ever shown. Marilyn responded by being more candid about her feelings. She admitted that she hated men and could develop no real relationship with them. She was worried about this and stated that any man worth going out with expected her to have intercourse with him on the first date and she complied to get it over with. She said, "What's the use of arguing with them?" "The longer you put it off, the more you get to hate the man, so you might as well do it the first time and then you can go ahead and have fun."

In the following weeks Mr. and Mrs. Narro reported that things were going well at home, emphasizing that Marilyn had been extraordinarily helpful and, in Mr. Narro's opinion, had become a more interesting person. They chatted about Mrs. Narro's parents, saying that even they had been easier lately. Marilyn commented that her grandparents were under the impression that the therapists were coming just for her, whereupon Mr. Narro said they had been told that every member of the family needed help. The therapists felt that he was only paying lip service to this principle and asked him what problems he had. He had difficulty in answering this question. He mentioned financial difficulties, then spoke of difficulty in reaching his daughters, and finally was able to say that there were times when he too would like some sympathy, but never got it, and that he found himself always caring for the other members of the family but getting nothing in return. Mrs. Narro felt she still had problems with her parents, and Jane was able, in a session when Marilyn was absent because of her vacation, to open up and talk at length about her clash over morals with her mother, her fear of death, her difficulty with schoolwork, and her lack of identification.

Although it was tempting to get involved with Jane, the therapists felt that after six months of treatment Mr. Narro was the one who had been reached the least and presented the major resistance to the family's changing in any way other than superficially. He provided no leadership in the house, was not respected by the three women, and was not the least bit anxious about this. The therapists decided to try to reach him directly by attacking his role as peacemaker and, indirectly, by stimulating Mrs. Narro sexually, so that she would either demand more of him or threaten to look elsewhere for some romance. To this end, they gave the family some sexually informative and provocative books, and encouraged them to explore a broader range of viewpoints, since neither Marilyn's extreme bohemian position, nor Mr. and Mrs. Narro's extremely conservative position were very satisfactory. As the reader might guess, the family walked out of the therapy room without the books. They did, however, eventually read them, and Mrs. Narro was stimulated sufficiently to talk about the fact that she had never been sexually attracted to her husband, that she had been in love with someone else when she had gotten married, and that she had kept track of this old boyfriend throughout the years, although she had not seen him. The male therapist said he felt her relationship with this old boyfriend was unfinished business and suggested she send him a card. Marilyn intervened to ask for help in how to handle her boyfriend. She said she was young, her life was ahead of her, and therefore it was more important that she, rather than her parents, be given help.

At the end of this meeting, Mr. Narro commented that it had been "an extremely interesting meeting," but by the following week he contended that he had forgotten all about what had been said. He did admit, however, to feeling anxious during the past week, saying that he had had fantasies of his wife being either killed or hurt in an accident. When the therapists pointed out the unconscious hostility underlying these fantasies, he at first denied it, but then said he had felt somewhat angry toward his wife for saying she was more excited by her old boyfriend than by him, but that he was even angrier at the male therapist for encouraging his wife to send a card to the boyfriend. His feelings of jealousy, however, had prodded him to lose some more weight, making an overall weight loss of sixteen pounds since the beginning of therapy.

The therapists felt their strategy was working. Mr. Narro did seem more anxious than he had been, and also seemed interested in becoming more aggressive. Soon after this, all three women complained long and loud about how mean they found some aggressive men to be. Jane showed up one week with a toy gun and said she'd like to kill everyone in the room but the female therapist. She intimated that the only beings she really cared about and who cared for her were the female therapist and a horse she wanted to buy. She said she didn't like the changes in the family, for now everyone considered Marilyn perfect and was more aware of Jane's shortcomings. She was angry at her mother for being so tight with money, and noted that both her mother and Marilyn had pretty, feminine clothes, whereas she did not. She also said she was afraid she could never love nor be loved by anyone. The therapists encouraged Jane to express all her complaints and angry feelings whereas her parents were generally content to have her remain silent. The therapists agreed with Jane that her appearance needed improving, whereas her father said he liked her as she was, i.e., fat, babyish, and masculine. Mr. and Mrs. Narro disagreed as to whether or not Jane should buy the horse, and they postponed making a decision for many weeks rather than coming to grips with their differences. The therapists confronted them with this and Jane said she no longer cared what decision they made so long as they delayed no longer. Mr. Narro then said she could buy the horse if she would assume a large part of the expense. The therapists stated their viewpoint that the arrangements were such that Jane would eventually feel overburdened. They also explored the homosexual and withdrawal aspects of her horsemanship. The family at this point were united by their angry feelings against the therapists and allowed Jane to buy the horse. They were particularly angry at the female therapist, who was more involved with Jane than was the male therapist and who had been more vehement in her confrontations.

Jane did get her horse, and following these stormy sessions, lost some weight and came to the meetings dressed in a more feminine manner. Moreover, after expressing her anger directly toward the female therapist, Mrs. Narro was able to be warmer and more personally interested in her than she had ever been, as illustrated by her voicing a concern that the female therapist, because she had to travel far to come to the meetings, might not have adequate time to eat her dinner.

With Jane doing somewhat better, Marilyn again took the spotlight by telling her parents that she thought she might be pregnant again.

Although this turned out to be a false claim, it led into a deeper exploration of her relationship with her present boyfriend, Al. She said she really wanted a man who could be strong yet kind, interesting, and intellectual, but was convinced she could never attract this type of man. She had enjoyed Al more than anyone she'd ever gone with because she could talk to him honestly about all her personal thoughts and feelings. However, he refused to talk about anything intellectual, had no money, and lacked ambition. She said she doubted that they could have a satisfactory marriage but, since she couldn't get anyone better, and since she wanted to have a baby (if it was true that she was pregnant), she planned to marry him. She also realized that she was smothering him by calling him as many as four times a day.

In the weeks that followed, the family was either quiet or produced trivia. The male therapist refocused on the sexual problem, pointing out that it was not just Marilyn who had a problem in this area — that Jane was afraid of sex and worried she could neither love nor be loved, that Mrs. Narro was frigid, and that Mr. Narro was much too passive. Mr. Narro said this was true, and that he could see how his and Mrs. Narro's sexual difficulties had affected the family. He then revealed that their marriage had not been consummated for two years because Mrs. Narro had complained that sex was too painful, and that finally, Mrs. Narro had gone to a doctor who had stretched her hymen. When Marilyn heard this she began to cry and showed more feeling that did either of her parents. She said she just couldn't imagine such a marriage, and stated that something must be very wrong with both of her parents to tolerate such a state of affairs. Mr. Narro said that, despite his wife's revulsion toward sex, he had never cheated, but the therapists pointed out that he had been overly seductive with his daughters. Marilyn had previously complained that she felt threatened when her father touched her and the therapists felt that her acting out was, at least in part, a defense against this incestuous threat. At the end of the meeting Mr. Narro said that he realized that he and his wife "had been particularly nice to each other on the surface all these years" because, basically, they hadn't been nice to one another.

The therapists had hoped that, following this session, the Narros would continue to work on their marriage. However, all the family members seemed to cooperate in an effort to avoid doing so. Marilyn broke up with Al and became despondent and difficult. After almost a year of therapy, Mrs. Narro reverted to her former pattern of hostile involvement with Marilyn to the exclusion of her husband and Jane. Some headway had been made in that Mr. Narro tried to dodge his role as peacemaker and complained instead that his wife was too preoccupied with Marilyn, was not providing the kind of social life he liked, and was not aware of Jane's needs. Jane picked this up, saying that she had been so depressed recently because of her overweight, poor social life and poor schoolwork that she had had suicidal thoughts and her mother hadn't even noticed. The therapists were able to help Jane discuss these problems, and in the following weeks Jane lost six pounds and began to feel better. Both therapists felt that this change in Jane was based on her positive relationship with the therapists, but regretted that there was no improvement in her relationship with her family.

Marilyn continued to wail about the fact that she was soon going to be twenty-one and was still single and childless. Mr. Narro said he was disgusted. For seven years he had listened to his wife complain about not having children and now he had to listen to his daughter's similar complaints. Marilyn said she wanted to go to New York to find a husband, and Mr. Narro took what seemed to be a firm stand against her going. Both therapists backed him in this. Mrs. Narro stated she liked her husband's firmness, but during the following week she undermined it by convincing him that, given some incentive, Marilyn would mature. Consequently, he had compromised and told Marilyn that if she would mature in two months she could go to New York with their aid. Maturity was defined as "becoming a member of the family, breaking up with some old boyfriends, helping with the dishes, and being a little nicer to mother." Even Marilyn admitted that this was a strange definition of maturity. The therapists confronted the family with the fact that the unconscious was ruling them. They made it very clear that Marilyn could not possibly function any better than she was functioning at present unless she continued therapy, which was not likely if she went to New York. Thus, Mrs. Narro's unconscious hostility against Marilyn had come into play when she persuaded her husband to back down. Also involved was her unconscious desire to keep her husband weak. Further, it was evident to the therapists that although on the surface Marilyn appeared to be uninhibited, unconsciously she was quite prudish. On the other hand, Mrs. Narro, who seemed to be a prude, unconsciously had many of the uninhibited attributes that Marilyn acted out. Marilyn was able to accept this interpretation, but Mrs. Narro was not.

Over the next six months, it became more and more clear that Marilyn and Jane were acting out their parents' unconscious wishes. The girls cooperated in trying to uncover and understand this pathological interaction. Marilyn talked about how disgusted she felt when her mother walked around the house nude and her father paraded about dressed only in his underpants. When Mr. and Mrs. Narro continued to deny any problems in themselves, Jane kept pointing out her father's tendency to be accident prone. Nevertheless, the more the therapists and the girls hammered at the unconscious sources of the family's behavior, the more resistant the parents became. The girls said there was much they wanted to discuss, and in anger at their parents' stubborn refusal to explore themselves, they asked for a separate session. The therapists, in an effort to break the impasse, complied with the wish, setting up one session with just the girls and one with just the parents.

At the beginning of the session with the girls, Marilyn announced that she was going to New York in a week and a half, but she agreed to come in for the sessions on an every-other-week basis. Jane told us she had had sexual intercourse several times, had not enjoyed it, and did not intend to do it again. Marilyn related that she had been sixteen, Jane's present age, when she first had intercourse. She said she didn't approve of what Jane was doing and went on to ask us how she could gain the respect of boys. She said she could not bear to say "no" to the boys because she saw them as worms who constantly had to ask for sex. The female therapist pointed out that this was how she saw her father and Marilyn agreed.

In the meeting with Mr. and Mrs. Narro, Mr. Narro blandly discussed Marilyn's going to New York and Mrs. Narro wallowed in her misery. The therapists pushed them to talk more about what they found unacceptable in themselves and Mr. Narro recalled that he had not been straightforward as a boy; that he had stolen a few things and had lied to his parents occasionally. He said this made him more understanding of the girls, but the therapists wondered if perhaps he did not also stimulate the girls in their behavior. There was further evidence, in the next few weeks, of his unconsciously stimulating Jane. After Marilyn went to New York, the Narros tended to concentrate on Jane. They forbade her to be alone in the house with a boy and when a boy unexpectedly visited her one night when her parents were out, she phoned her father to ask his permission to go for a walk. His response was, "Where are you going to go — to the golf course?" She said she hadn't thought of doing so on her own but was almost tempted to go there after he made this statement. The therapists again pointed out how the parents stimulated the girls to act out; Mrs. Narro by being ultraprudish and idealistic and Mr. Narro by phrasing his statements in such a way as to make them suggestions.

During the next several weeks Jane continued to complain about the cold, distant atmosphere in the home. Marilyn came in biweekly and reported that although she was quite lonely in New York, she was determined to form a relationship that would be meaningful rather than just continuing to sleep with everyone who came along. Mr. and Mrs. Narro both produced dreams revealing sexual problems. Mr. Narro's dreams seemed somewhat disguised, while Mrs. Narro's were extremely primitive. In one dream she and Marilyn were in New York and were attacked by a lecherous old man. All three were destroyed in such a way that she saw different parts of bodies including a stomach and a four-foot-long penis. In associating to the dreams, she said she was concerned about Marilyn's being hurt. She added that although she herself had never consciously feared being attacked, her mother had had so much anxiety over the possibility of being attacked that she had had to be hospitalized.

While Mrs. Narro was dreaming of violence, Marilyn was associating with people who acted out their violent impulses. She reported that her new boyfriend, Curly, had hurt his hand punching someone. In response to the therapists' inquires, she said he tended to punch someone about four times every week. She went on to say that she liked him very much, despite the fact that he drank, fought, stole, and was engaged in the rackets, because she knew he would protect her. This was particularly important to her, she said, because her father had never protected her. She also recognized that there might be a connection between her mother's dreams and her choice of friends.

A few weeks later Jane called the therapists aside to say she thought she might be pregnant and, if so, she intended to commit suicide. Actually, Jane was not pregnant, but the therapists were struck with the fact that after one and a half years of treatment, the girls were still acting out sexually in angry response to their parents' unconscious wishes and also for the purpose of hurting their parents; in the process, they were badly hurting themselves. The therapists also were aware of the fact that although Mr. and Mrs. Narro reported that they had enjoyed their vacation together and had improved their sexual relationship, they were still unable to give of themselves to their children and were completely ineffectual in dealing with them, tending to talk about the "disgrace" Marilyn brought on the family and ignoring Jane's problems rather than showing either girl they cared.

Marilyn had turned to Curly for solace and the family was convinced that, though she was very much aware of Curly's weaknesses, she had no intention of giving him up. It seemed futile to continue seeing her on an every-other-week basis, and the family was told that either Marilyn must come in weekly or the therapy would continue with just the parents and Jane.

It was the therapists' feeling that Marilyn would not be satisfied for long to remain completely out of the therapy. Indeed, it took only two weeks before Marilyn wrote that Curly might have to go to jail for robbery and that she was thinking of coming home if this happened. Jane said she didn't want Marilyn to come home because she had just started to do better. Jane's marks had improved, her art work was improving, she was not pregnant, and she had been pleased at a recent birthday celebration she had had with her parents. She was afraid Marilyn would take all this away from her. The therapists directly advised the family to make Marilyn's coming home conditional on her regular attendance at therapy sessions. They also advised them to shift roles in that Mr. Narro and Jane should be the ones who would stand up to Marilyn and Mrs. Narro should not argue with her but, instead, should join her and even outdo her in being daring both sexually and aggressively. The latter was suggested in an attempt to loosen Mrs. Narro's defenses as well as a way of mobilizing Marilyn's superego.

Curly did go to jail and Marilyn came home and attended the meetings regularly. Mr. Narro and Jane did not let Marilyn control them, and Mrs. Narro was able to relate to Marilyn in a friendly, hands-off manner. Marilyn insisted she was going to marry Curly in six months when he got out of jail. When no one argued with her she became depressed and complained of headaches. The male therapist said he thought she had a big headache with Curly — that the odds were against his ever changing. In the following months, he somewhat playfully teased her about her relationship with Curly and would suggest that she find other outlets for her unconventional strivings — going with hippies or living in a loft. She seemed to enjoy these interchanges and, instead of rebelling and arguing as she had formerly done, she became more and more willing to reveal and explore thoughts, fantasies, and feelings. In one meeting, she told the therapists how fascinated she was with crime, and how she liked to read the descriptions of crimes in the newspapers. She said she often fantasied herself fighting with others, going so far as stabbing somebody in the stomach. The similarity between this fantasy of Marilyn's and Mrs. Narro's dream in which a man was dismembered provided further evidence that Marilyn tended to act out her mother's dreams.

Jane, too, was more willing to talk about herself. She told us about a dream she had had in which she, her mother, and sister were all kings who were about to die. Marilyn then related a dream she had had in which she had used a big rubber hose to squirt someone. Both girls revealed that they have been carrying knives in their pocketbooks for "self defense."

The male therapist commented on the masculine identification in both of these dreams. Marilyn admitted this was true in her case and added that she really felt contemptuous of men and was more aggressive than most girls. Jane denied a masculine identification, but went on to describe her new boyfriend in such a way as to make him sound quite similar to Curly. It seemed to the therapists that recently Marilyn was acting out less whereas Jane was taking over her acting-out role.

The following week Mrs. Narro told the male therapist that she was angry at him for making her feel like a freak when he had said the women in the family had some masculine traits. The female therapist said that her colleague's remark had not come out of thin air, but had been based not only on the therapists' perception of the family in the sessions, but also the content of the dreams (the three kings and long rubber hose). Mrs. Narro pooh-poohed the symbolization in the dreams, arguing she had read an article saying that dreams were not necessarily to be interpreted as Freud had stated. The female therapist asked Mrs. Narro why, after almost two years of therapy, she continued to act so naïve and to remain so distant from the therapists. Mrs. Narro replied she had always been on the periphery of a group, holding herself back from being part of it. She admitted she was stubborn in not accepting the therapists' ideas. The male therapist told her that he had rarely seen such a stubborn person; he suggested she go on being stubborn and continue to refuse to accept other people's ideas, particularly those of the therapists. Mrs. Narro laughed at this and seemed to loosen up.

In the next few sessions she and Mr. Narro were more open in discussing their marriage. Mrs. Narro explained that she loved music and complained that although her husband had promised to take her to concerts or operas, he had not fulfilled his promise. He said he'd been willing to and she called him a liar and then burst into tears. The therapists agreed that Mr. Narro had been a liar, and had promised many things he had not fulfilled. This led to some introspection on Mr. Narro's part and a few weeks later he was able to connect his fears that his wife would be hurt or killed in an accident with his hostile thoughts about her. He said he felt she still inhibited and controlled him, but recognized that, because he had a great need for approval, he allowed her to do so. He said further that although he was still struggling to become master of his own home, he had been helped, through the therapy, to become more aggressive and self-assured in business and was going into business for himself.

Soon after this, Marilyn, who had been complaining of a urinary tract disorder, went into the hospital for some tests. Jane, who always seemed to talk more freely when Marilyn was not present, used this opportunity to talk about herself. She reported that she was doing much better in school but that, nevertheless, she seemed to have a heavy heart. Since she was unable to put her finger on any specfic problem, the therapists encouraged her to associate to her dream in which she, Mrs. Narro, and Marilyn were all kings who were about to die. She talked then about her fear of death, and her fantasies that her real parents had been rich, her mother very beautiful, and her father very handsome, and that they had died in an airplane crash. She went into detail about her fantasies and then added that, actually, they had probably been quite poor because rich people either have abortions or get married. This led to a discussion of her tendency to feel sorry for anyone who she felt was poor or downtrodden. She then admitted that she was seeing a married man, not because she was interested in him, but because she felt sorry for him.

The following week Marilyn returned and told us that the doctors had not found anything physically wrong with her. The therapists related her physical symptoms to her fear of getting married. They also brought her up to date on what Jane had discussed in the previous meeting. She then focused, as had Jane, on her tendency to identify with the underdog. She told how she had cried when she had read about the lives of drug addicts in *Life* magazine. She said she was crying for them and for herself, for if she did not marry Curly, she did not know what would become of her. She said she believed she could easily become a prostitute. She also said she felt guilty because she had urged Curly to act antisocially. In fact, one of his arrests was related to her insisting that he take part in a robbery so that they would have money.

The therapists pointed out that all the women in the family tended to identify with the underdog and to bring home "stray dogs." Mrs. Narro said she did this literally — that she loved to care for helpless creatures. She reported another dream in which she had two girls and a baby boy. Marilyn then told her mother that it wouldn't be too long before she'd give her a baby because she planned to become pregnant as soon as she was married. Again, the therapists pointed out how Marilyn was doing this *for* her mother and how she persisted in acting out her mother's unconscious.

Mr. Narro also reported a dream which, he said, had been very disturbing to him. In this dream someone sneezed, he said "gesundheit," and the female therapist was scornful of him for having said it. He said he'd felt angry toward the female therapist after the dream — that here was another woman telling him what to do. Despite his resentment of this, he said, for several days after he had the dream he had been unable to say "gesundheit" and finally, when he resumed saying it, he could only do so when he sincerely meant "good health." He said he was more direct and aggressive in the office than at home and felt the female therapist would like him better there. The female therapist said that Mr. Narro's perception of her attitude toward him was fairly accurate; that she was very disappointed in him; that she had hoped for and expected more from him and that perhaps his wife was satisfied with his progress but she was not. He responded by saying that he was aware recently of being angry at everyone, but particularly at his daughters, for he felt he had given them a great deal but they had not reciprocated. He mentioned, for example, the fact that Jane had dyed her hair despite the fact that she had promised him not to do so. As he talked, however, it became more and more evident that he was stressing the superficial aspects of her action, — her appearance — and was ignoring their relationship and what it had meant to him that she had broken a promise.

The therapists pointed this out and the male therapist suggested that Mr. Narro might give his family less materially, but more in the way of understanding. Marilyn agreed with the male therapist, saying she never felt that her father understood her or wanted her to be happy, but was only interested in her complying with his superficial standards.

The following week Mr. Narro said he'd been so angry at the therapists during the past week that he had wanted to stop treatment altogether. He had thought it over, however, and realizing he was confused, wanted to know exactly what he was doing wrong. The male therapist began by saying that Mr. Narro did not express feelings but tended instead to intellectualize. Since he couldn't express feelings he was unable to relate to his children. The female therapist agreed, saying that it had not been difficult for the therapists to relate to the girls and wondered why it was so difficult for their parents to do so. Mrs. Narro defended herself by saying that she didn't hear the female therapist say anything different from what she said. Marilyn disagreed with her mother, pointing out that the therapists really listened to them, whereas neither parent ever really listened but responded mechanically with hackneyed answers. The therapists went on to say that both Mr. and Mrs. Narro stressed superficialities so much that they talked about stereotypes rather than about real people. Mrs. Narro seemed not to understand what the therapists were saying. Mr. Narro, on the other hand, said he could see these faults in his wife but not in himself and wondered what was wrong with him. The therapists replied that if he recognized his wife's faults, it was wrong not to discuss them with her and to go along with her in her carping, critical attitude toward the children.

In the sessions that followed, the therapists focused on the "emotional divorce" between Mr. and Mrs. Narro, and although Mr. Narro attempted some introspection, he tended to revert to denial of difficulties in the marriage, citing, as an example, the fact that he and his wife had recently spent a pleasant day together in the park. Fortunately, Mrs. Narro was more honest in stating that she had not enjoyed the day because she had sensed that her husband was impatient and preoccupied. She had not, however, communicated her feeling to him at the time.

This honest expression on her part made even clearer the fact that Mr. and Mrs. Narro were unable to talk to one another. In the therapy sessions they related to each other through the therapists and at home through the children. The therapists decided, therefore, to try to force them into communicating with each other by having them come to the following sessions without their children.

The therapists informed Mr. and Mrs. Narro that they would observe the sessions through the one-way mirror and directed them to use the sessions to discuss their own relationship.

The first few sessions in which the Narros were by themselves were quite productive. They admitted that they were talking to each other for the first time since they were married, and Mr. Narro later said that he had always avoided being alone with his wife for fear they would have nothing to talk about. This session was also helpful to the therapists in that they too had an opportunity to be alone – to listen, observe, and talk to each other more freely than in the therapy room where they were more exclusively preoccupied with the family. The therapists were somewhat surprised that Mr. and Mrs. Narro, when alone, were more accepting of the therapists' ideas than when they had been together. Moreover, since they no longer were occupied with fencing with the therapists, they were forced to turn to and deal with each other.

Mr. Narro opened their first discussion by saying "You and I have to learn to enjoy life together. In the past twenty-five years we have given 90 percent of our energy to the kids and not to us." Mrs. Narro responded by suggesting that "Maybe we should go back to when we first got engaged. I said I didn't love you and you said you had enough love for both of us." She then spoke quite honestly about how scared she was of marriage and how afraid she had been of sex; how she was mad at herself for not having been able to enjoy sex more, and how she had become so ambivalent to her husband that she had poured all her feelings onto Marilyn when she had come along. Mr. Narro said she'd done the same with the dog before Marilyn arrived. He said he wanted no more of that; that from now on he wanted her undivided attention. He seemed more forceful than ever before in his assertions of what he wanted from his wife in their day-to-day living. On the other hand, he dodged any attempts she made to discuss sex, saying that he'd never heard a man say that his sex life was good. By the third session, they'd run out of conversation and asked the therapists to join them to discuss Marilyn's problems. The therapists refused, saying that Marilyn would probably marry Curly and they should continue to talk about their own relationship. It became apparent that they had little more to say to one another, and were quite dull. The therapists sent them a note suggesting they talk some more about sex. Again Mrs. Narro talked of her lack of interest in sex, and Mr. Narro pompously played the part of a therapist. The female therapist commented to the male therapist that she personally found Mr. Narro repulsive and couldn't imagine being interested in him sexually. Not only was he fat and flabby physically, but his blandness and lack of passion and excitement made him a most unattractive person.

The therapists decided that, since Mrs. Narro protected her husband by not revealing her true feelings about him, it might be helpful if the female therapist did so. They then joined Mr. and Mrs. Narro and the female therapist repeated to Mr. Narro what she had said about him to the male therapist. She added that this was doubly disappointing to her because she felt he had the potential to be sexier and more exciting if he'd only get rid of some of his armor. Mr. Narro glanced at his wife and asked her if she felt the same way, and she then recalled that when she'd been most upset about Marilyn, all he could do was pat her on the back and say, "Don't worry, dear." Mr. Narro told the therapists that he wanted to get rid of the armor but didn't know how. He asked the therapists to help him and in the next few sessions they did help him to explore some pertinent areas. He talked a great deal about his disappointment at never having achieving the feeling of having pleased his father, and, in retrospect, realized that he'd been a mama's boy and that his mama had shielded him from his father and so over-protected him that he never had learned to be interested in others, let alone assertive with them. He had had very little experience and no deep relationships with girls prior to marriage. His wife had always been protective of his feelings and the female therapist, therefore, was probably the first woman who had confronted him with his shortcomings and stated that she expected more from him as a person.

Shortly after this, the team had to inform the Narros that because of administrative reasons the treatment woud have to end shortly. Both Mr. and Mrs. Narro were disappointed, and Mr. Narro said he was particularly disappointed because he felt he'd only been reached very recently. He wondered if one of the therapists could see them privately.

Mr. Narro then related two dreams he had had. He interpreted the first dream as meaning that he had some fear of exposing himself further to the therapists. In the second dream some dogs chased him up to a revolving door. He managed to manipulate them into fighting with each other and in this way escaped. He said he realized that he manipulated the women in his family into fighting with each other so that he could escape involvement. The therapists pointed out that he had attempted to split the therapists' team when he had asked if the family could be seen by just one of them, and Mr. Narro was able to see the validity of this interpretation. In the last month of treatment, Mr. and Mrs. Narro continued to work quite intensively on their sexual problems. During this month Curly was released from jail and Marilyn went to live with him. The Narros were, for the first time, more concerned with her welfare than they were with appearances. They supported Marilyn in her attempts to help Curly get a job and accepted the fact that she was living with him in a trial marriage despite the fact that this might prove embarrassing to them.

Mr. Narro even took the initiative in telling Mrs. Narro's parents about the situation. The grandparents accepted it and were sympathetic with the Narros' point of view. Marilyn, although willing to marry Curly because she thought she would be more acceptable to the community and her parents if she did, was much happier at not being forced into doing so prematurely, and was most appreciative of her parents' new attitude.

The Narros reported that Jane had recently gotten a summer job on her own and was going out with a more appropriate group of boys. She still, however, was functioning protectively with one boyfriend, much as Marilyn functioned with Curly, and as Mrs. Narro had functioned as protector for Mr. Narro.

Mr. Narro said he was now more successful in his business, having expanded into a couple of private enterprises. He felt his loss of forty pounds was a reflection of some of the deeper changes he had made. He stated that, best of all, he found it much easier to communicate with his wife. They both felt, however, that there was more they still wanted from therapy and, since individual family treatment was no longer possible, they would be willing to joint in a multi-family program which was soon to be started at PPC.

In the last individual family session, both Mr. and Mrs. Narro said they had liked the order of treatment, i.e., going from family treatment to couple treatment (alone, with the therapists watching), to couple treatment with the therapists present. Mr. Narro said that he had only been reached in the last few months of treatment. He felt his defenses were so strong that nothing short of the full treatment could have worked with him.

Mrs. Narro spoke mainly in terms of her relationship with the two therapists. She expressed great admiration and love for the female therapist, and although she could not verbalize feelings of love for the male therapist, she kissed him good-bye quite sexually and lovingly. She was able to tell him how angry she had felt toward him for the way he had handled Marilyn — his suggestion that she had had homosexual relations, or that she wasn't getting nearly enough sex and should move to a loft and live with hippies. Mrs. Narro had kept quiet at the time, however, because she sensed that the female therapist had supported the male therapist in this. In actuality, both therapists felt that the technique the male therapist had used with Marilyn had been quite successful. He had definitely established a strong relationship with her, and rather than becoming more promiscuous and homosexual, she had become concerned about her morality and, for the first time in her life, admitted that she cared what others thought about her. During the last eighteen month of therapy there was marked diminution in her sexual acting out. In the last six to eight months of therapy, although involved in a masochistic relationship with Curly, she had grown enough to relate on a deeper, more meaningful level.

In summary, the techniques used with the family varied with the phase of treatment. In the early phase, the therapists worked hard to establish control. This involved their insisting that there be no secrets, refusing to be put into the role of judge or of siding with either the id or superego side of the family. They positioned themselves, instead, as observers, noting the pathological structure, the poor communication, the excessive reliance on the defense mechanisms of intellectualization, denial, and projection, and the emphasis on superficiality. As the therapy continued, the therapists more actively encouraged the family to express their feelings — the unacceptable ones as well as the more acceptable ones. They made efforts to strengthen the father, attempted to focus on the emotional divorce in the marriage, and explored the sexual problems throughout the family. In all of these efforts they met with tremendous resistance. It became more and more obvious that to effect any changes the unconscious would have to be explored and made more conscious. Family members were asked to talk about their dreams and fantasies and these were interpreted both individually and as shared fantasies. At every opportunity the therapists pointed out the correspondence between the girls' conscious fantasies, their acting out of these fantasies, and their parents' unconscious fantasies. They pointed out the ways in which Mr. and Mrs. Narro unconsciously stimulated the girls' acting out. At a still later phase of treatment, the therapists became even more involved with the family. The male therapist formed a strong relationship with Marilyn and the female therapist with Jane. Both therapists soon realized, however, that they were adopting the children instead of really helping the parents to be better parents. Before they could be better parents the Narros would have to have a better marriage. With the idea of forcing them into dealing with their marriage, the therapists suggested that they meet alone. These sessions were helpful in opening avenues of communication between Mr. and Mrs. Narro, but Mr. Narro was still unable to be aggressive or sexual. The female therapist, in contrast to his wife and mother, intervened by confronting him with her negative feelings. This enabled Mrs. Narro also to express her negative feelings more openly. These confrontations seemed to be somewhat successful in finally breaking down Mr. Narro's defenses and by the end of treatment he was becoming more involved in his marriage and his family. Neither therapist felt, however, that treatment was completed; although the Narros were doing somewhat better in their marriage, and were less superficial in their reactions to their children, they still needed help in exploring themselves more deeply, and in helping their children to give up their masochistic mode of relating and to find healthier means of gaining satisfaction. Hopefully, this will be accomplished in the multifamily sessions in which they are going to participate.

Concluding Remarks

The fears of parents can become the preoccupation of the children. Mr. and Mrs. Narro's sexual fears were acted out in real life by Marilyn and Jane. Much of the excitement and liveliness in the Narro family revolved around Marilyn's sexual escapades. As such, Marilyn might be seen as a family "healer."

Both Mr. and Mrs. Narro felt that through therapy they had made significant changes as individuals and in their marital relationship. They were prevented from making further changes by their own satisfaction with each other and with their relationship, and this satisfaction prevented the mobilization of the pervasive anxiety which is one of the hallmarks of individuals who are undergoing deep changes within themselves. The Narros were also, by their own admission, frightened of upsetting the homeostatic balance in their marriage. It seemed easier to them to aim for lesser goals of change than to blast to the root of their conflicts which centered around Mr. Narro seeing his wife as his mother and constantly trying to please her, and Mrs. Narro seeing herself as her mother's little girl and constantly trying to please her mother rather than meet the needs of her husband and her two daughters.

Our, at times, somewhat unconventional approach with this acting-out family was successful in modifying the symptomatic behavior of both daughters. Jane, who had shown signs of incipient schizophrenic fragmentation on psychological testing, was much more outgoing, much more feminine in appearance and behavior, and seemed better integrated. Marilyn, although caught up in a sado-masochistic relationship, was no longer promiscuous and could see herself as more lovable and more able to engage in a meaningful intimate relationship.

Therapists' commentary on a marital dialogue

Ross V. Speck and Geraldine Lincoln

Chapter 14

This verbal interchange between the Narros occurred in a session referred to in the previous chapter (Chapter 13) when Mr. and Mrs. Narro were instructed to talk with each other about themselves and their relationship. The therapists were present and tape-recorded the interchange from behind a one-way mirror. The therapists also passed notes to the Narros at intervals during the Narros' dialogue with each other. The chapter on this family describes in some detail what was transpiring during that period of the therapy.

The authors are well aware that there are serious shortcomings in subjecting a dialogue between two or more people to interpretation. We regret that we did not have facilities for filming this dialogue, for both authors agree that repeated reviews of the dialogue together with a film would have provided us with a good deal of additional data and understanding. However, we were impressed with the amount of agreement between us when writing up our commentary on the transcription of the dialogue which follows in this chapter.

The authors had worked together as co-therapists on two research projects as well as in private practice over a number of years, and shared a point of view about pathology in human systems which included the importance of both the past and the present, the intrapsychic and the interpersonal, and the personal involvement of a heterosexual co-therapy team with the family group.

The reader of this transcript and commentary will find that there is much directness and personal involvement at the points where the therapists speak to the marital pair. We wish to reassure the reader that this was done deliberately and is quite in keeping with our belief that the therapy of a couple or a family is best accomplished by the therapy team first encountering the relatively "closed" system of the unit being treated, forming a relationship with the family, and then moving in and becoming part of the family system (working from within). This means that the authors feel that there is little or no value in passive neutrality and that the co-therapy team must be interacting, experiencing, "alive," and affective human beings throughout the therapy experience. A degree of frankness, direct confrontation, and emotional responsiveness which is rarely seen in work with individual patients is the rule rather than the exception in family treatment.

For most of the treatment of the Narro family we worked with the parents and the two daughters conjointly. Following the brief period of time during which we worked with the parents alone (and from which this transcript is taken), we once again began working with the four family members as a unit. What we learned from seeing the couple alone was not treated as confidential information when the family returned as a unit, and some of the new therapy material that came from the sessions was presented by the therapists and by the Narros in the sessions with the whole family.

We feel that the following dialogue between Mr. and Mrs. Narro (and the therapists' commentary) captures accurately and perhaps painfully the locked nature of the "gruesome-twosome" relationship in this marriage. Both daughters (Marilyn and Jane) were easier to motivate toward change. When this dialogue was transcribed with therapist commentary, only one similar approach had been published.[1] Since then, Ackerman, Haley and others have published commentaries on verbatim family dialogues.[2,3]

We are publishing this chapter — with all the repetitious, "spiralling," "no exit" quality of the marital interaction, which may be somewhat frustrating to read through — because it is basic data which the experienced clinician-researcher may compare with the clinical course in Chapter 5. The neophyte family therapist may compare his own responses to the marital dialogue with the therapists' commentaries.

Verbatim Transcript	*Therapists' Comments*
She: You are so immersed in what's going on now with the business that I don't think you have room for any other kind of thoughts.	Mrs. Narro is unable to ask for something for herself.
He: Well, let me assure you that I do; I do very much.	(Mr. Narro needs to reassure her and himself.)
She: Well, I'm not complaining.	This is highly complex. Mrs. Narro, in her first statement, said in essence, "What's the use of complaining since nothing can be done about it?" When he says or implies that something might be done, she fairly adroitly denies that she wants anything. In these three brief statements a collusive, dyadic alliance between Mr. and Mrs. Narro is demonstrated which has some of the qualities of mutual double-binding in which each of the pair is really asking for the other to nullify a will-of-the-wisp type of need which both seem to have.
He: Complain if you want to complain. (Angry tone of voice.)	Mr. N. says angrily, "Complain if you want to complain." His tone of voice belies his statement. Thus,

he is giving contrasting and mutually nullifying messages at different levels.

She: I didn't say that in the form of a complaint; I just know that right now this is an all-pervading occupation.

Because of her own personal dynamics, she cannot ask for anything directly for herself. (We remember Mrs. Narro's relationship to her mother.)

He: It isn't. It takes up most of my time — it takes up all my thinking during the day — I'll agree with you — and at night sometimes I think about it —

He is responding to the tone of complaint in her paralanguage rather than to the verbal content of what she says.

She: Aw, come on now —

She calls him to task because she realizes that he is being phony.

He: — and we'll talk about it, but every once in a while things run through my mind about the family — about you or the girls — every day — every day. Well, what I am trying to say is that I don't want to be — I want to be open — I want to tell you exactly how I feel, but by the same token I want you to tell me, because then I know just what our relationship is. I don't know whether I am making myself clear.

He continues to insist that he is interested in his wife's welfare, but he also accuses her of holding back in their relationship, and of not making any clear statement of what she wants from him.

She: Well! I thought I was always open, but you never were.

She counterattacks and throws the ball back to him.

He: Well — (long pause) — there are times when there are things that you want to tell me but you are afraid to tell me — because you've admitted it — because you are afraid you will be considered a nag or your mother did this to your father, or your father to your

He tells her to be open and honest, but then adds that she must be careful in the way in which she communicates her needs to him. The effect is again to preclude any real open communication between the two of them.

mother, or you don't want to be the same way. I think it's bad to have something on your mind and you are afraid to say it for any reason at all. (Emphatic.) At least say it once — maybe it is the wrong thing to keep saying some things, but if you never say it you won't know. Maybe the way you would say it wouldn't bother me, but the way your mother would say to your father bothers him. Do you see what I mean?

She: Yes.

She willingly enters into another collusion with the husband so that again nothing gets clarified.

He: Many times you've said things to hurt my feelings — don't think you've never hurt my feelings. First I may be angry, but then I may be hurt, then afterwards I realize you are right or you are wrong.

He tells her that she is able to hurt his feelings, and he is so vulnerable that it is not until afterwards that he can formulate his own opinion on what she was telling him. This is another plea not to be direct with him.

She: (Laughs). That was funny.

She enjoys being able to hurt him. She has a sadistic component in her personality which finds ready satisfaction in his passive and masochistic submission. She is also uncomfortable that he has recognized her attacks upon him.

He: The first thing when you bother me about certain things or talk to me about certain things that don't appeal to me — I get angry or I get hurt — I don't stay angry very long — and then afterwards I'll think about it and try to figure out whether you are right or wrong. I can't help myself — I always come back to being the guy who looks at the other guy's side of the question.

He is confused and caught in the web of her bind. He gets angry but then submits that he must be wrong and she right. (From our psychotherapy contacts with him, this is a direct carryover from his earlier relationship to his mother.)

She: So what's wrong with that?

She maintains the status quo and does not want to shake up the system (the collusion). She wants to maintain control of him in her mother role.

He: I think it's done me harm at certain times, but not in our relationship — in other relationships with other people — not in a personal relationship — I think I'd have been a lot better off if I hadn't worried about how the other fellow

It becomes even more obvious how he wants her to become his mother and how lost he is if she gives him no clue. His narcissism shows in his feeling that everything is related to him.

wa˙ or thought or felt. But where you are concerned I would much rather know — no matter what it is that you have to say to me — than guess, because I can read it — I can tell by the look in your eyes, or you won't let me look in your eyes and I know that there is something bothering you — it might not be anything to do with me, but my first reaction is that it does have something to do with me. Now this may not be a normal reaction, but this is the way I feel. (Sounds sincere.)

She: You mean that every time I'm disturbed you think it has to do with you?

Even she is surprised at his narcissism.

He: This is my feeling, unless something has happened.

She: You never come to me and say "There's something bothering you, come on, spill it" — you never do that. You just walk around and look at me funny.

She still wants him to be interested in her, and he can be interested only in her response to him. His "looking at her funny" is his way of getting her to respond to him — to make him be — rather than his genuine interest in her as a separate person.

He: That's right.

He admits to his tremendous dependency on others for personal identity and shows how needful he is.

She: Why don't you come out and say —

He: Well, I think I have been doing it more lately, maybe not. I have a supersensitivity that I think is misplaced. Somehow when people say things or act in a certain way I immediately take it as a personal — as something personal — they may forget about it a minute later, that they said it or thought it or whatever, it may not have meant anything as far as I was concerned, but sometimes I'll go around for days being concerned about a word dropped here or a. . . .

She: I think I'm pretty much the same way.

She has a similar narcissistic problem.

He: Maybe everybody is but I don't think so. But I think this would be the greatest thing that we could get out of this whole program — if I would feel completely comfortable with you and you with me — no guessing.

Is this a beginning awareness of the value of a separate identity or does he want to simply get out of the bind that he must have experienced with his mother?

She: No, I could understand that, but I think every wife keeps certain things to herself and every husband keeps certain things to himself — isn't that right?

She seems to fear he will swallow her.

He: I imagine so.

She: Because sometimes what bothers you in the morning, if you don't say anything, by the time the evening comes it does not bother you any more.

She sounds frightened and may be saying, "Don't get too close."

He: Yeah, but I'd hate to think I'd opened up some Pandora's box and we'll start bickering about every damned thing that came up. I think there are certain things if allowed to simmer for an hour or so, pass away — I'm not talking

Although she has made him somewhat afraid of disturbing the marital system, he nevertheless puts in a plea for better communication and threatens her with the possibility of his escaping her control.

about those, but if something is bothering you in the morning and is still bothering you at night I'd rather you told me. Now you know I can say to you this is the fact or you have the facts wrong or I don't think your feeling's right or wrong for this reason or other — or this is the way I am, what are you going to do about it, but at least give us a chance to talk about it. Like I said, there was a long time there, which I realize only now, that I didn't want to really be alone with you.

She: Well, listen, I've been very disturbed for a long time. (She's resisting.)

He has admitted to a problem and she immediately assumes that it is her problem. His statement must have made her anxious because it implies that she does not have as strong a hold on him as she has thought.

He: That isn't the reason — we've both been disturbed — I'm disturbed.

She: You're disturbed — I'm disturbed.

He: I'm disturbed — I probably don't react the way you do — this bothers you, I know it does. I think I am a little more willing to accept certain things and figure to myself the world isn't going to come to

He is beginning to reveal his ambivalence about his relationship with her. She tries to make a joke out of it, but he persists in exploring whether or not he can tolerate differing with her and hearing the consequences. Can he be a separate person? He is also saying her intensity bothers and overwhelms him.

an end — I think you are a lot
more intense about certain things
— I don't know whether it's because I have less feeling or —

She: Do you really have less feelings or are you just afraid to let
your feelings come out?

> She keeps control by acting the
> part of the therapist and focusing
> on his part of the problem, rather
> than on their relationship.

He: I don't think I'm afraid to
let my feelings come out — not
any more — I used to have an idea

> He goes along with her talking
> about his need to protect his feel-
> ings.

that I was a big brave guy if I
didn't show anger, I didn't show hurt, I didn't show pain — I used to
think it was the greatest thing in the world when I'd go to a doctor
to have a wound bandaged or a dislocated finger, and he'd fix it and I
could laugh while he was fixing it with the most excruciating pain.
I don't think I'd laugh any more — I think I'd yell. This business of not
showing how you feel doesn't pay.

She: Yeah, that's right. It doesn't.

He: I don't particularly want to be
classified as a sissy, and I had to
show them I wasn't a sissy.

> He opens up and talks about his
> fears of being seen as a sissy . . .
> that therapists see him in this
> way. . . .

She: Were you a sissy?

He: I don't think so — I wasn't as
fast a runner.

> She challenges him, accuses him
> of really being a sissy, and does
> not accept his rationalizations. He
> becomes more and more defensive.

She: You looked like a sissy.

He: I wasn't able to keep up in certain things with the rest of the gang
— I couldn't run as fast, but I wasn't a mama's boy.

She: Did you roll in the dirt and —

He: Sure — we used to fight on the street — come home with our clothes
torn — stagger home from Elm Street with a dislocated hip from playing
football or a broken nose.

She: Oh, that's when you were older.

He: Thirteen or fourteen years old. When I was seven or eight years
old my mother had an iron fence around me after I got over the flu, and
I got the reputation I think, then, if I remember correctly, that I was
a sissy so I had to prove that I wasn't. I think that this is one of the
reasons at least that I have been reluctant to show feeling — that might
be considered — you know—to cry —

She: Maybe to cry — but there are other feelings that you don't show too. Like anger — you don't show anger.

He: Yes, I do.

She: No, you don't.

He: I may not show it — you know damned well when I'm mad, don't you?

She: Yes, but you don't let it out.

She continues to challenge him while he defends himself and finally he observes her non-verbal communication when she scratches. ... He readily enters into collusion with her to divert his attention from this line of thinking.

He: Well, that's different.

She: No, that's important to let it out.

He: Well, I show it.

She: Not to any great extent — maybe you just keep quiet and walk away. That's all — but that's not showing anger.

He: I don't keeps quiet and walk away any more to anybody. Do you have a bite?

She: I don't know — I've had it for three days and it itches like mad — I don't know if it's a bite or what it is.

He: I'll kiss it.

She: (Giggles). And I've been concerned about your health because you get no exercise and fresh air whatsoever. Running around in town from one office to the other is not walking or exercise. I think you are doing yourself harm — you are losing weight and your muscles have no tone

She switches the topic and takes control of his activities. He allows her to do so and pledges his loyalty to her. This is another collusion in the service of maintaining the status quo in their relationship. This is a tightly locked system.

whatsoever — they're all saggy and I don't think that's good. I don't want you to play handball because that's too strenuous, but if you could just get out and play golf one morning — one Sunday a week — one day a week.

He: I'd like to but I don't know where the hell to play.

She: Where do the other men play?

He: I don't feel like getting up six o'clock in the morning to. . . .

She: Do you have to get up at six o'clock to play at Fairview?

He: Sure, you can't get a starting time and most of the men want to play eighteen holes — I'll play nine holes — I'll play with you — play nine holes of golf — I'd rather not — I'd rather play with men.

She: Oh sure, I'd think you would.

He: Yes, I'd like to go out and play golf once a week.

She: It would do you good.

He: I wouldn't go out and garden 'cause I despise it.

She: How about just walking?

He: No, I don't like that. I'd get bored to death — I have to be doing something.

She: How about bicycling?

He: I never learned how.

She: — or go to the Y and swim.

He: I don't like indoor swimming. I'd rather play golf or tennis.

She: No tennis, I wouldn't want you to play tennis.

He: I agree. I think you are right — I ought to get out and do something with my Sunday afternoons.

She: No, Sunday morning before it gets hot — you can always come home and take a rest and — you don't want to get up at six to play golf, but you've been getting up at six thirty or seven every Sunday anyway. You could get up at seven o'clock to go to work down in the basement on Sunday.

He: This is terrible — I'm not doing that any more.

She: It's no good. It would be the best thing in the world for you if you could just go out and play.

He: What I've got to do is get a fixed date with a foursome and go out every Sunday.

She: Well, that shouldn't be too hard to arrange.

He: I'll have to do it.

She: — 'cause usually by this time of the year your complexion is brown — now you are gray looking.

He: I'm going to do it.

She: Will you?

He: Yeah.

She: Promise?

He: Yes, I'm going to call Bob or one of the other boys.

She: Don?

He: Maybe — maybe not. (Laughs)

She: Well —

He: He bores me.

She: Well, once in a while you could play with him.

He: I'll get a foursome to play on Sunday — I think I'd look forward to it, because some of the pressures come off. Even this Saturday — I'm only going in for a little while — I'm not going to spend the day there — I don't have to anymore — I'll have my weekends back again. That I'm definitely going to do. (Silence) I also think we have to spend some weekends with Jane.

He is lost. He capitulates. She tells him what to do, when to do it and with whom to do it. The degree of her control is impressive.

She: She doesn't want to do anything with us.

He: I think if we planned things she'll do it.

She: For instance.

He: She's perfectly happy to go camping with us. We ought to every once in a while include her in our plans, and then some weekends we don't include her in our plans. I'm not saying we're going to go running away every weekend. I think we ought to do something together — we haven't been doing things together at all — this is something — we start out — we plan. Well, from now on we'll do this, that, and the other thing — but we do it once and then things seem to fall back into their old rut — you got a match? My lighter is out of fluid.

While this part of the dialogue is taking place, we become increasingly aware of her resistance, blandness, collusion, and of her control and desexualization of him and his willingness to allow it. At this point we knock on the door and send in a note suggesting that they talk about sex. This is done in order to refocus their communication on a central problem which they share.

She: Weekends she never wants

(Knock on door)

to be anywhere except with Ed.

She: (Laughs) I love these love notes. I don't seem to have a match, dear.

She is laughing because she is in control. She enjoys the sex which we have introduced because she feels at this point it is not really threatening. Her statement, "I don't seem to have a match, dear", is open to many levels of interpretation, of course. Even though we are outside, behind the mirror, Mrs. N. seems more tuned in to us than she is to her own husband who is in the room.

He: (Reading note) "Sex – it's better than you think – it's even better than thinking."

She: (Laughs)

He: Oh, I thought you were going to take your dress off.

She: (Laughs) Oh God (Silence) So what do you do with a wife who doesn't feel sexy? Get another wife?

They reassure each other that they will keep on playing the game of reassurance, with her taking the blame for the poor sexual relationship and with him not really either blaming her or looking under the surface for his part in the problem.

He: Maybe I haven't been a good teacher.

She: I remember ___ used to say it was the greatest winter sport she knew – but she hated it in the summer time. I never felt it was any kind of an indoor sport that I particularly enjoyed or looked forward to.

(Silence)

He: Well you know – (clears throat) I really don't know how I can – I can't analyze you because I'm not an analyst.

She: Don't try – I don't want you to try.

He: No, but I mean – I don't think that you are a cold person or frigid or anything like that.

She: No, I have feelings, but I'd be just as happy if I didn't have sex at all.

He: Well, I wouldn't.

She: I know you wouldn't – no man would.

He: Oh, I guess there are men that would.

She, No, I just – I don't know – it goes against me – let's put it like that – there's a – and something – the aesthetic part – it just goes against me. (Irritation?)

He: Do you think this would be true if it was me or any other man?

She: That's right.

He: Do you really feel that way? (Said like a little boy — pleadingly)

She: Yes.

He: You are not trying to make me feel — ?

She: No.

He: — because very honestly this is something that bothers me.

She: I am sure that it bothers you.

He: Not necessarily your lack of deep interest in it, but the fact that it's my fault.

She: I don't know if it's your fault since I haven't had experience with anybody else.

He: I feel that as we've brought out here — that this is something that goes way back — before you and I ever got together. Your feelings toward sex generally — maybe some other man might have changed your attitude toward it, and I was never able to for some reason.

She: This is something I'll never know, will I?

He: I hope you won't. (Laughs)

She: No.

They are reluctant to change this situation. The dialogue does not sound real at all with so much intellectualization and resistance.

He: You may find out some day by something that I may do to change your attitude — I don't know. Maybe I ought to send you to a teacher.

She: A geisha girl.

He: I wouldn't send you to a geisha man — maybe I ought to go to a geisha girl — maybe I haven't learned enough.

She: It might be helpful — you haven't had much outside experience either.

He: But I certainly wouldn't want to go through life without sex — as you well know.

She: Well, that's normal — I guess I'm not normal.

He: See, this reaction upsets me — when you say "I'm not normal."

She: I say I guess I'm not normal.

He: Well, why should you think you're not normal?

She: Because I don't think sex is — because I don't look forward — once I am aroused that's a different thing.

He: I know.

She: But I would be perfectly satisfied to just not be bothered with it at all.

He: The thing that has always struck me is — so many men have told me this about their wives.

She: You've said that before — maybe you think it's normal.

He: I don't know — it may be normal amongst a certain class of people — or a certain type of person — I'm not willing to —

She: With the times we were raised in or —

He: I don't know — this is something I have never done — discussed it — I find it difficult to do here, let alone amongst strangers, but I have never been able to discuss my sexual relationship with other people — and yet, as a matter of course, a bunch of men will be around, and one man will say that if he never touched his wife after the first year they were married she'd never miss him, and I've had men tell me they don't bother with their wives — they look for their sexual release elsewhere.

She: Well, that would worry me, too. If they never bother their wives, their wives must either close their eyes, or —

He: They probably do — they are probably so relieved that they don't have to respond that they figure to themselves, it's like he goes off to play poker — he's not with me that night either. I have asked men — I have said "Have you ever — your wife knows you must be getting sexual satisfaction somehow — doesn't she ever ask you how?"

This is an example of his curiosity about others, his willingness to be a voyeur, to ask others to reveal their thoughts and feelings, but his unwillingness to share his own thoughts, feelings and experiences with others.

She: What they don't know don't hurt them.

He: They say they don't ever ask them and they don't tell them.

She: I know. —— told me she has never gotten undressed in front of

She is saying, "See I am not so bad, other women are worse." On her husband — never in all the years they have been married.

He: And yet this doesn't bother you.

She: No, you know that.

the surface, it might seem that two inhibited people are gently feeling their way into a discussion of their sexual difficulties. However, these people has been married twenty years and they are still looking for rationalizations as to why they have a poor sex life. Actually, they are satisfied with a little boy — little girl relationship and are not really seeking change. They are using the treatment to seek approval from us and not to obtain a more mature man-woman relationship.

He: I say, I know that — it's not a question of being shy or — (Sigh) I don't know — I don't know whether it has to do with me — I have to confess that I think possibly part of it is me — if not all of it — at least part of it.

No one ever takes responsibility for long. It shifts too fast for anything to be accomplished.

She: It may have been because you were so heavy always; that might had something to do with it.

He: I wasn't heavy when we were married.

She: You weren't light.

He: I weighed less than I do now by ten pounds.

She: I was scared then anyway.

He: (Relieved) I think you're still scared for some reason or other. (Pauses) I also think that even

He is relieved at this point to shift the responsibility back to her.

when we are having sex you are not completely immersed in it — you are thinking of — is it good or is it bad — or could it be better or this isn't all it's cracked up to be, or something like that — but you are not just — your mind isn't completely devoid of —

She: I'm not carried away.

He: I get that feeling — I'm sensitive to that — once in a while — not all the time, but sometimes I'm sensitive to it — I wish I knew how to tell you to —

He becomes very hostile and doesn't help her, but just baits her.

She: Let myself go —

He: Let yourself go — you let yourself go when you are angry — when you get angry you let yourself go without any strings attached — which indicates that you must be full of anger. (Laughs)

She: Oh, not as full of anger as I was.

She becomes defensive but does not get angry at him overtly nor does she look at herself more deeply.

He: No, I let myself go when we have sex. I'm full of sex.

Some mutual hostility.

She: You're full of love, eh?

(This is where we knocked on the door a second time and handed in a note saying "Stop playing the therapist and be a passionate lover." This intervention was possibly ill-timed as we did not hear the foregoing in leaving the observation room and walking in to the next office where the couple were talking. However, during several hundred hours of work with this couple, their momentary angers with each other never did escalate to a full-fledged battle. We had often hoped that this might occur.)

(Knock on door)

He: You are a nuisance.

She: Oh, my God.

He: (Reading) "Stop playing the therapist and be a passionate lover" — right here?

We see here rapidly shifting dyadic complementarity. They now shift to us, just as at home they shift their focus to the children.

She: Is that note to you or to me?

He: Apparently I'm being the therapist here. This becomes impossible — I can't be a passionate lover with that great big plate-glass window and with the sound box on. I just can't.

She: I can't either.

He: I don't know anybody that can.

She: You're too inhibited.

It might have been better had we been more direct in our expression of hostility. At the time we were responding to Mr. N.'s projection of the blame on to his wife. His refusal to express himself more was part of this. Our effort was to separate them, going after the husband to attempt to break up the symbiosis.

He: Oh I don't know — anybody —. First of all I don't quite understand what they ask — what they want us to do — discuss the techniques of sex — I wouldn't do it if I had to walk out of here and never come back again — it goes against my grain — what we do when we are in bed together — that's our business. If they'd like to come and join us and maybe help us over this thing — I think it would be a good idea — because I don't know where to go from here.

She: They want us to solve these problems between ourselves.

He: I'm not going to solve it in front of this window.

She: Oh, they don't want you to get sexy. (He laughs.) They want you to express love — I don't know. (Sounds sad.)

He: Last week when you mentioned you had a dream and I didn't pursue the dream with you and I said that I'm not a psychiatrist — I can't explain a dream, they criticized me because I dropped it — and now we're talking about sex and I am trying to find out how you feel and what I can do or what you can do, and I'm being criticized. So, I'm confused.

He does not respond to her sadness. He is so narcissistically involved with himself that he cannot perceive the needs of another person. They are locked in a repetitive communicational bind.

She: I thought we were getting along fine.

He: You mean in this conversation?

She: Yes.

He: I think we can reserve the passion for our bedroom but maybe we can discuss the other aspects here. They don't know how far along the way we've come when we can sit here and talk about it.

They were not asked to have sexual relations and to be observed through the window. They use concrete thinking to defend themselves from involvement on an emotional level with each other.

She: I think they know. Now you feel bogged down, huh?

They each defer to the other. It is obvious that she is in a powerful position and he is the angry little boy, particularly with us.

He: Well, all I can say is just don't lie there — do something. (Laughs)

She: You have to be aggressive. Be aggressive.

He: Now? I really thought we were getting somewhere in that conversation — are they at the door? (Knock) I thought I heard somebody at the door.

She: Hi; well, come in.

He: It's about time.

Mrs. L (therapist): We thought maybe you could do it all yourselves.

COMMENTARY ON A MARITAL DIALOGUE

He: Apparently we can't—I thought we were getting along real good.

The statement that they are doing real well is the statement that the status quo is their habitual role relationship. Nothing is being shaken or changed.

Mrs. L (therapist): Well, I've been sitting and trying to put myself in Mrs. N.'s position and I am sure that she has problems with sex, but you couldn't make me excited either—you're bland, you're flat, and you are smug. This may be pretty hard but I was saying to Ross, maybe if he'd cry, maybe if he'd break down, maybe if he'd scream—I don't mean just the anger—I've seen you get mad at the kids—but you are so—its like somebody was describing a patient today and they said about her (flatly), she says "I am so excited about this or I am so angry about this"—who can feel for her? I can't feel with you, Mr. N. I am sure you must have feelings—but, boy, I wouldn't want to go to bed with you—I wouldn't feel like it would a bit of fun. Now (to Mrs. N.), you haven't been saying it, but I am sure you must have some of these feelings—you've been talking—about the weight—what does he do to get you to feel—well, gee, this is the most romantic, exciting evening of our life.

This is a non-analytic technique, *direct confrontation,* by an affective therapist who is trying to supply a live model of human response when dealing with annoyance and frustration. The therapist is taking a position which is different from the more protective, hypocritical position both Mr. N.'s mother and wife have taken. This statement of Mrs. L.'s is made in the context of the positive working relationship with both Mr. and Mrs. N. It had been discussed by both of us prior to entering the room to join the dialogue between the husband and wife, and it had also been discussed with our colleagues in the research group. It was used as a possible technique to meet an impasse.

Mrs. N.: I never felt that way about sex.

Mrs. L.: Well, it's up to him to make you feel about it—does he tell you how beautiful your body is—does he make it an experience that's worth remembering? You won't discuss details, but something is wrong in the detail that's going on, and you are not living.

This is an effort to break the system by going after one person rather than having the problem passed back and forth from one participant to the other.

Dr. S. (therapist): I think they could discuss details. I heard him say that he'd just pick up and walk out if he had to — if he had to go into details — maybe we have to do that — there is something missing.

This is an attempt to make Mr. N. stop, and not run away from the confrontation but face it.

Mrs. L.: There is no spark. Life is sex — there's no — I'd like to flirt with you but I don't know where we'd go.

The female therapist could not think of anything which she would enjoy doing with Mr. N. She could not envision enjoying a conversation, a dinner, a drink, or any kind of encounter with him. The male therapist had previously described him in a direct confrontation as "Piggy" in *Lord of the Flies*, and this is as close a representation as we could think of. There was no place for "Piggy" and there seemed to be no place for Mr. N. It seemed that no woman in his life had demanded that he be a man. Instead, both his mother and his wife had supported his sexlessness. In contrast, the female therapist and some of the female social workers who had observed the sessions, had been either revolted or dismayed by his complacency. Consequently, as a therapeutic maneuver, in this context, in the continued meetings between the family and therapists, the female therapist confronted him with her own reaction to his lack of manliness.

Mrs. L.: Why did you look to your wife then?

Mr. N. looks to "mama" for approval. There is the constant "eye monitoring" which is commonly observed in dyads. *The therapists must pay as much attention in dyadic or family therapy to the nonverbal communication as they would to the verbal material in individual therapy.*

He: What? I just looked.

Mrs. L.: Well, why did you look away from me to her?

He: I really don't know — maybe I wanted to see what her reaction was to what you just said. Whether she feels that way.

Mrs. L.: I'll tell you this, Mrs. N. If you can't come out more honestly about how you feel, you are never going to get a thing that you want.

She: We had sex relations the other night and my reaction was that I was a pretty poor sex partner.

Mrs. L.: What did your husband do to make it marvelous?

Mrs. N. takes her usual masochistic position and joins in a collusion with him; she supports his pathology by taking him off the hook.

She: He got very upset — he said I was too introverted about it and I should shut up and stop talking about it so much.

He: And just enjoy it.

She: I can't relax and just, you know, just give.

Mrs. L.: Was it all your fault — was it all on the side of your being unrelaxed?

The female therapist makes a strong bid to break up the collusion between Mr. and Mrs. N.

She: Well, I don't know. Like I've said — since I've never had sex experience with anybody else the only sex experience I know is with him. I don't know whether it's good, bad, right, or wrong. I don't know.

Dr. S.: I guess with Marilyn and Jane — there's been a lot of disapproval there about the fact that they have had sexual experiences, particularly Marilyn, but in a way you really missed something, didn't you? Here you are saying — at whatever age you are — that you don't know, and that, gee, this is what it's supposed to be like, and that's pretty terrible.

The male therapist is feeling sorry for Mrs. N. She is far behind the girls (despite the pathological behavior which they have shown). He wonders if she might have been different with a different man. However, we tend to think her own conflicts make her what she is. She shows very little searching for change-directed behavior. The male therapist tries to get her to move to the point where she will want something more. As it is, she is not even ambivalent.

She: Well, when I first got married and some of my friends were married, and they were saying, oh, boy this was the greatest, I thought, gee whiz, I wish I could feel that way, but I don't. I didn't know whether it was because it was that I wasn't madly and passionately in love with him, but as the years went by I think I realized that that's just me, I would be that way with any man, I think.

Mrs. N. tends to blame herself and does not let her husband be despondent for a minute. She is the over-protective mama who will not let her son grow up and become a man. The therapists must be relentless to keep such a husband and wife on the track of constantly examining their relationship or they very readily slip off in a collusive effort to avoid dealing with the real issues.

Mrs. L.: With that other man you went with —?

She: I don't know — he never tried anything with me, so I don't know.

He: Did he ever arouse you sexually?

She: No.

He: Well, believe me, I had girls that I went out with that aroused me sexually although I never tried anything.

She: Well, he never tried anything, that's what I mean.

Mrs. L.: Well, how did he make you feel?

She: I was always excited when I was with him — always.

Mrs. L.: Why doesn't your husband make you excited?

She: I don't know.

Mrs. L.: How do you feel when I say this to you? (to Mr. N.)

He: Very inferior — I'm trying to find the word — I feel like maybe the whole thing is my fault.

Mrs. L.: Do you feel like you'd like to cry? Does it hurt you to know — I've thought a long time before saying this — I don't know how to reach you; apparently your wife hasn't reached you.

He: Yeah, right now I think I could cry.

Mrs. L.: Why don't you?

He: Because I — I — there is something that keeps me from doing it — I don't remember crying more than two or three times since I was a grown man — maybe twice.

Mrs. L.: Maybe this is what's wrong.

Dr. S.: What were the two occasions?

He: Well, I remember crying when I was — after we came back from my father's funeral — not before — not when he died but on the way back from the cemetery, I cried.

Dr. S.: What kind of feelings did you have and what were you thinking about?

He: That goes back a long time — I was seventeen years old.

Dr. S.: Well, what thoughts did you have when you came back — what made you cry — did you cry for joy — what made you cry? Did you miss him? Did you feel it would be nice to have him back? About what?

He: I think I was probably feeling sorry for myself. I remember the comment that made me cry. We were in the limousine that the undertaker provided and I was sitting with my grandmother and grandfather, and my grandfather said to me, "Well, now you are going to be the man of the family," and I started to cry and I remember so well now, and I don't remember whether my mother put her arm around me or somebody told me not to cry, and my grandmother said "Let him cry, it will do him good." I didn't cry when my mother died – do you remember me crying when my mother died?

She: No, I couldn't cry when my mother died, either – she was sick so long it was a blessing when she passed away.

He: But I remember another occasion – the only other occasion I can remember is that I was with my wife and it was before we got married, and I said to her "I wish my father were alive, I think he would like you," or something like that, or, or "He would love you."

She: And you said you missed your father very much and you cried. I remember that. It was when we were engaged or dating –

He: It seemed to me that the several times that I cried it always had to do with my father – I don't – in all of the escapades that Marilyn – the mischief that she has gotten involved in, and all the terrible hurt that we have had and all the tears that my wife has shed I don't think I ever cried – even to myself. You know there are times for some reason that your masculinity forbids you to cry in front of other people or you think that's the reason – and you go off by yourself and shed a couple of tears – I don't recall – maybe I got a little moist in the eyes or something like that – but, believe me, I didn't cry. I felt like it many a time.

Mrs. L.: It would be swell if you could let yourself go.

He: I felt like it had been such a waste.

Mrs. L.: What's been a waste?

He: Marilyn's life has been such a waste.

Mrs. L.: Marilyn has had more than either one of you. When you said that, my reaction was – your life, not Marilyn's. Marilyn has at least had some feelings of excitement and passion. You block them all off.

He: What I was going to say before you finished, before you interrupted – was that in thinking that her life has been a waste, sometimes a flash comes through that so has mine where she is concerned – and I'll go further and say maybe it has been a waste in other directions, too – there are certain things that are missing, and I recognize that there are certain things that are missing, and something in me says stop thinking that way, such thinking will make you despondent – forget about them – push them aside and go about living every day.

Mrs. L.: What's missing?

He: I don't know what's missing.

She: Maybe I am not exciting – I am not an exciting person – maybe I am too bland.

Mrs. L.: You've got other faults but you're not bland.

He: You are not bland. I said to you before that you show passion when you get angry, so you do show it. I don't show it at all.

Mrs. L.: You are hopeless about him, because you don't go after him to give you what you want. Have you ever gone out in the woods and had intercourse in the woods?

She: Are you kidding?

Mrs. L.: No, I am not kidding.

She: (Laughs) Yeah, when we go — no, not even when we go camping — there is no privacy there.

Dr. S.: Not even when you were camping?

She: No.

Dr. S.: It's in a tent, though — it's probably better than in a house but it's still not quite in the woods.

Mrs. L.: Have you ever gone off to a motel, the two of you, just to get away and feel like it is an escapade — it's fun, just for the two of you?

He: No, but I always feel more excited about sex when we go to a hotel or we're away somewhere or the kids are out of the house completely and we are home alone.

She: I always feel inhibited when somebody is in the next room.

He: I just feel that there's more — not more privacy. I don't know what it is — I enjoy sex more when we go off out of town or something like that.

This is confirmation of our theory that sex is too incestuous for them.

Mrs. L.: Don't you think he has enough potential to become more exciting and more passionate? Are you writing him off completely?

She: Maybe I am writing myself off.

There is more collusion as Mrs. N. takes him off the spot.

Mrs. L.: But then you're writing him off.

He: Well, this is what bothers me about my wife — she's always

He now comes to her defense.

writing herself off in certain areas — she's lousy at sex, she says, therefore she will never be any better — or maybe, "I've been a lousy mother so therefore I won't be any different," or "I've been a lousy this or that." She knows she's not lousy. I don't know whether she is asking for me to prove it to her that she's not, and I haven't risen to the occasion, I don't know, but it makes me angry that she deprecates herself.

Mrs. L.: She deprecates you if she deprecates herself.

He: Yes.

She: Yes, I got angry at him the other night.

The collusion has not been broken. Future sessions will continue this arduous task. In the next few sessions Mr. N. began to explore the relationship with his father. And he was more ready to examine why he could not let himself go more.

REFERENCES

1. Jackson, D. D., Riskin, J., and Satir, V. Method of Analysis of a Family Interview. *Arch. Gen. Psychiat.* 5:321-339, 1961.
2. Ackerman, N. W. *Treating the Troubled Family.* New York: Basic Books, Inc., 1966, pp. 3-292.
3. Haley, J. and Hoffman, L. *Techniques of Family Therapy.* New York: Basic Books, Inc., 1968, pp. 3-471.

Autonomy and responsibility in family therapy

Jerome E. Jungreis

Chapter 15

Observations of a family made by a family therapist can be systematized along a number of parameters. The problems for which the family seeks treatment can be meaningfully conceptualized in a variety of ways. These conceptualizations give access to the lines along which change can be produced in a family, and can suggest forms of family intervention. A family diagnosis in this sense is not so much a diagnosis of a disease entity as it is a clue to a course of intervention into a family system to produce change. It is a treatment-oriented diagnosis rather than a descriptive or genetic diagnosis of an objective state in a family.

Let us consider now some of the parameters along which a family can be meaningfully conceptualized. The family can be viewed as individual personality isolates in a series of relationships extending from each individual to the others in the family. In terms of treatment, then, the therapist would focus mainly on the needs and conflicts of each individual member of the family. Those who focus on family structure see the family as component parts that fit together well or poorly, e.g., parents and children, men and women, the sick and the well. These parts fit further with the therapist, the community, etc.

Therapy would attempt to reintegrate the differences and distinctions between the component parts. Some therapists view the family with regard to specific issues that are in the forefront of the family struggle, such as intimacy and distance, control and permissiveness, giving and taking, domination and submission, etc. The family problems can also be conceptualized in terms of channels of interaction: verbal and non-verbal communications, distortions in communications, physical exchanges of concrete items, use of space, etc. In this instance the family therapist will attempt, through a variety of techniques, to reorganize the communication patterns. His main emphasis will be on restoration of appropriate communications in the family. In therapy, the therapist may well heighten the issues and possibly dramatize them to achieve their resolutions.

Dynamically, a family therapist may view the family as fixated at various levels of psychosexual-social development. For example, the family can be viewed as a series of people who are extremely dependent and who are fighting to make the other one the parent figure on whom they can concentrate their dependency needs. Or a therapist may view families as fixated at a particular level of psychosexual development, with all the various permutations involved in such fixations. Here, the therapeutic encounter would involve the use of family system analysis to make regressions and fixations conscious with the ultimate aim of simultaneous family development of more mature levels of adjustment. A therapist may tend to tune in more to the faulty transactions that are a function of family egos deficient in appropriate adaptive mechanisms. He may focus on conflict resolution, for example, and, through a variety of imaginative techniques, literally teach the family how to resolve conflicts. One with a primary interest in roles will tend to view the family along such dimensions as role complementarity and conflict, evolution and change of roles, generational roles, etc. The family therapist in this instance may attempt to assist the family in becoming aware of their role distortions and in assuming more appropriate roles.

The above list can be easily expanded, depending upon one's previous training, biases, interests, and theory of diagnosis and treatment. Since all these parameters are slices from the same cake, they may seem to be overlapping and at times redundant. The significant concern to the therapist is that view of the family which permits access to intervention, facilitates positive changes, and provides a criterion to judge such change. Accordingly, we believe that the versatility and effectiveness of the family therapist is enhanced if he does not adhere to a single view of the family. Much depends on the level of entry most suitable to a particular family initially, on the type of family "pathology," on family defenses, and on family expectations of the therapy. Subsequently, changes in the family in therapy may call for changes in therapeutic orientation.

Since concepts lead to or reinforce techniques, we shall discuss both as consistent aspects of conjoint family treatment. We have found the parameter of autonomy and individual responsibility an effective operational concept in the middle phases of treatment, and one which can be usefully added to the therapeutic armamentarium. By autonomy and individual responsibility we mean that members of a family are aware of their own internal needs and goals and take responsibility for using other members of the family to fulfill these needs.

A conceptual model of healthy family life would ideally include a concept of the family serving its needs as a unit. The individual needs his family to truly be himself and meet his deepest needs and, conversely, the family needs the cooperation of its individuals to sustain itself so that individual needs can be met. Few would agree that this "social contract" always works smoothly. It takes working at and effort like any other task. Also, since the relationships are in some state of dynamic balance, complicated by changes in the family over time, i.e., birth and growth of children, aging of parents, job and school changes, and others, adjustments and accommodations of one to the other must be made continuously. Families exhibiting "pathology" may be viewed as having a problem which obscures or distorts the individual in relation to his family, or vice versa.

Murray Bowen has talked of pathological families in terms of their being an "undifferentiated family ego mass." [1] The individual identity and autonomy has become submerged and blurred in the identity of the family as a unit. Warren Brodey has furthered this concept by what he calls "narcissistic externalization." [2] He defines it as follows: "A network of narcissistic relationships of which ego-dystonic aspects of self are externalized by each family member . . . The constellation of roles allows the internal conflict of each member to be acted out within the family rather than within the self, and each family member attempts to deal with his own conflicts by changing the other." This concept of families as having a problem with their own sense of autonomy is particularly relevant to the families in which "acting out" is a major problem. We have observed that in families where there is a sexually promiscuous teenage girl, the identity struggle persists as a serious obstacle to satisfying family life and to therapy. We would, however, add a dimension to the work of Bowen, Brodey, Rafferty, et al [3] by noting that not only do individuals in these families deny their own feelings and project them onto other family members; they also actually (but unconsciously) construct family situations so as to obtain cooperation from the others in their family for their projections. What we as therapists usually see are the partial or end-products of such activities. What we would like to add here to the phenomenon which Brodey has described is another significant dimension which occurs when families cooperate in the projections of their members. The projector's own sense of autonomy is blurred and he need not take responsibility for his feelings. Nor need he take responsibility for his actions as self-motivated, for, as we shall see, the projections are no longer a fantasy in someone's mind. *They are true.* For example, A goes to a party and meets B, to whom he takes an instant and unreasonable dislike. A then acts in a manner, subtly or otherwise, to indicate his dislike of B. B responds appropriately and is cool to A. A then says to C, "B dislikes me." C observes the ensuing interaction between A and B, comes to A and says that he agrees with A. "Yes, B doesn't like you." This operation requires cooperation from B. Here, B is acting appropriately. B has done nothing to elicit any kind of negative response from A.

Another example of fantasy verification occurs in a child guidance clinic where the presenting problem is a child's underachievement in school. The child guidance worker takes note of the fact that the mother exerts considerable pressure upon her child to do his homework, checks his work carefully, and asks many questions about what happened in school during the day. It seems clear that the child's underachievement is related to the mother's domination and pressure. Quite logically, the worker may tell the mother to reduce her pressure on the child, and obediently, the mother refrains from interfering in her child's schoolwork. Now, what sometimes happens is that the child gets worse, does no homework whatsoever, and his marks drop even further. The mother now in all justification can tell the guidance worker that it is clear that she must exert control over her child or his marks will decline further. The reality at this point is with the mother. But what may be lost sight of is the dynamic interplay between child and mother collaboratively to maintain the status quo in which neither takes responsibility for their own actions. The mother points to the reality of the child's poor marks as justifying her intervention and intrusiveness, and thus never confronts herself with her own need to dominate, to control. The child, on the other hand, can continue to deny a need for a special relationship with his mother and his fear of personal inadequacy.

In the family, these types of operations, persisting over time and between people who are deeply involved with each other, produce parallel, internal, intrapsychic, characteriological representations of these transactions. To the extent that these internal reflections of family transactions are embedded in the personality structure, invested with libidinal energy, and unconscious, they are relatively inflexible. The individual, after a time, no longer needs the original family to carry out these transactions that are the outward expression of his inner self, but he can help mold a new family or environment to reach a correspondence between his perception of self and the life of people around him. This chapter addresses itself to this lack of awareness on the part of the family members of their responsibility in family conflicts as well as their inability to see their own needs and their attempts to meet them in family life through continuous, interlocking, mutually cooperative unconscious mechanisms.

Let us move now to some data revealing how individual identity and responsibility manifest themselves as we observe families in treatment. Here are some typical therapist-family experiences that betray the existence of a poor sense of autonomy and cooperative nonindividualization.

In the initial call the parents say that their child will not come in to see you. In many instances, the attitude of the child quite justifies the parents' concern as to whether the child would come. What neither child nor parents see is the interplay of communications and transactions in which each assists the other in focusing upon the other, not themselves. The family members are united in placing responsibility upon the therapist to resolve their dilemma, which is based upon their perception of each other. The child may see the parents as coercive; the parents may see the child as recalcitrant and negativistic. By asking the therapist to take responsibility, they are asking that he be allied with one or the other family member, perpetuating not only a family split, but, equally important, blurring the autonomous needs of each member.

Here are some other instances, some very typical, that point up nonindividuation:

The therapist asks the daughter a question relating to an experience she has had, and another member of the family answers. The daughter accepts the answer, though obviously the experience has been filtered through the perception of another member of the family.

An explosive or uncomfortable topic comes up for discussion, and after a few moments, the topic has changed. No one knows why or how this has happened.

A parent or child asks the other to change, ostensibly for the benefit of the other. In reality, the change requested is for the benefit of the one who asks for it, or for the benefit of both.

A member of the family has suffered some hurt; another member of the family insists he or she feels the pain more. Conversely, a member of a family engages in self-destructive activity and seems to be unconcerned about it while the others are all worked up and anxious.

A family acts as though it is up to the therapist to "prove" that they are having problems, no matter how gross these problems may be.

The family reacts to questions concerning family life with defensiveness. The members of the family can then relate to the intrusiveness of the therapist by feeling that they are being attacked, rather than to the content of the question of family life and of themselves as individuals.

The parents claim that all they want from their life is happiness for their children. They are unable to talk about what they want for themselves.

There are many more such examples. But let us go on to some more complete experiences with families in which the richness, complexity, and interwoven threads of inner needs and transactional manifestations reveal themselves and highlight the therapeutic task of making known to a family each member's autonomous needs and individual responsibility in getting the family to meet them.

A family, for instance, came in for family therapy because of their daughter's sexual behavior which had resulted in a pregnancy. At the end of the session, it seemed quite clear that they were highly ambivalent about wanting treatment. They seemed to want the therapist to insist that they come, so that they could either frustrate him by refusing to come, or else continue to feel that this was something imposed on them to which they needn't commit themselves. Each individual member in the family exhibited severe symptoms that had gone on for many years, without anybody having been concerned about them. They could only express concern about the daughter's sexual problem. For example, the mother had suffered severely from insomnia for many, many years, pacing back and forth and talking to herself half the night. Both parents had been emotionally divorced for many years, and only seemed able to communicate sporadically when some practical issues came up in the life history of the family. The family viewed the daughter's pregnancy as an accident, and felt that once the baby was delivered and presumably given up for adoption, all would be forgotten and life in the family would go on the same. The daughter thought that possibly family therapy would be a good thing because this would be one way to get the mother to have psychiatric treatment. The mother thought that possibly family therapy would be a good idea because the daughter was not doing well in school. The father also shared his daughter's belief that his wife needed psychiatric treatment, and that this was the way to get his wife into treatment. At the same time, both parents presented themselves as bearing much more pain than the daughter, so that it ended up with the daughter being squeezed out and not getting any consideration either regarding her future or regarding her feelings about what had happened to her.

In another family consisting of mother, father, a son, and a daughter, the daughter had some sexual experiences and had become pregnant. A note in the case goes as follows: "In general, there was a mass of denial on the family's part that they really need help. The mother thought originally that the daughter needed help to 'forget what had happened to her.' Although there were many family problems, such as a previous long separation between the parents, their constant bickering, mother's deep depressive episodes and gross psychosomatic symptoms, her irritability, father's alcoholism, the son's extreme reticence and withdrawal, his isolation from the family, plus the daughter's sexually acting-out episode and poor schoolwork, it was explained to the therapist that this was their concept of what life was like and that they had little expectation things could be improved. Thus, the entire responsibility for an awareness of family problems and change in the family was placed upon the therapist. All the symptoms had been put in such a perspective that no one in the family needed to take any responsibility for or concern himself with what was happening to them."

Here is a case of two very drab, ordinary looking parents, a nondescript son, and, by contrast, a daughter who dresses in colorful clothes and has a kind of dark beauty and graceful bearing. The mother attacks her daughter and constantly disapproves of practically everything about her — her clothes, her friends, her hair, and her ways. Father approves of the daughter and the son adopts the mother's critical attitude. The parents are divided with regard to the parental role and the marriage role particularly. Mother accuses the husband of not being part of the family, never helping her with the problems, being self-centered and interested only in the pursuit of his own pleasure, which is drinking on weekends. She feels that she carries the responsibilities for everyone. The husband rebuts that he is involved with family members, denies that drinking is a problem, and sees himself as a good husband and father. Despite the family's protestations to the contrary, the therapist feels that all they are saying is that they lead a rather dull life and that the parents are only able to relate to each other through their arguments over the daughter. In addition, she provides the only excitement in the family and if she were not around, family life would become deadly and isolated.

The following is an example of a husband and wife relationship in which the mates use each other to prevent any awareness of their own needs. (*Note how they chose each other and how they perpetuate a system which on the surface is actually true.*) The father had been a lonely, somewhat isolated man all of his life, and had always had highly ambivalent feelings about wanting to be part of his own family. He tended to be withdrawn, but was afraid of becoming too removed. He married a woman who had always been concerned about being left out of things and who was very anxious about any kind of withdrawal by another person. In their marriage the two of them bickered constantly. The husband felt that his wife couldn't leave him alone, and she felt that he withdrew himself and denied her a relationship. The fact of the matter was that each was correct. The husband was always trying to get to the top floor attic room by himself; this made his wife anxious and she went after him, demanding some kind of communication. This actually met father's need for some kind of communication, but at the same time enabled him to see himself as strong, independent, and needing no one. His wife, on the other hand, did not have to face her anxiety about her inability to be self-sufficient because she had a husband who was withdrawing himself all the time, and who would make any woman demand some kind of more affective relationship. Neither assumed any responsibility for his own needs and feelings, but could project them onto the other, with a very strong sense of reality backing him and reinforcing the situation.

Another case deals with a poor Negro family consisting of a mother and four children. The oldest is a son, 17, the next a daughter, 15, and then a son, 12, and a daughter, 10. The family mood is one of hopelessness and depression but this is denied. While each member of the family sees himself as reacting to a hostile environment, he is really reacting to an inner depression and hopelessness. The hostile environment may be seen as another member of the family or some source outside it — the school, police or whatever. When members of this family want something for themselves, they try to get it in such a way that they end up by losing. This serves three functions:

1. They do not get the satisfaction they want and can thus perpetuate their feelings that satisfaction is denied them because others won't give it to them.

2. The person offering them help is discouraged from continuing to do so.

3. They need never face the fact that they *cannot* enjoy life.

For example, when the mother was concerned about her older daughter's school performance, the daughter wanted her mother to help out. Mother went to the school to inquire about how she could be helpful. It turned out that her daughter had given her the wrong information, so that what started out to be a way in which mother could have helped ended in the mother's frustration and anger at her daughter, and the daughter's anger at her mother for misunderstanding her. When the second son needed an eye examination, the mother took him to the clinic. He proceeded to break his glasses a day or two thereafter. He didn't get the benefit of the glasses, and mother was discouraged from trying to help him. Situations like these, then, led the members of the family to feel that real satisfaction couldn't be obtained inside the family, but must in some way be obtained outside it. They then reacted to the external environment in much the same way, which led to further frustration, whereupon they turned back to the family and went through the same cycle again. For example, the older daughter was responsible for preparing the evening meal, since the mother worked. The meals she prepared were good, but not exactly the kind that mother wanted. The daughter maintained that she was cooking appropriate meals, and that mother was unappreciative; mother felt that, since the daughter was able to cook good meals, she ought to cook the kind of meals mother really liked.

Each saw the other members of the family as powerful and denying. Mother truly was a powerful person in this family, attempting to assert control, giving and withholding. Nonetheless, she saw all of her children as having power over her. For example, she would have liked sometimes to go out with friends on Saturday nights, but was afraid that if she did the children would run off and get into all kinds of mischief. Since this is what the children actually did, she was concerned with good cause and was justified in feeling that she could not go out. This reasoning prevented her from being aware of the fact that she could not really enjoy life and that she was a depressed person with no goals except somehow to persevere. Each of the children saw the other children and the mother in the same fashion.

The younger brother was already getting into various minor problems in school and in the neighborhood. He constantly did things to provoke attention and when attempts were made to clarify this he cried and acted helpless. The younger daughter saw all the older siblings as having privileges which they could, but would not, share with her. Everyone in the family seemed to feel that everyone else was getting a bit more of the pie than he and together organized themselves in such a way as to reduce the size of the pie. Mother was angry and complaining and feeling deprived. When the children tried to gratify her, they were rebuffed, and when she tried to gratify the children, they rebuffed her. Thus, the whole family had a sense of being deprived by others and by the world, and not one member was able to take responsibility for himself. Each one denied his need to be given to or to be cared for. Thus each one gave up autonomy and had a part in perpetuating the blurred family system.

In another family of four, consisting of parents in their late forties, a son in his early twenties, and another son in his late teens, there existed persistent mechanisms of projection and denial reinforced by the others. Father said that if his wife would leave him alone he would be able to manage his functions as the head of the household. His wife said that if he would take over the masculine functions, she would have no problems. Thus both parents had a problem with their masculine and feminine identification and denied this problem by projecting it onto the other, with the clear realization that there were sufficient elements of truth in their accusations to reinforce their own defenses.

In another family, which consisted of parents in their forties, a daughter in her late teens and an older and younger brother, the daugh-

ter was going with a man about her father's age who had been married
and divorced several times and had the reputation of being promiscuous. He looked like the father in the family. The daughter told her
mother about her exciting escapades with this man with whom she
almost but not quite consummated the sexual experience. Mother promised to keep the matter confidential but then told her husband, who got
very angry at his daughter, alternating between blaming her and
blaming the man. A number of times he threatened to beat the man
up, but he never really threatened to punish his daughter. Each one had
a hidden fantasy which was worked out against the reality of the
other members of the family and their interaction with them. For example, the father was very curious about his daughter's experiences with
men. Since he could not face this part himself, he evidenced it by
becoming upset whenever his daughter had any kind of relationship
with another man. He saw the sexual or possible sexual experience as
predominating in the relationship. His own jealousy of his daughter's
relationship with other men was never faced. To adapt to father's
conflicts, his daughter had an ongoing relationship with a man who
was her father's age and who even looked like him. The father knew
this. The daughter herself was never able to face the attraction she
felt toward her father; she projected her fear of loss of control onto
her father, whose threats and anger she said kept her from being able
to form stable relationships. The mother, who assisted at this game,
was never able to face up to her own vicarious pleasure in her daughter's activities with this man who looked like her husband. It was
quite clear from the mother's identification with her own father, who
had also been promiscuous, that this was an issue she had never fully
resolved for herself. She had been quite faithful to her husband since
her marriage, but there was no doubt that she was giving her daughter
messages that she was very much interested in and enjoyed the problem her daughter had — all this under the guise of a concerned mother.
Her own identification with the daughter in this process was clear.
She also felt that it was perfectly acceptable for men to be as promiscuous as they wished, but not women. In this context, she gave her
older son all the permission in the world to have sexual experiences,
but he had deep anxiety about girls. He projected this onto his mother,
saying that she was constantly pushing him toward sexual experiences
and that this made it difficult for him to relate to girls. Again, there
was considerable truth in this, but what he was unaware of was that
he had an internal fear of normal relationships with women as well as
other fears relating to heterosexual experiences. In this game the family plays of going around and around, with no one taking responsibility
for his own actions and feelings, the reality of the family situation is
such that all members must maintain the postures that they have
assumed.

Another case exemplifies the father-son relationship. A twenty-year-
old son had a car which broke down periodically. On one such occasion
he called his father to let him know the situation and to tell him not

to expect him home on time. He insisted that he wanted no help from the father. The father took the message (correctly) to mean that his son was asking for help, and he came charging down and took over. The son reacted by feeling very resentful of his father's intrusiveness and control. In both cases, their interaction prevented them from being aware of and responsible for their own feelings. The son was unable to confront his dependency upon his father and his fear of having to assume responsibility for management of the car. He was fixed on the objective reality that father was intrusive and controlling and prevented him from taking this responsibility. The father, on the other hand, felt that he was not at all a controlling person but that his son was always asking for help. Actually, in this case, the entire family created various problems and needs for the father either to resolve or fulfill. In this way, he was able to feel wanted, and the infantile needs of the other members were gratified. However, on the surface, father acted as though he were angry at the family for being unable to assume more independent responsibility. The rest of the family were quite angry with father for his interference. None focused on their own real needs.

Having accepted the hypothesis that the families in question had problems with their sense of autonomy and with their ability to assume personal responsibility for their own feelings, behavior, and motivations, we approach the question of technique in terms of level of entry and points of intervention along these dimensions. We accept the fact that a disruption of the usual communication lines is essential, not so much to disrupt abnormal or pathological communications, but as a take-off point in attempting to help the family become aware of their problem with their own sense of autonomy. These therapeutic techniques of disruption of existing family patterns and transactional pathways in the family are seen as 1) attempts to involve the entire family rather than one or two members (usually the identified patient or the mother), and to help the family become aware of the abnormal nature of their relationships, and 2) as a phase in getting to the deeper levels of change in family life. When it becomes clear to the therapist that there is a heavy overlay or blurring of ego autonomy among the individual family members as well as an inability to assume personal responsibility for their own behavior, it is time to think of the techniques which we will now describe.

We have found that it is important, not only to change the transactional rules of the game, but also to have people talk about what it means to them to have to play the game a new way. There is a definite attempt to link the intrapsychic with the transactional, going back and forth between the two to achieve maximum leverage and maximum capacity to change. We have found it very difficult for members of a family to undergo intrapsychic change if there is no change in the transactional field. Conversely, families are apt to consider changes in the transactional field without corresponding internal representational changes as mere annoyances, as something that pleases or placates the therapist or, even more subtly, as different ways of transacting which result in approximately the same distortions as before.

Some of the simple and preliminary techniques we use when the family problem is a need to individuate seem appropriate here. In some families a spokesman for the family, say the father, will insist on including the entire family or parts of it when talking about himself. He will refer to his own feelings as "we" or "my wife and I." He will not say "I" feel such and such a way. The therapist carefully delineates that he is talking about himself, and encourages him to use the first person singular. Simultaneously, he urges other members of the family to describe their own actions, feelings, and fantasies in relation to the father's statement. Another method that we have found helpful is to ask members of the family to talk about something relating to themselves which does not involve other members of the family. At the end of a particular experience in therapy, the therapist summarizes what various persons have said about themselves, what they have revealed about themselves, and asks them to act upon these statements. For example, if members of a family have seen a movie or television show that seems meaningful to them, you may want to ask them what in particular has interested them, which characters they liked, why, what they thought of the motivations involved in the story, and similar questions. Point out the differences in the way different members of the family perceived things and, if possible, relate these differences to the family and inquire why they do not freely talk about their uniqueness as it relates to their problems. In this way, by repetition and "working through," you establish patterns whereby members of the family are expected to talk about themselves, their own autonomy and responsibility for their own activity. Simultaneously, as the family gains more experience with this procedure, the fear and anxiety surrounding this kind of self-awareness will become apparent. It has frequently been my experience that when a member of the family reaches this stage, he pauses as if standing at a brink. A mother, for example, who started to get a sense of her own autonomy in relation to the family became quite frightened; she talked about the fact that she didn't really know who she was and expressed a variety of fears of impulses and her inability to control herself. This woman was considerably overweight and, with the onset of this feeling of autonomy within herself and her ability to handle her life, she started to reduce. With this then came the fear of sexual promiscuity, of attractiveness to men. This could never have been dealt with had she not been able to disassociate herself from feelings that she was forced to be the kind of person she was by her husband, her children, her parents, her in-laws, uncles, aunts and many other people, including the school counselor, and, initially, the therapist. She had even felt that she was unable to control herself because some significant parts of herself had become identified with externalized objects. That is, she experienced a sense of hopelessness about being able to control herself because she perceived her impulses not as the "real" her, but as alien forces.

Another technique leading to development of autonomy in family life is to assist the family in determining who it is who makes the decisions in the family. At times, one member will take complete responsibility. This should be noted carefully since deeper probing sometimes reveals that, although this person said that he had taken this responsibility, he also indicated that it was forced upon him. One should be on the lookout, then, for signs of lack of autonomy on a deeper level, open protestations of individual decision-making notwithstanding. It sometimes puzzles the therapist, when a family reports something happening in their lives, that no one is able to say clearly how the move began. In this process of tracing the responsibility for a decision to the person who finally made it, who actually started things rolling, we frequently find the family struggling with their own autonomy in the here and now. This can be dealt with, reinforced, made more explicit, and heightened by the therapist, so that a greater sense of autonomy and responsibility prevails in the family.

In one particular family, for example, the doors to all the bedrooms had been removed by the parents who feared some sexual activity among their children. At some later point, the father put the doors back, but had considerable difficulty in being able to state that he had done it because he felt it was the appropriate thing to do. Had the therapist accepted the fact that the father had taken the responsibility, as the latter said he had, he would never have learned that the father felt it was the pressure from the therapist and the rest of the family that made him put the doors back on. However, the attempt to determine how the decision was reached and how the father saw himself in relation to the family helped everybody to realize how the other members of the family felt, and how what he was doing was projected as something necessary because of the needs of the others, but without awareness of his own participation in the process.

Another technique that is helpful is to encourage the family to talk about their dreams. This is something that is difficult for one member of the family to project onto other members. People in general, and our clinic families in particular, frequently deny any responsibility for what occurs in their dreams, the attitude being that the dream was unconscious, and therefore not under the control of the person dreaming. By emphasizing not the interpretation of the dream, but the fact that a member of the family has had the dream, and that consciously or unconsciously it was his dream resulting from some internal process of his own, a sense of reinforcement of a person's uniqueness and motivation can be heightened and delineated. As this occurs, members of the family, particularly the person who has had the dream, will frequently associate to the dream and be able to talk more freely about their own feelings.

Another technique that we have found quite useful is to choose the member of the family who seems to be most able to cooperate with the therapist, point out over and over again how much he is missing in life because he has been unable to really be himself, and wonder when is he ever going to be the kind of person that he fantasies himself to be and would like to be. This theme, reiterated over time, frequently brings good results. Simultaneously, the rest of the family will try to prevent this person from achieving or working toward attainment of autonomy; this should be carefully pointed out, and the patient struggling for this autonomy should be encouraged. For example, in one family we chose the father for this technique. As he spoke more and more freely about himself and his own needs and started to become more autonomous and to develop his own particular interests, his wife simultaneously became quite depressed, irritable, and rather difficult to live with. The father struggled for a considerable amount of time with his own guilt about this, with his inadequacy as a husband since he was making his wife unhappy, and in other ways felt strongly impelled to pull back into his old way of transacting with the family. However, the therapist encouraged him to attain his autonomy and to realize himself as he would like to be and had imagined it all his life, while simultaneously insisting that if the wife was depressed or irritable she should talk about it and what father's change meant to her as a unique autonomous person.

Another helpful technique is the assignment of "homework" to a family, which means that the members of a family must continue to work on a change in their transactional relationships that began during the previous therapeutic hour. The emphasis is on the transactional change as well as on helping the family to come the following week to discuss their difficulty in accepting this transactional change. The therapist often provides a recommendation, a course of action. If the family itself has asked for the recommendation, it is difficult for them to say that they are not getting anything from the therapist. It is in the exploration of the individual's difficulties with the assignment that we find the parallel intrapsychic representation of the transactional field. This is where we must push for more material to widen the path to the specificity of each family member's individuality and to bring about internal changes that would correspond to the different transactional arrangements that have been suggested in the "homework." A simple example of homework is a situation where one finds father and child, usually a son, unable to communicate directly, and therefore having to deal through the mother. After this difficulty is discussed during the therapeutic hour, the family are encouraged to continue to emphasize mother's disengagement from the father-and-son interaction, and to report the following week on what happened. Without question, the family will attempt in a variety of ways to indicate the impossibility of their task and the threat it presents to family life should it succeed; they will probably report a variety of subtle techniques by which the mother and father and son have attempted to hamper this operation. Most obvious will be the mother's attempts to undermine the effort, but a closer scrutiny will reveal the father-son collusion.

There exist numerous other examples in the published literature on family therapy which indicate the necessity for breaking up the transactional field. We would like to stress here the importance of asking the family to continue to work on their problem and to report the following week each member's difficulty in carrying out the assignment in terms of his own needs and fears. Not only is continuity and momentum maintained, but the family is in effect in treatment twenty-four hours a day for that next week. This tends to intensify the meaning and experience of the therapy for the family, and the impact of the transactional change will be more profound. Frequently, this change will not occur immediately, but with the continuing emphasis of the therapist on its importance, many families eventually manage to "do their homework" and discuss their difficulties with the transactional changes, their own personal discomfort with these changes, and the fantasies lying behind them. Sometimes we have found that asking one member of the family to assume primary responsibility for himself makes it difficult for the family to disperse and attenuate the family responsibility. The following case is an example which highlights some of the techniques which we discussed above.

The B family consists of a father in his early fifties, a mother in her late forties, a teen-age daughter of about seventeen and a son close to sixteen. The mother had had a premarital affair which resulted in pregnancy and an abortion. She was unconsciously encouraged in this affair by her own mother. The husband knew nothing of this. In the marriage, there were no children for some years. Both parents then said that they would like to adopt a child, with the mother being the one bearing most responsibility for the adoption. (In the initial exploratory phases of treatment with this family, both parents insisted that they had really wanted to have this child.) Adoption application was started, and the parents were accepted by a child welfare agency as potential adoptive parents. However, the mother conceived about a month before they were told by the agency that they were to receive an infant girl for adoption. At this point, the parents no longer felt the need to adopt a child, but could not bring themselves to tell the agency about their change of mind. Overwhelmed by guilt over wanting to reject the proposed infant, the mother accepted the little girl who was given to her by the adoption agency; she still did not tell the agency of her pregnancy. The mother then gave birth to a son (whom she infinitely preferred) and found herself with two infants on her hands, approximately eleven months apart. Since her early childhood the daughter had been troublesome. With the onset of her teens she became somewhat of a problem because of her many flirtations with boys which bordered on sexual promiscuity, with the family never knowing whether or not she had actually consummated a sexual experience. The son was a rigid, constricted boy who seemed much younger than his stated age.

In the therapy, it became clear that the mother was the spokesman for the family, and all communications went through her. The father was taciturn, resistive to the therapy, and felt that talking was a waste of time. He was ineffective in controlling his daughter who would continuously provoke him to set limits for her. It reached a point where he realized that if he did attempt to control her, he might kill her. The truth of the matter was that she had goaded him to this point, but neither daughter nor father recognized that the father was responsible for allowing the situation to deteriorate so. The daughter saw the situation as one in which the father attempted to be domineering. She constantly referred to him as "the boss," and in other ways undermined his sense of being a father who could act. She made him feel that he was a tyrant. Because she sensed the rejection of her parents, particularly her mother, she constantly provoked them into seeing her as a nasty girl, and this helped her to externalize her own feeling, which had long become a part of herself, that she was unworthy and no good. She could justifiably point to her parents as constantly accusing her of being worthless. The parents in turn had good reasons for their accusations, and there was no doubt that her behavior justified her parents' attitude. While she constantly accused her father of being overbearing, she talked at other times as though she could run the family better than anyone else. This mechanism of provoking her parents into being hostile and punitive served to maintain her illusion that she didn't have any bad or inferior feelings about herself, but that it was her father or mother who were making her out as "bad."

The son felt that his parents, particularly his mother, would use anything he said in therapy against him or in order to control him. Thus he was never able to talk spontaneously about his own feelings, only about his reactions. Even when he seemed to be talking about an action he had taken, or some feeling he had had, a deeper exploration and intensified inquiry revealed that they had occurred in reaction to a member of the family or frequently someone in the community. The father's taciturnity constantly led the mother into making conjectures as to what the father was really thinking and feeling. Since she found it much more comfortable to analyze others rather than herself, it was natural for her to do this with her silent husband. Simultaneously, it was natural for the father who, like his son, was a reactor, to get angry, deny what his wife was telling him, and insist that these were her ideas and not his. Although he would not state his own ideas and correct his wife, he berated her for attempting to interpret his thoughts and feelings and denied that her interpretations were correct. This only led his wife to a further intensified search into what he was "really" thinking or feeling. The father's extremely constrictive and puritanical attitude was related to a need on the mother's part to have such a person control her. She did not see her husband clearly in this role, nor herself as needing controls and therefore being attracted to a man like him. Instead, she was constantly furious at her husband because he established controls not only for her but for the children as well. Thus, while she felt the need of controls, at the same time she rebelled against them. Father felt that, with regard to his family, he was in a deadlock from which he could see no way out. He felt it was up to his wife, the therapist, his children, and everyone else to change because he could see no way out for himself. Further exploration revealed that every member of the family saw the therapist and every other family member in exactly the same light. Typically, too, the daughter attempted to relate to her brother through a series of teasing maneuvers. She was unaware that she really was starved for interest and companionship from him. Instead, she set up a situation in which she simultaneously teased and denied him, constantly feeling that she was attempting to reach out, but was rebuffed by him. In this process, the mother usually sided with her son, who did not start the provocation. Thus, daughter was again "bad," and mother and son were close to each other.

For a number of sessions preceding the one we are about to discuss, the members of the family had been asked to talk about their own feelings, to stop weaving everyone else into their own autonomy and responsibility, and to talk about the uniqueness of themselves and what they wanted for themselves, from the viewpoint of the family as well as the world in general. In this particular session, the father was typically silent. His wife said that he was awaiting a report from his doctor concerning a possibly serious physical condition. The father said nothing, but looked worried. As a matter of fact, he had not said anything to any member of the family, denied having any worries, and insisted that the lab studies would turn out all right. I found myself being drawn in by Mr. B.'s silence, and attempted to do a lot of talking and evoking, suggesting possible feelings he might have. It was Mrs. B. who pointed out that I was doing with father exactly what I had told her she had been doing. I agreed with her and acknowledged the force of the husband's power over me.

It was at this moment, when the parents were able to talk about how I had been "sucked in," that they discussed this aspect of communication between them in somewhat more detail. The father said that, because he would like very much to please his wife, he listens to her talk about the various things that come up in her daily life and also attempts to converse with her. He then stated that actually he didn't have the slightest interest in what his wife was saying, and had no desire to talk to her; that it was a tremendous effort for him to listen, but that he was prepared to listen (suffer) or talk because he loved her and because he felt she did so much for him. Simultaneously, the wife reported that she knew how much of a sacrifice it was for him to listen or talk, and that she went out of her way to perform a variety of small tasks to please him out of her own sense of guilt because he tried so hard to do what was difficult for him just to please her. He listened patiently to her, he attempted to converse with her, neither of which was easy for him. I then suggested that, as an experiment, Mr. B. not talk unless he had to, unless he really felt that he had something specific to convey to his wife, and that he not try to please her. I suggested to Mrs. B. that she not talk to her husband unless there was some practical need to do so, and if she did, not to be disappointed by her husband's lack of interest or by his cutting her off. In other words, I was suggesting a change in the transactional field. When they came in the next session Mr. B. was absolutely furious with me. He indicated that things between him and his wife had been going along rather well until I, the therapist, came between them and tried to bust up their marriage. He had been absolutely miserable the past week and stated quite strongly that he really *did* want to talk to his wife. He almost tearfully indicated that he wanted to tell her the things that had happened to him, and that conversely, he was very much interested in having her talk to him.

This discussion then led into Mrs. B.'s feeling that what her husband was saying was really a trap. Actually, she had the feeling that he didn't want her to have any kind of meaningful relationships outside of the one with him. He didn't mind her having the kind of superficial relationship she had with the neighbor who lived a block away and for whom she didn't care much one way or another, but he always made some kind of nasty crack when she had a long phone conversation with a good friend. As I pushed this a bit further, Mr. B. admitted that he didn't really want to share his wife with anyone. Somehow he had always felt she might care for others more than him. As Mr. B. was able to verbalize with increasing clarity his own needs, he became aware of significant changes in the way he had seen himself. He had seen himself as constantly making sacrifices for his demanding wife and children, and as either having to provide what they needed or else feeling totally inadequate. He could now see clearly that in his own way he was making demands upon the rest of the family in terms of conformity, in terms of leaving him alone when he wanted to be left alone, in terms of wanting his wife to do a lot of talking and of feeling extremely lonesome and distant when she did not.

In the next session, however, the father became quite obdurate and stubborn, insisting that he had never wanted to come to therapy in the first place, that it was his wife's idea, and that this was another demand now being placed upon him. Family life, he said, was nothing but a series of demands with which he felt he had to comply, and here was another one. It was at this point in the therapy that I felt the family was ready to test this theory. I suggested to Mr. B. that he didn't have to come any more if he didn't want to, that I would be glad to see his wife and children alone. I left it to him to decide whether or not he would come. He could test what he really wanted for himself. I strongly insisted that if he did come, it be only because of his own desire to participate in the sessions, and not to please his wife or children or me. I thus delineated his area of responsibility for himself, and resisted being incorporated into the pathological transactions of blurring the autonomous ego lines.

For the next few sessions the entire family continued to come, with the father being quite angry at being placed in an autonomous position. His wife reported her extreme discomfort with her husband's verbalizations. As she increasingly had to fall back on her own needs and talk about herself rather than about her husband and her interpretation of him or the children, she started to talk more clearly and distinctly and with much more conviction. She was able to speak more clearly and directly also about her fears of self-confrontation. When she talked about herself and her own needs, she constantly found herself feeling stupid, childish, guilty, and bad. This was extremely painful for her and the crystallization of the changed family transactions clearly revealed how the rest of the family had been structured to help Mrs. B. avoid these feelings about herself.

In the next few months, I used some of the techniques mentioned earlier, such as asking each member of the family to talk about himself and to use the pronoun "I" rather than "we"; attempting in a variety of ways to trace who was responsible for what and who initiated what; asking each to present nonfamily experiences; and intensifying the family-therapist relationship. I culminated with the "homework" technique. The latter revealed sharply and clearly the interlocking relationships in the family that kept each member from self-recognition and self-awareness, and it enabled the family to make rather dramatic shifts. During this period of shift, the family went through extremely painful episodes in which the daughter was confronted, for example, with her own autonomous feelings of being extremely bad, worthless, unwanted. She was able to say that she had an image of herself, an adopted child, as somehow born unworthy. The mother was able to talk of the period prior to the adoption, her preference for her son, and to reassure her daughter that not being wanted was related to her own needs, not to the daughter's being "no good." The father talked of his fear that he could not be a good husband and father unless he was forced to by the rest of the family. The son mentioned his fear of being overwhelmed by the women in the family, and fighting them off by passivity and withdrawal. Each member of the family was helped to verbalize his own needs, and to stop using the other members to reinforce the projections and denials which had reality when the therapist entered the family experience with them.

We did not have the opportunity of continuing with the family to the point where we could explore in depth their individual responses to their own intrapsychic needs once the pathological transactional relationships had been weakened. However, the awareness of the uniqueness of each individual member of the family seemed to have a dramatically therapeutic effect which served to release the members of the family into fuller development of themselves as autonomous persons while simultaneously absolving them of guilt and a variety of other psychological responses in answer to the needs of each other. This rather complex change in a family in which the changes in the transactional field are related to intrapsychic exploration and change always seems to have a beneficial effect upon the family. Surprisingly, these kinds of changes tend to weld the family closer together, based upon the real communality of need between the different members and the transactions based upon realistic expectations of themselves and others rather than on a series of infantile, binding, mutually guilt-provoking, hostile, and destructive family relationships.

We have pointed out in this chapter the importance to many families of helping each member of the family to liberate himself from the effect of narcissistic externalization which had become reciprocally cooperative among various members of the family. What each had been facing in their externalization was a true experience validating him, but overlayed and involved and initiated by gross distortion on the part of various family members. These mechanisms help to bind families together, to perpetuate distortions from the family to society outside the family, and to prevent growth and maturation. Using the techniques described above, families can be assisted to want to struggle. With their liberation from the use of interpersonal transactions to maintain a pathological homeostasis and a pathological balance between the intrapsychic and the transactional, comes a freedom to grow and mature.

REFERENCES

1. Bowen, Murray. Family Psychotherapy, from The Family as a Unit of Study and Treatment. Amer. J. Orthopsychiat. 31(1):40-60, January, 1961.
2. Brodey, Warren M. Some Family Operations and Schizophremia: A. Study of Five Hospitalized Families Each with a Schizophrenic Member. AMA Arch. Gen. Psychiat. 1:379-204, October, 1959.
3. Rafferty, Frank T., Ingraham, Blanche, and McClure, Sally M. The Disturbed Child at Home. Paper presented at Annual Meeting, American Orthopsychiatric Association, 1965.

The use of external social control in family therapy

Ivan Boszormenyi-Nagy

Chapter
16

The therapist of families with a juvenile delinquent member cannot avoid dealing with issues that assign him certain functions of an agency of social control. Many therapists would like to avoid such implications of their role; others may defensively over-identify with these role expectations; still others may enter into a battle with courts and law enforcement agencies, trying to make them more understanding of the therapeutic point of view. I would like to explore in this chapter certain implications of the therapeutic leverage that stems from the therapist's recognition of the usefulness of authorities for his traditionally non-authoritarian goals.

Families were referred to this project by the court. It was clear that many of these families would never have taken the initiative to get psychiatric help whether as individuals or as a family. The family therapist has to give his own answer to the question: can enforced therapy succeed? Szasz devotes considerable attention to the intrinsic contradiction between motivation necessary for psychotherapeutic change and "treatment" enforced in the interest of the convenience or safety of others.[1] Since family therapy often results in the avoidance of forcible hospitalization or other forms of detention, the practical and therefore the theoretical implications of enforced family therapy are different from those of enforced individual psychiatric treatment. It would indeed amount to an implicit scapegoating of the delinquent family member if the court didn't demand the expert examination of the silent contributions of all family members to what appears manifestly as one member's doing, particularly since the family as a whole can be considered an entity or a shared motivational system producing delinquency.

The right of families to raise and control their minor members has been an unchallenged basis of all major civilizations. On the other hand, in cases of obvious neglect, children have traditionally become wards of the state, a fact that is often symbolically expressed by referring to kings as *parens patriae*. Contemporary court practices allow for detention and special trial of delinquent children and for termination of parental rights if parental neglect or misconduct is found (Sussman,[2] Neumeyer[3]). In some instances judges order parents to have their child undergo some form of psychotherapy. I believe that the development of the family concept of psychiatric disturbances will produce major changes in court philosophies and practices.

Family therapy and the underlying family concept of pathogenicity require clear concepts of suprafamilial societal dynamics. The individual member is subordinated to the norms and social reality of the family, often of the extended family. The child can act out impulses with an implicit or conscious expectation that the family will ultimately control him. One of the main findings of family therapists confirms the formulations of Adelaide Johnson regarding the importance of covertly deficient moral value systems — "superego lacunae" — in the parents of juvenile delinquents.[4] Frequently, parents covertly condone those actions of their children which they find overtly most objectionable.

To the extent that parents can be assumed to be at least covertly sharing the delinquent motivations of their children, their role shifts from that of the controller to that of one in need of control by more powerful agencies. Society has to assume the role of controller toward the child and implicitly toward the family. The pathogenic family motivational system which leads to the delinquent act in the child appears in the final analysis to be aimed at testing society at large as a quasi-parental personification. Often it appears that the superego lacunae have formed a multigenerational chain. Each new generation may become emotionally progressively orphaned and more dependent on vicarious acting out. The parents have to test external controls because as children they were not given sufficiently strong parental controls for internalization, at least not in certain specific areas of impulse manifestations.

The deficiency of internal structural value orientations in parents has to lead at the least to a certain degree of role and norm disorganization in families. I suggest that this disorganization can be called an anomic property of the family. The term anomic is used here as descriptive of a quality of social systems in which there is insufficient motivating force deriving from a meaningful configuration of appropriate normative values. For instance, parents may act fundamentally infantile rather than parental, and they may force their children into a position of responsibility through their dependent behavior. The anomic quality may be restricted to circumscript areas of function or it may manifest itself as a pervasive state. In any case, the anomic aspect of any organization may give rise to role diffusion, to diminished control of impulsivity and to subtle, collusive, often ultimately destructive scheming.

At the same time that I am stressing the importance of the family therapist's clearly delineating the way in which the family system challenges external controlling authorities, I would like to stress the need for spontaneous self-asserting therapeutic goals for every family member as an individual. No genuine psychotherapeutic approach, including family therapy, is thinkable without at least an inner core of autonomous choice to undertake and continue therapy. In fact, the family therapist is well advised to test and try to clarify as early as possible the available spontaneous motivation of family members for therapy. In order to change, members must have some desire to give up the systems of stagnation, to grow emotionally, and to form new systems on a level of increased maturity for all.

Questions of the relationship between individual motivational formulations and multi-person, system-based motivations will continue to puzzle therapists for a long time to come. Who is responsible for a member's system-determined actions? Is the symptomatic member a captive or a perpetrator of the system? What is the ultimate goal of treatment: simultaneous treatment of all members individually or a therapeutic exploration of their interaction system with none of them treated as discrete individuals?

There is little doubt that the ultimate outcome of family treatment depends on whether or not a therapeutic engagement of the pathogenic system forces is possible. For instance, as long as the family members keep coming only to help Johnny have better control over himself, the outcome is quite dim. As soon, however, as his mother begins to examine her own memories of her corresponding childhood difficulties, family therapy appears more hopeful.

However, regardless of the family therapist's convictions about the relevance of the parents' past, the "superego lacunae," and other more or less unconscious or latent delinquent propensities, it was Johnny's behavior problems and not the members' complaints about their family system that brought the particular family to treatment. Futhermore, society may be willing to "coerce" the family to seek help, but only because of manifest problems and not for latent mechanisms which reside in the family as a unit. The individual psychotherapy patient may be resistant enough to face unconscious motivations in himself but these are at least referring to the same physical individual who is suffering or symptomatic. In family therapy, though, the most important motivational obstacles may reside in an outwardly symptomless member. Often the "well" sibling is just as much an unprotected victim of thwarting forces as the symptomatic one.

Even if he succeeds in enlisting the court or another authority to support his work, the family therapist will have to face the difficulties inherent in a paradoxical situation in which people need coercing to become freer and more responsible. His own attitude to life, the degree of sincerity of his own innermost respect for growth and responsibility are constantly being tested. He has to make the choice again and again whether he will play his role as an agent of the court and moral order or as an agent who extricates each member from captivity in the pathogenic system.

To produce autonomy by way of authority may sound paradoxical. Yet therapeutic disclosure of parental weakness ultimately tends to result in increased parental strength. However, with increasing disclosure and pain goes an increase of resistance against therapy. The therapist's real strength will be needed when he breaks into the family's systems of repetition, stagnation, chaos, and destruction. He will have a greater portion of resources left for his struggle if he can enlist the overt help of outside authorities in the task of external control. If this is not possible, his authority remains an indirect one, covertly depending on the implicit court authority which made the referral.

Illustrative Clinical Material

The H. family was referred to the project by the court. The reason for the referral was an apparently minor and transitory acting out on Betty's part. It was reported that she ran away from home, stayed away for two consecutive days, and was found by police in what her father described as a "house where continuous parties go on and kids come in and go out day and night." Mr. H. went to court with Betty and approved of her going to a detention home since this was what he had told her he was going to do. For the first two months of treatment Betty was actually brought to family sessions from the detention home and returned there after each session.

The H. family consisted of seven members: Mr. H., 42; Mrs. H., 40; Mabel, 20; Bertha, 19 (married, lives out of the home); Joseph, 17; Betty, 16; and Susan, 14. Both parents came from a rural farming background and their educational level did not seem one that would make them suitable for white collar jobs. Mr. H. worked as foreman with a small building contracting company and Mrs. H. has been doing unskilled factory work for the past few years. He was working on out-of-town jobs Monday through Friday and she did most of the housework, with little success in getting the children to help out. A larger house in a good residential neighborhood indicated the family's upward-moving aspirations toward middle-class living.

The initial impression that the family therapy team received was that this family would not last too long in treatment. The essentially non-introspection oriented family was headed by a sullen and passively aggressive, martyrlike mother and a somewhat garrulous, manipulative father. He seemed to be capable of agitating one family member after the other by teasing, rewarding with warmth, and referring to his authority and earning power. The mother appeared left out, mumbling, and silently angry. Overtly, all children sided with father and were critical of mother's compulsive ways of doing housework and of her inability to accept anyone else's contribution as satisfactory.

The family seemed to be chaotic and structureless as far as role differentiation was concerned. The parents were acting generally non-parental, either by omission or by childish behavior on their part. The children seemed to be confused between values of goodness and reliability on the one hand and clever exploitation on the other. No one seemed capable of committing himself to any genuinely meaningful position on any issue. The only exception was Betty, who cried in the first session and admitted fears that since she had done wrong, she wouldn't be taken back into the family.

Betty's role in this family appeared to be misleading. Despite a quasi-retarded, generally dull appearance which fitted in with reports that her school progress was definitely slow, she seemed to occupy an important, implicitly parental role vis-à-vis her parents. She was the only child who was willing to help Mrs. H. with her housework, and seemed to be acting out through her delinquent behavior some of Mrs. H.'s inexpressible resentments toward Mr. H. Yet Betty must have played an important, warmly reassuring, feminine role where her father was concerned, for he liked to sit next to her and fondle her in a longing rather than parental fashion. It also appeared to the therapists that Betty was in a parentlike position due to her "good listener" capacity. It is quite possible that Mrs. H.'s emotional demands on Betty increased in the two years since Bertha had married and moved out, because Bertha had for many years been her mother's ally and chief companion.

As therapy progressed, Mrs. H. began to be more expressive. She started to talk about her past and described the deprivations of her early childhood. Her mother died when she was small and she was raised first by another family and later by her stepmother. Her father was very strict and a person who believed that he possessed spiritual powers of healing. Throughout the early phase of therapy Mrs. H.'s slow and somewhat self-deprecating manner of speech made her a target of the entire family's more or less explicit contempt.

Toward the end of the second month the content and structure of family sessions changed considerably. Gradually, Mrs. H. became the person who had a great deal to say, mainly about her disappointment in both the marriage and the whole family's attitude. This openness of talk obviously threatened to tear open painful wounds in her and probably in Mr. H. as well. In one session she made an explicit statement that if she was going to get hurt this much, she would terminate the therapy.

It has to be noted at this point that by the time these rearrangements began to take place in the sessions themselves, Betty had been out of the detention home for several weeks and she was showing no evidence of sexual or other types of delinquent acting out. Instead, she appeared what she basically must have been: a shy, socially isolated, homebound teen-age girl. In the same session in which her mother threatened possible termination, Betty talked about her fear that her parents might want to separate. Perhaps it was an unconsciously programmed "solution," a way of her keeping therapy even at the expense of becoming the "patient" again, that she collapsed one day. When the alarmed family rushed her to the hospital, however, the doctor could not substantiate any physical illness.

In the meantime, the debate between Mr. and Mrs. H. intensified. The key issue seemed to be whether Mrs. H.'s contribution to the family's income was significant enough to justify her making Mr. H. feel inadequate as supporter of his family and making the rest of the family feel that she was an overworked martyr. Mr. H. was most angry with his wife's use of her income for these purposes, and when she asked the family to vote on the issue, they unanimously voted that she stop work. In the subsequent session Mrs. H. stated that the family intended to discontinue therapy because of the inconvenience it caused to the time and work schedule of more than one member. Mr. H. gave apparent verbal support to the idea of continuation, but he obviously let Mrs. H. handle it for the family and thereby his actions proved his own ambivalence about continuation. The team, consisting of a psychiatrist supervisor and a social-worker trainee in family therapy, told the family that they did see further goals for the treatment but that the final decision should come from the family. Both therapists shared the conviction that should they have insisted on continuation the family would have defied them anyway, even if not in the same session.

At this point, in the thirteenth week of the treatment, the therapists were forced to take stock of the treatment. They realized the limitations of this family for verbal progress toward insight and noted the family's unquestionably hostile ambivalence toward them as "bad" parents. The next move came in the form of a phone call from Mrs. H., who asked to cancel the next meeting for the entire family, ostensibly because of the uncertainty about whether her husband could make it. The therapists interpreted this message as a further ambivalent move in a series of testing games and decided on a stronger course.

First, Mrs. H. was called back and encouraged to bring the family anyway. She responded with insisting on the cancellation and announcing that the family could not possibly continue because of her and Mabel's work schedules. Thereupon the therapists sent out a letter advising Mr. and Mrs. H. that the announcement of discontinuation was not acceptable in this form, and that the two parents were to appear for the next appointment. They neither responded nor showed up. Yet, when called again, Mrs. H. promised to come in with her husband the following week. However, she called the office on the day of the appointment and cancelled the session for that day as well as all subsequent ones. The therapists now decided to call the court probation worker and asked her to put pressure on the parents, realizing, of course, that court personnel could only exert a limited pressure, especially in view of the fact that Betty was not behaving badly. From the point of view of existing law practices, parents (or other family members) cannot be assumed to be responsible for delinquent tendencies of a child. In this case, however, the approach worked, as proven by the events that followed.

When Mr. and Mrs. H. came in after three missed appointments, they had a lot to say, and this time exclusively about themselves. Mr. H. reported that in the previous week, for the first time in many years, he almost had a serious traffic violation. Mrs. H. reported an incident that happened the previous weekend during a party the family was giving for Mabel's birthday. At one point in the evening, when the kitchen door opened, Mrs. H. saw Mr. H. making a pass at one of Mabel's girlfriends (grabbing the girl "in the front"). In a strikingly impersonal fashion she stated that the glass she was cleaning at that time began flying and smashed across the room. She was fuming with rage when she described the incident. He denied the action but was not too forceful in claiming that his wife was mistaken. At any rate, in this session Mr. and Mrs. H. appeared like two different people from what they had been as far as motivation was concerned. They had a lot to explore and talk about.

Many subjects emerged in the ensuing two months, at the end of which the treatment was to be concluded for administrative reasons. It turned out that Mrs. H. had been disappointed for a variety of reasons ever since the earliest days of her marriage. Her husband had left her home alone while she was in labor with her first child; he spent most of his savings on drink, and he sought the company of gay women. He, on the other hand, complained that his wife had never wanted to go out with him and that she had been a housebound, perfectionistic, nagging person, who took out her revenge finally by taking a job and constantly reminding him of the things she was able to buy for the family because of her extra income. Many violent verbal battles were fought over the topic as they marked the emergence of a new, more assertive style on Mrs. H.'s part.

There was a noticeably growing realization on Mr. H.'s part that his wife was gradually becoming a much more assertive person. Many new occurrences were reported in the last four weeks of treatment. For the first time Mrs. H. went to the beach with the children, spent a week there, and enjoyed every hour of it. Mr. H. joined the family for the weekend and took them out for dinner to celebrate his wife's birthday. For the first time in many years the two parents went out together to a restaurant.

At the time of the termination the parents were still greatly involved in clarifying their feelings about increasingly meaningful and well-defined issues. There were more talks about what the value of Mrs. H.'s job and salary was for Mr. H. and the family. Mr. H. was able to state that his pride was hurt by Mrs. H.'s constant references to the importance of her financial contributions to the family budget. Mrs. H., on the other hand, was able to emphasize her own need for functioning independently from her husband, who would not give sufficient credit for competence. It seemed that Mr. H. appreciated the opportunity to talk about his alleged flirting escapades, partly because he hoped to deflate the myth of their significance in return for more intimacy between himself and his wife. Both parents were still interested in exploring memories of their childhood as well as of the early years of their marriage. They seemed to be quite motivated to go on for a long time and in fact did ask for referral to another agency for further conjoint treatment after the conclusion of the project.

The children were in the meantime moving out of the family. Mabel was engaged, Joseph joined the Navy, Betty began to regain her capacity for peer relationships without a need for acting out, and Susan became more outgoing and outspoken.

Considering the overall picture of their performance, this family had been basically motivated for treatment and even for change. Paradoxically, however, their capacity for sustaining the continuity of treatment needed the support of external authority. This support amounted to external control and seemingly, at least temporarily, it diminished the spontaneity of free choice. The complexity of the situation was further increased by the fact that the court was in no position actually to enforce the continuation of family treatment and that the parents must have been partly aware of this circumstance. Perhaps the parents needed the *illusion* that someone else was responsible for changing the family system.

In view of the theoretical implications of the maneuver we utilized with this family, it might be in order to summarize the essence of the pathogenicity existing in this family.

Mr. and Mrs. H. were, at the time of the referral, two adults who had not mastered the basic difficulties inherent in a close relationship. They settled on certain defensive relational and characterological positions with a great deal of constriction of self, and a resultant irresponsibility of action as far as the parental role was concerned. The clinical material strongly suggests that both parents had childhoods in which adequate parenting was missing, even though they both received indoctrination of responsibility for work.

As these hungry, emotionally unmarried, and nonparental parents found themselves committed to the responsibility of raising five children, they began to act out their childish rebellion through the family system in a fashion that led to one child's behavior bringing on external control by police, court, and psychiatric treatment agencies. The total experience of therapy with this family was at least suggestive of the viewpoint that Betty's delinquent behavior fitted into the parental expectations of indirectly obtaining help with their marriage. The H. parents obtained parents for themselves through the acting out of their child, the subsequent external control functions by society through Betty's temporary detainment, and their being urged to continue conjoint treatment. It seems from the pouring out of memories and explorations that the parents were greatly reassured and freed by the experience of being controlled from the outside. Perhaps the most important therapeutic clue in the therapists' decision to ask the court worker's intervention was their impression that the parents made their statements about their intention to quit in the context of manifestly ambivalent acting-out behavior.

Our work with families of school-phobic children has led us to a similarly active, often externally controlling approach. School authorities frequently interpret the role of the therapist as one that stands for a maximum of permissiveness to achieve the best therapeutic results. School officials were often surprised at our request to put on the parents all the legal pressure so that the child and parents could become involved in family therapy. The results again showed that these parents and children needed external control to gain strength to face denied problems and confidence in the value of constructive effort. They needed to be extricated from their pathogenic symbiosis so that they could move toward autonomy and responsibility.

Lack of cooperation by the authorities did apparently undermine family therapy work in a number of cases. In one case involving a sexually delinquent young girl, the parents started to show increasing signs of resistance after initial promise of therapeutic progress. At the same time the girl showed renewed signs of minor acting out, quite obviously to prevent the discontinuation of the therapy. The parents, however, pushed toward termination and began to miss sessions. The therapists, recognizing the need for external support, contacted the probation officer, a policeman. After listening to the therapists' request for his intervention, he decided not to support further therapy, because he felt that the girl was being rehabilitated under his guidance. His evidence was that she had contacted him for obtaining a part-time job as a waitress. Conceivably, competitive prestige reasons and deeper resistance to the idea of therapy made this man reluctant to give his support to the therapists. The therapists had to quit despite their distinct optimistic impression about the family's basic underlying motivation for therapy and further progress.

In another family, which was not a court referral, the acting-out behavior became more and more focused within the parental couple. They became grossly negligent of their children and alarming reports began to come in about the emotional and even physical deprivation of the children. The family stopped coming to therapy sessions. The therapists sent out letters and made phone calls, none of which were answered. It was decided that the only way to have this family return was to report the case to the Philadelphia Society to Protect Children in the hope that their workers would put pressure on the family by threatening to bring the case to court unless the parents assumed their responsibilities.

The attitudes of the authorities sometimes differ from the concepts held by the therapists. The court may adhere to certain conceptions which the therapists may find reminiscent of pathogenic familial attitudes. A sexually acting-out girl was told by the court to come in for treatment, yet the court workers agreed with her mother that her stepfather should be kept uninformed of her delinquent act and its consequences, even though the case became public in the form of court records. The family therapists felt that by this misplaced respect for the girl's and her mother's right for privacy, family therapy was denied a chance right at the start. The pathogenic system of unreality and dangerous uncontrol, manifested in the acting out itself, was permitted to remain hidden behind the cloak of respect for individual rights for secrecy.

The fact that most common types of delinquent behavior have a root in familial interaction leads to the logical conclusion that intervention should be directed not at the symptomatic member but at the sustaining multi-personal dynamics. Yet the school systems are filled with counseling cases where two, three, or more children of the same parents are grossly disturbed and the parents remain uncooperative in the face of salutary efforts planned by schools or by agencies. Similarly, court probation workers often feel that they can put a behaviorally disturbed child under psychiatric probation but that existing law practices make it extremely difficult to bring serious pressure on the silently destructive and uncooperative parents.

Concluding Remarks

It is one of the most fundamental implications of Freudian psychology that certain family influences may create and determine the deleterious conditions which thwart the autonomous (healthy) emotional development of individuals. Family psychiatry in general, and family therapy in particular, have brought out the significance of ongoing, current, collusive patterns of multi-personal interactions that prevent change and emotional growth.[5]

At the same time, one of the most fundamental values of all major civilizations lies in respecting family ties and parental rights and duties to shape the life values of children. By becoming a protector of maturation and healthy personality differentiation within families, the law could become an agent of both free society and free individuals. It could compel the coercing multi-person systems of captivity to yield and to support the right of individuals for autonomous life goals and responsibility.

Ultimately, these implications of family therapy will lead to new thinking concerning the motivational boundaries of individuals, and the concept of family as a value, ideal, or norm, as it is most often treated, will have to shift toward one of a live process to be examined. In this light, and as a result of the experience of family therapy, we can conclude that the phenomenon of juvenile delinquency should be viewed as a danger signal which indicates the lack of a sufficiently solid grounding of contemporary nuclear families. Ideally, the protectively controlling influence of therapeutic and authority agencies should balance their respective contributions toward stabilizing anomic nuclear families. On a deeper level of meaning, therapeutic use of external authority does not curtail the freedom of the nuclear family; as a matter of fact, it supports the anomic family's right for protective external control.

REFERENCES

1. Szasz, T. S. *Law, Liberty, and Psychiatry; An Inquiry Into The Social Uses of Mental Health Practices.* New York: Macmillan, 1963.
2. Sussman, F. B. *Law of Juvenile Delinquency; The Laws of the Forty Eight States.* New York: Oceana, 1950.

3. Neumeyer, M. H. *Juvenile Delinquency in Modern Society*, Third Edition. New York: Van Nostrand, 1961.
4. Johnson, A. Sanctions for Superego Lacunae of Adolescents. In *Searchlights on Delinquency: New Psychoanalytic Studies*, K. Eissler, ed. New York: International Universities Press, 1949, pp. 225-245.
5. Boszormenyi-Nagy, I. A Theory of Relationships: Experience and Transaction. In *Intensive Family Therapy, Theoretical and Practical Aspects*, Boszormenyi-Nagy and Framo, eds. New York: Hoeber/Harper and Row, 1965, pp. 33-86.

An evaluation of training in family therapy, family counseling and family system concepts

Alfred S. Friedman

Chapter 17

Our demonstration of family counseling and treatment with families of sexually acting-out girls was conducted in the context of a training and "curriculum development" project. We had, accordingly, a commitment to make a systematic effort to evaluate the success of the training program and to assess the learning of the trainee family counselors. For this purpose we had our own subjective impressions of the potentiality of each individual trainee for becoming an effective family therapist and our estimate of how much progress he or she had made during the training program toward that goal. We could if we chose, use as a rough subjective criterion the degree to which each trainee approximated, in insight, attitudes, and skills, the ideal image of the effective family therapist as developed jointly by the training staff. We also had available the trainees' own subjective impressions of how much they felt they had learned and how well equipped they had become to conduct effective family therapy. Obviously, we needed a more objective means of assessment than any or all of these, and we therefore conducted a pre-training and post-training evaluation of the trainee group and of a control group, on relevant variables, based on a battery of performance tests. We then compared the pre- and post-performances to obtain an objective measure of the effectiveness of the program. The test battery was planned by the project coordinators and two research clinical psychologists. At the end of the training program an independent scoring of the test results was conducted by the two research clinical psychologists.[*]

Our testing of the trainees proceeded in three general areas: 1) factual-theoretical, 2) personal-attitudinal, 3) family counseling competence. The first two parts of this assessment were conducted with the larger theoretical seminar group, including the smaller core practicum group, and the third part of the assessment was conducted only with the core practicum group. The larger didactic seminar group met

---

[*] The author is indebted to Joseph Friedman, Ph.D., for development of the methods of analysis of the results of the trainee test evaluation reported in this chapter.

weekly for the duration of an academic year, and included, in addition to the core trainee social case workers, school counselors, clinical psychologists, and ministers of various denomination. This seminar benefited from the varied professional backgrounds of the participants who contributed insights from their own professional and personal experience.

The following is a brief description of the procedures employed for evaluating the trainees in each of these three areas, and the results that we obtained:

FACTUAL-THEORETICAL

Our seminar curriculum contained an array of factual and theoretical data and concepts that we expected each of the trainees to learn. For the purpose of measuring this learning or change, we developed a fifty-item multiple choice examination intended to sample the factual material presented in the seminar. The subject areas covered by the examination included: psychology of adolescence, problems of female sexual adjustment, psychopathology of family functioning, social and cultural factors related to family dynamics, and aims and assumptions of the conjoint family counseling method.

We obtained the following results in the pre-testing of our seminar trainee group ($N=80$) on this multiple choice examination: The trained social case workers answered, on the average, 60 percent of the questions correctly, and the ministers answered, on the average, 54 percent of the questions correctly. Thus, there was a smaller difference than perhaps might have been expected between these two groups in regard to the amount of factual and theoretical background they brought with them to this training program. This pre-testing result indicated that while the trained social casework group might be more sophisticated and experienced in family counseling techniques, they still could make use of a certain amount of theoretical material in order to better conceptualize the conjoint family approach and the other relevant issues.

On post-testing, the mean correct score for the whole trainee group was 69.4 percent compared to a mean score of 55.5 percent on pre-testing. The degree of improvement was found to be statistically significant to the .05 level of confidence ($t=2.1$). Only six trainees out of the total group of 80 did not improve their scores to some degree on post-testing. Nevertheless, the amount or degree of improvement was in most instances not dramatic or impressive. We would like to believe that this examination did not adequately reflect the amount of actual learning which had taken place, and we tend to rationalize that the extreme difficulty of the examination, including as it did a number of subtle or controversial items, was a factor in maintaining the low ceiling of scores on post-testing. It should also be noted that no effort was made to review the specific questions of the examination during the seminar discussion sessions. Another possible reason for the relatively low-test post scores was that the trainee group had less interest in the many theoretical examination questions which did not relate directly to technique of conjoint family counseling, the latter being, after all, the specific mission of the seminar.

We recruited a control group which consisted of 18 social case workers employed in family service and children's agencies; these constituted an appropriate control group for the trained social case workers in the seminar program. This control group answered, on the average, 55 percent of the questions of the multiple choice examination correctly on pre-testing, which almost exactly matched the performance of the seminar group. The post-testing was conducted at approximately the same time that the trainee group was post-tested. But the control group did not, of course, have the training seminar in between. They might, however, have derived some learning as a secondary effect of discussions with the fellow case workers in their agencies who were members of the trainee group. This control group answered correctly, on the average, 57 percent of the questions on post-testing. This does not represent a statistically significant increase over pre-testing. Accordingly, we can conclude that the multiple choice examination demonstrated an increase in factual and theoretical knowledge as a result of the training seminar, to a statitiscally significant degree, but not to a very impressive degree.

In addition to objective or performance testing, we conducted a survey toward the end of the first year of training in which we obtained the trainees' subjective evaluations of the effectiveness of the seminar. The percentages of the trainees who reported that they had gained increased understanding of the five main topics of the seminar were as follows:

Psychodynamics of family life relationships	100%	(3)
Psychopathology in family life relationships	100%	(2)
Psychodynamics of female sexual promiscuity	95%	(1)
Issues and principles of family unit counseling and family treatment	95%	(4)
Social and cultural considerations in female sex behavior problems	91%	(5)

The modal rank order assigned the topics according to the relative amount of new information and understanding gained, is indicated in the column at the right.

The second procedure employed for the evaluation of the factual-theoretical content of the curriculum was a one-hour essay-type examination consisting of the following five questions:

1. List three possible advantages and one possible disadvantage to counseling with the whole family in the home compared to working with the maladjusted or mentally ill member alone in the hospital or office.

2. Pathological families, or families with mentally ill members have been characterized as "closed social systems." Explain the meaning of this term, give some examples, and tell how such a closed system might contribute to the mental illness of its members.

3. What misperception of the father's role in the family would be added by an arrangement in which he was the only disciplinarian in the household?

4. a) Explain one way in which female sexually promiscuous behavior can be conceptualized in psychoanalytic or psychodynamic terms.

   b) Explain why each of the following conditions is not in itself a safeguard against promiscuous sexual acting out: 1) masturbation, 2) a pious, religious atmosphere in the home, 3) candid discussion of sex in the family, 4) uninhibited attitude toward exposure of the body and nudity in the home.

5. a) List at least four possible determinants of sexually promiscuous behavior in girls.

   b) Since no one really knows which is the most important or critical single factor, make your own guess regarding this, and defend your choice.

The scoring procedure for this essay examination was as follows: Two clinical psychologists functioned as independent raters and evaluators. They conferred with the training coordinator and the teaching staff and developed model or best answers to each of the five essay questions. They also listed, in rank order, responses considered to be of lesser quality. In addition, two psychologists, working from a random inspection of test answers, constructed a number of additional valid answers to the questions. The range of possible responses were then assigned point values, resulting in a total of 88 points, and 12 points were added for organization and style of expression, making a possible "perfect" score of 100 points. This maximum or "perfect" score was computed by ascribing a number of credit points to each of several possible good answers to a question, and then summing these points. Thus, if there were three possible good answers to a question, all equally valid, the trainee would be required to produce all three answers completely before receiving maximum credit. If he wrote only one of the answers he would receive only one-third credit for the question. It may not have been too reasonable to expect a trainee to write all the possible valid answers to a question within the alloted time inasmuch as the questions were not worded specifically to elicit all possible valid answers. We shall see from our results later how this original scoring procedure had the effect of maintaining a low ceiling of scores on this test.

Next, working jointly, the two psychologists conducted a brief reliability training procedure, and scored twenty of the essay examination papers jointly in order to gain communality of approach. An additional ten papers were scored separately by each and the degree of agreement was examined. There was found no consistent tendency for either scorer to systematically assign either higher or lower point values. Discussion to resolve the differences followed and resulted in a joint final score for each of the examination papers. The pre-testing examination papers and the post-testing examination papers of the trainees and of the controls were mixed randomly together in one group for scoring, and the scorers were unaware as to which of the groups a particular paper belonged.

Results

The mean scores for the trainee group increased from 35.4 on pre-testing to 48.6 on post-testing. This represents a statistically significant degree of improvement, by "t" test at the .01 level of confidence ("t" ratio=2.81. The mean scores for the control group were 35.5 on pre-testing and 38.5 on post-testing. This difference was found to be non-significant by t-test.

The quantitative results of this essay examination appeared to demonstrate the results of the training seminar somewhat more conclusively than did the results of the multiple choice examination. Perhaps the open-ended or less structured type of examination provided more opportunity for the trainee to demonstrate his improved ability to conceptualize and to make constructive use of the curriculum material in the examination.

Nevertheless, we are still faced with the fact that the trainee group achieved only about one-half, on the average, of what the independent evaluating psychologists considered to be complete and perfect answers. The highest score achieved by any trainee on post-testing was 65 points. The large unfilled gap of 51 points between the mean post-testing score of 48.6 and the ideal score of 100 is explained partly by the original scoring method developed for the test, as described above. It might have been more realistic to have developed a scale of 75 points instead of 100 points for this test. It is, of course, difficult to determine how much change or improvement on an examination is required to demonstrate that a training program is successful, or how much change is required to justify the training program. Furthermore, while these changes proved that the trainee group learned curriculum material, the factual-theoretical form of test does not tell us whether the trainee is able to make constructive use of the material he learns in the actual helping and counseling work with clients, or whether his agency permits him to implement these changes into a new role function.

A second procedure for evaluating the results of the essay test was applied: One of the evaluating clinical psychologists reread the examination papers a second and third time for the purpose of identifying areas of general improvement which were manifested in a qualitative way. It was considered possible that an improved response, which might only be reflected quantitatively in an increase of a few points, might appear to be more significant in a qualitative sense as an indicator of the trainees' increased understanding and approach to the problem. The review was also meant to serve the purpose of highlighting areas that needed further explication and further emphasis in such a training program and to reveal the gains that were made by the trainees. Accordingly, we were alert to the weaknesses that were evident in the trainees' post-testing answers.

Following are some of the observations from this qualitative analysis of the answers to the essay questions:

Question 1 asked for both advantages and disadvantages of family therapy in the home. On both pre- and post-evaluations, the trainees handled the advantages quite well, reflecting some prior knowledge in this area gained, presumably, from their own independent reading and from their recent interest in the new method of conjoint family counseling. However, in regard to the disadvantages, most of the trainees could deal initially with these only in such practical terms as the additional cost of travel to the families' homes. After training, they were 1) able to discuss such possible disadvantages as the use of the home setting by the family members to resist treatment (by leaving the session for a brief visit to the kitchen, etc.), and 2) to consider that there might be less opportunity in the home setting for uncovering and elucidating the early emotional development of family members.

Example: In regard to possible disadvantages of family treatment, one trainee referred in pre-testing in a vague manner to the complicated problem of dealing with several persons at once and the anxiety generated in the helping person by this. Upon post-exam, the trainee was able to specify the problems of coping with multiple transferences and counselor countertransferences, and to point out the possibility that in the family treatment setting the designated patient might feel relieved of the responsibility for working on his problems and changing.

On Question 2, it was found that, on pre-testing, the trainees did quite well in referring to the concept of the pathological family as a "closed social system," but that, on post-testing, they were more adept in giving appropriate examples of this concept.

On pre-testing, the trainees spoke in generalities, mentioning only the importance of the family members' conflicts with each other. After the training period, the answers included mention of the homeostatic balance of family dynamics, their effect in holding one member "ill," and their exclusion of extra-familial influences which might serve as corrective experiences.

Example: A trainee reasoned on pre-testing that the term "closed social system" must imply that the family members were inextricably involved with each other, but he could not elaborate. Compare this with this excerpt from the same person's post-exam response:

A closed social system is one in which the family effectively shuts out influence and relationships from outside the family which must interfere with the sick needs and relationships within the family. An interdependence is set up with the children so that they are safe only within the family group. A child in such a family is isolated from normal friendships and can develop various twisted perceptions of other people.

On Question 3, in regard to the arrangement in which the father is the only disciplinarian in the household, on pre-testing the trainees focused on the effect that the perception of the father as a harsh, unloving figure would have on the children. On post-testing, a number of trainees, but still only a minority, were able to introduce the broader concept of the effect of such an arrangement on the whole family system. They discussed how such a one-sided discipline served to reduce the mother's role as a parent, or how the mother might be quietly using the father to do her bidding as the disciplinarian, or how the children might have great difficulty in resolving Oedipal problems and attachments, in learning self-control, and in maintaining adequate boundaries between the two generations, as a result of the failure of a smooth and cooperative functioning of the parental team vis-à-vis the children. The trainees "knew" at one level the advantages of a total family approach (as was indicated in their answers to the first question), but when asked to respond in terms of the interactive effects on all the family members of a given situation, as in this question, some of the trainees were still not able to apply the family system concepts readily. We must assume that this ready application of concept to the practical situation develops only after a certain amount of experience in working with whole families and in discussing the problems and approaches required in this practical work.

Example: One trainee, on pre-testing, pointed out that where the father is the only disciplinarian the boy's identification with him would be hampered and that the possibility of seeing the father as loving would be negated. On post-testing, this trainee added to the above as follows:

If the father were seen as the only disciplinarian, one of the misperceptions would be in the mother's role. She would be seen as perhaps another child or sibling, as ineffectual, having no status of her own. The mother in this role would compete with the children; depending on her relationship with the father, she could undermine his discipline, sabotage him, set up scapegoats for the father to punish and thus intensify sibling difficulties.

Questions 4 and 5, regarding psychodynamic formulations underlying female promiscuity, were in general dealt with in a weak fashion by the trainees in the pre-testing. For example, a fair number of trainees did not even attempt Question 5-b, which requested them to select one important or critical determinant of sexually promiscuous behavior in girls and to defend their choice. Many of them stated that they lacked knowledge in this area, making it clear that they did not omit the question simply due to lack of time. Also, in the pre-testing, a number of trainees discussed the moral and religious issues in relation to promiscuous sexual behavior. On post-testing, they discussed psychodynamic factors in addition to the moral issues, or, in some cases, replaced the moral issues with psychodynamic factors.

There was clearly an increase in the psychodynamic sophistication of the group in general. Many of the pre-testing answers discussed ego defects in the girl as factors in sexual delinquent behavior. The girls' hostility was most often considered to be the result of socio-economic and cultural deprivation rather than the result of family relationships. On post-testing, such additional dynamic factors were added to the responses as: frustrations in affectional and love relationships within the family, unsatisfied needs in early childhood, and the use of sex in a "pseudo" fashion to gain essentially childish and non-genital aims. Others pointed out that the girls could be responding to subtle or unconscious invitations by the parents to act out the parental fantasies and the unsatisfied parental wishes.

Example: On pre-testing, one respondent could only acknowledge her lack of information and list several non-specific factors, such as family pathology, inadequate sex education, and socio-economic conditions. On post-testing, the same trainee developed such ideas as: the unconscious stimulation of the girl by her parents to act out their sexual urges, hostility directed against the parents for rejection, the possibility of sexual acting out to ward off homosexual desires, and the threat of the increased sexual drive of puberty, resulting in a flight into pseudo-mature maladaptive heterosexual activity.

Question 5-b, which referred to selecting and defending the most important determinant of promiscuous behavior, received a large variety of answers encompassing many points of view and a wide diversity of quality. A few merely offered generalities about poor family relationships as a cause of the problem, but many others offered good explanations buttressed by appropriate case examples. The case examples adduced were excellent and indicated a general increase in the understanding of the problem.

PERSONAL-ATTITUDINAL

We were interested in the personal and emotional attitudes of the trainees toward sexually acting-out adolescent girls as being relevant to their perception of their role and their goals, as well as to their competence in counseling. We were also interested in the changes in these attitudes which might develop as a result of the training program. Accordingly, we used as our assessment instrument the *Osgood-type Semantic Differential Scale,* which we developed for this purpose.

This scale consisted of 26 bi-polar adjective descriptions, on each of which the subject is asked to rate concept-figures on a seven-point continuum scale. The two concept-figures rated in this instance were: "The average adolescent girl," and "the sexually promiscuous adolescent girl." The order of presentation of these two concept-figures for rating was counterbalanced. The scale included such items as "Sad-Happy,"

"Foolish -Wise," "Dirty - Clean," "Cold - Warm," "Insincere - Sincere," "Worthless-Valuable," etc., in addition to the original semantic-differential items required for deriving the three major factor scores developed by Osgood: 1) Evaluative, 2) Potency, and 3) Activity. The usefulness and "validity" of this type of scale has already been established by the basic research with the instrument.

Results

The total trainee group, on pre-testing, perceived sexually promiscuous girls as generally described by the following adjectives: "foolish," "sad," "tense," "sick," "self-rejecting," "hating," "untrusting," "lacking in self-control," "self-centered," and "masochistic." They did *not* perceive them as generally being "ignorant," "poor," "worthless," "dirty," "bad," "insincere," "lacking in conscience," or "masculine."

An interesting serendipitous finding on pre-testing with this scale was that the male trainees had a rather different picture of, or attitude toward, the sexually promiscuous adolescent girl from that of the female trainees. The female trainees, compared to the male trainees, perceived the promiscuous girls as significantly (by chi-square test): 1) more "foolish" (rather than "wise"), 2) more "active" (rather than "passive"), 3) more often "good" (rather than "bad"), and 4) less "submissive." In regard to this latter item the male trainees perceived the promiscuous girls as being very "submissive." In regard to some items, a complete reversal occurred: the males perceived the average girls as being more "active" than the promiscuous girl, and the females perceived the average girl as being more "passive" than the promiscuous girl.

The male respondents presented generally a more positive picture of the adolescent girl than did the female respondents. This was particularly true in regard to the "average adolescent girl," but the tendency was present to a nonsignificant degree statistically in relation to the promiscuous girl as well. Some of the items on which the male respondents' picture of the adolescent girl was more positive were: "fast," "happy," "healthy," "trusting, "sincere," and "loving." Perhaps the males tended to romantically idealize the young female, while female respondents tended to be more realistic or more circumspect regarding members of their own sex who were younger than they were. The findings suggest that the lack of knowledge and of objectivity regarding the sexually promiscuous girl is so pronounced that a personal factor, such as whether the professional observer is a male or female, overrides the effects of a common professional training.

As a measure of the effect that the curriculum had on the trainees' attitudes toward, and perceptions of, the sexually promiscuous girl, we calculated the post-minus-pre-change scores, on our semantic differential attitude scale: We then corrected these change scores with the changes that occurred in the perception of the "average adolescent girl." The differential change score thus became our measure of shifts in the perceptions of how the promiscuous girl differed from girls in general. The results indicated that the trainee group now perceived the promiscuous girl as significantly less "foolish," less "weak," less "untrusting," less "passive," less "self-rejecting," and less "self-centered" than they had perceived her originally (to at least .05 degree of confidence). It was interesting, as in the pre-testing, to look more closely at the response to the "submissive-dominant" item. The bi-modal distributing of ratings on this item in pre-testing that resulted from the difference in the attitudes of the male and female groups of respondent now disappeared in post-testing. The promiscuous girl was now perceived both as being less extremely "submissive" (by males) and less extremely "dominant" (by females). There was accordingly no significant difference found overall between the pre-test mean rating and the post-test mean rating.

The male trainees now corrected for some of the unrealistically ideal picture they had had originally of young girls in general. Their absolute ratings of the promiscuous girl did not change as much as the female trainees' ratings did, but when corrected by the somewhat lower and more realistic ratings of the average young girl, their ratings of the promiscuous girl still showed a tendency, though non-significant, to change to a higher opinion of them.

FAMILY COUNSELING COMPETENCE

An excerpt of a tape recording of an actual family counseling session, conducted by a teaching therapy team, was adapted to form one of the practicum test procedures to evaluate the trainees' knowledge of technique. In the particular excerpt selected for this purpose, the father was arguing with his sexually delinquent 21-year-old daughter, who claimed that she was actually completely independent, and should be, since she worked and supported herself. Although she lived with her parents, she stated that her behavior was her own business. The father said to her, at this point, "I am willing to accept loss of control over you, if you are willing to accept responsibility for your independent behavior." This sounded on the surface like a reasonable statement and reflected the father's typical intellectualized and somewhat emotionally detached approach. The therapist had intervened at this point and made an observation directed to the father. The tape was stopped, however, before the therapist's statement was played, and the trainees were asked to write what they themselves might have said or done at this point if they had been handling the session. For the second question the playback of the tape recording was resumed so that the trainees could hear the statement which had been made originally to the father by the family therapist. The trainee was asked to comment on this intervention and to discuss it in relation to his own response which he had already written. The third and final question on this examination was to present some dynamic formulation of the five minutes of family interaction which had preceded the father's statement referred to in the first question.

The therapist's statement on the tape (which provided the basis for the second question) was to the effect that the father really felt that he had no control or influence in the situation, and why not talk about his feelings about himself, about why he lost control, etc., rather than try to arrange a fair deal; that his proposal sounded reasonable, but that he was apparently in no position to state any conditions until he and his daughter worked through their feelings toward each other. Under the father's apparently affectless statement, there were subtle tones of pleading with, and carping with, his daughter.

Results

In pre-testing, a minority of the trainees had, in their responses, touched on, with more or less sophistication, some aspect of the same issue that the therapist raised. A majority responded at the more superficial level of the interaction, and dealt with the father on his own terms and on the same superficial level that he used in dealing with. and relating to, his daughter. They said, for example, that they would try to get the daughter to clarify in detail what she thought her duties ought to be in the home, and what her responsibilities for her sexual behavior ought to be so as not to get pregnant and present her parents with a crisis situation. These pre-examination responses were nearly all reasonable, sensible, and meaningful for the particular family problems presented on the tape. Nevertheless, a clear shift was observed in the trainees' response on post-examination to a more dynamic and more affective level of family interaction. All the practicum trainees improved their performance to some degree. The degree of change and improvement in the responses on this practicum test was much more marked and impressive than the changes obtained on the factual-theoretical tests with the larger seminar group. While no statistical test of significance was conducted, due to the small size of the sample, "blind" comparison of the pre- and post-test responses of each trainee resulted in a rating of greater sophistication of the post-test response every case. (Incidentally, this particular question and excerpt of family therapy interaction was not discussed with the trainees by the teaching staff during the course.)

Following are some examples of post-test responses, comments on the father's statement above, which indicate the level of sophistication of the trainees in the understanding of the family dynamics:

If father were to say "If you'll accept the *consequences of your behavior*," it would make more sense, but not much. Actually, acceptance by him of her lead in the situation is not taking a responsible position and the license to do as she pleases is pretty well conveyed. Even more confusing (when you hear it on the tape) is the forcefulness and air of conviction with which this statement is voiced.

Not only does the statement not make clear sense, but the affect accompanying it conveys the message that father is making a clear positional statement. How could one possibly get a clear message? Actually he makes loud, meaningless statements and then steps aside and undoes everything he previously stated, while mother and daughter pick up the fight.

In responding to him I might say something about how confusing this statement is, but odds are it would only precipitate more double-talk. A much better approach would, I think, be to pick up on the implied license. "No wonder she acts out — she has your full permission!" (This would be direct, but catalytic. For this man anything less would be shrugged aside.)

A key issue in this excerpt concerns itself with this father's impotent, ineffectual and passive role in this family. It is interestingly related to his very first statement in which he makes the daughter the active one in the acting out, i.e., "I am willing to accept loss of control over you, if you are willing to accept responsibility for your independence."

Obviously, he left to mother and mother-in-law the responsibility for decision making, etc. He abdicates to mother the active role in the family.

It sounds as if father is giving daughter tacit permission to act out sexually. It also seems clear that he seems to be giving permission for her to lose control with him. The statement "I am willing to accept loss of control" implies his lack of responsibility.

I would say that father is acting out through daughter in an attempt to resolve his Oedipal conflict, and that daughter is complying, and that this is complicated further by the fact that they are not natural father and daughter (since the daughter was adopted), so that the more usual and natural incest taboos are not so available to them.

Index